'A Journey.'

John

THE EDGE OF TIME

THE EDGE OF TIME

War time child to accidental retailer

John Pellowe

Matador
9 Priory Business Park
Kibworth Beauchamp
Leicestershire LE8 0RX, UK
Tel: (+44) 116 279 2299
Fax: (+44) 116 279 2277
Email: books@troubador.co.uk
Web: www.troubador.co.uk/matador

ISBN 978 1780880 822

British Library Cataloguing in Publication Data.
A catalogue record for this book is available from the British Library.

Typeset in 11pt Bembo by Troubador Publishing Ltd, Leicester, UK

Matador is an imprint of Troubador Publishing Ltd

This book is dedicated to Mum and Dad,
for great opportunities. Also to my super, loving family.

Contents

Foreword

Dyslexic and turned seventy, when systems and memory are failing, is not a good time to consider writing a book but the idea had been ticking over in my mind for some time. I was always conscious I was never told why my Grandfather Pellowe left sunny Falmouth to come and set up a business in grey, polluted Oldham. No one ever mentioned anything about it; was that the way of things then? I wanted to ensure that my own kids and grandchildren knew about my life and I also began to realise I had a bit of explaining to do about some testing personal times. Consideration turned into actuality the night that my mother died. I had visited her in the nursing home every morning and evening but that night the nurses told me not to bother visiting Mum as she had received lots of visitors and was very tired. To this day I don't know what drove me to do it but with a little spare time now on my hands I sat down and started the first chapter. Perhaps it was just coincidence, we'll never know, but later that night Mum died.

As time went on I found I was struggling with the embryo book so one day I wandered into Lees library to talk to a friend who worked there. Celia had helped Viv and I to sort out the garden at Dyehouse Cottage way back and I asked if she knew of any books that would help me to write my autobiography. Armed with two or three tomes I returned home to continue but a year after their return date the books were still with me and I hadn't made a lot of progress. I called on Celia again: 'I have played around with some notes but I really need someone to type and edit, do you know of anyone?' It was then that I was introduced to Lynne Lowes who had never written a book before although Celia assured me that she had the right qualifications to fit the bill. And so it came to be Lynne who now knows more about me than she bargained for whilst patiently transcribing the notes of the moron she was to meet. We have slogged on, 'not too fast and not too slow', and to Lynne I am sincerely appreciative.

This book is also a way of crediting the people who have influenced and helped me along life's way, both directly and indirectly. It is also a vehicle to mention friends I have made; fun, parties, and happy times over the years; huge sadness and yes, mistakes. Unfortunately many good folk and lots of great tales do not get a mention and this is entirely due to Lynne who can be a ruthless editor and is punishing on the word count! She has told me constantly that we are not writing the *Encyclopedia Britannica* but hopefully the people and stories she has cast aside will make it into my next book!

Overall I would like to take this chance to say how I really appreciate the opportunities life put my way. I would like to think I have used them to their full advantage and in turn created opportunities for others, but let's not kid ourselves; timing, good luck and an element of faith did not go amiss either.

To my grandchildren - time passes so quickly kids, believe me, so do your best by trying to *CATCH THE MOMENT*, or the train before it leaves the platform as your great grandfather and I did. Along the way keep notes on the trip, save sketches, notebooks and diaries and you will be glad in later life.

And finally to the reader - do a favour for me, keep a box of jottings, postcards, holidays, photos, bits and pieces because one day someone will want to look in that box!

Cheers
John Pellowe

Starting Point

As unconvincing as the boy who tells his teacher the dog has eaten his homework!

A cast iron lamp post can be a safe haven if you happen to be out of control, on a pair of roller-skates, at the tender age of ten. Unfortunately it was my head that made contact with the lamp post and although I did indeed stop, I sustained a terrible injury. What followed was just one of many childhood visits to be stitched up in the casualty department at Oldham Hospital. To be accident prone seems to be my lot as this unfortunate characteristic dogged me all of my younger life and I have the scars to support my claim. However some would say that rather than being accident prone maybe I am a just a daft risk taker for I have always liked to take things to the edge.

One of my earliest recollections of a self inflicted injury happened at Werneth Primary School when I was aged about seven. One day, during playtime, curiosity led me to a corner of the play ground where there were lots of abandoned cast iron manhole covers leaning against the wall, eight

or so deep. I decided to amuse myself by inventing a game with these 'toys' and so I started to pull the first one forward onto my body and then another and another, the aim being to see how many of them I could hold. My knees began to quiver with the weight of the third manhole cover and by the fourth down they all came like a pack of cards and hey presto my hands were under a couple of hundredweight of very heavy steel. My memories are of lots of blood, a posse of teachers galloping to the rescue, an ambulance and a lot of pain. Upon my return to school I was sporting a terribly impressive sling and giving off a strong odour of iodine, which incidentally stung like hell. I was not able to write for a good while but, as I had never been one to shine in class, nobody noticed except perhaps a girl called Vivienne who, despite my apparent lack of intelligence and general buffoonery, was my friend. Meanwhile the bloodstained area of the playground became a permanent no go area and curiously the manhole covers vanished overnight. What they were doing there in the first place god only knows, but imagine the fuss if such a thing happened now. In those days my drama just added an extra dimension to playtime but the lasting legacy of this early episode is some adjustment, shall we say, to the little finger of my right hand which now lies 45 degrees to the right.

Disfigurement, however, did not put me off and somehow the accidents continued. My mother became more and more annoyed with each calamity but things just seemed to happen to me. I felt I had no involvement in the cause of my mishaps although she blamed me entirely. Normally I was punished in proportion to the wounds and injuries I incurred but on at least one occasion I managed to escape the punishment that Mother meted out because I was too badly injured. I was in Werneth Park one day with an evacuee from Guernsey called Donald Falla who was living with us during the war as Oldham was considered to be far safer than German occupied Guernsey. Don was a few years older than me and Mother hoped that an older, more responsible friend would teach me how to avoid the many accidents and scrapes I seemed to find myself in. I was, I suppose, eight or nine years old at the time and Don was about fourteen. The park was surrounded by a ten foot high wall which had cast iron benches all the way along in order for people to sit down and watch the world go by. Don and I decided to have a race, he running from bench to bench on the ground whilst I raced along the top of the wall. We were competing well initially but the coping stones on the top of the wall were uneven and so I had to take more care than Don. Consequently he pulled ahead and recklessly I stepped up my own pace not wishing to be beaten. Unfortunately I tripped, taking a header onto the top of one of the benches and poor Don had to pick up the pieces, blood everywhere. Desperate and fearful, he took me to the nearest place for help which happened to be Werneth Fire station. The Fire Chief was peacefully and innocently enjoying his morning brew but he took one look at me, quickly wrapped a few pads round my head and put me straight into his car and off to casualty. I had to have stitches in both of my eyes and also to a large part of my head, around fifteen stitches in all. The kindly Fire Chief then took Don and me home and now the pair of us began to feel really worried. My whole head was bandaged up. What on earth would Mother say? Old Don was really shaking; he knew he would cop it so we sent the Fire Chief into the house ahead of us asking him to tell my mother that it was not as bad as it looked for I believed that even she could not lose her rag with a uniformed, peaked capped, terribly smart Fire Chief. My mother, at only five foot, was not a large woman but she was the main authority figure in my young life, the strap she kept behind the door being her final card. As Dad was out working most of the time discipline fell to Mother and she took her duty very seriously as Don and I knew only too well. The Fire Chief, having prepared Mother, beckoned us into the house and I can still recall how stunned Mother looked as she was confronted with what appeared to be a 'Mummy' as I was covered in bandages which revealed only my eyes! This had been a very bad fall; apart from the extensive damage to my head I also had a badly bruised shoulder and a great wound on my arm. As the Fire Chief departed we braced ourselves and maybe for a moment Don felt that he should have stayed in Guernsey to take his chances with the German Army rather than be confronted with Mother's wrath. The outcome of it all was that he got confined to quarters for a week, as well as having his daily chores stepped up, whilst I got away with it on this occasion due to the extent of my injuries. Believe me, the injuries were preferable!

Later that evening when Dad arrived home from work he was lambasted with the latest episode of my wrongdoing whilst Don and I listened, invisible in the wings. As usual Mother ended her sorry tale by asking him: 'what are you going to do about it?' Dad always tried to slide out of these quarrels, he was a very easy going chap, but even he couldn't lightly pass off such a bad head injury. Although his words were much more restrained than Mother's they had more effect, so I took note and really tried to be more responsible but my mishaps continued. The 'balloon' inevitably went up each time I was returned home from my friends at the hospital, wearing bandages, plaster or stitches. Mother was not impressed at all and made it clear she couldn't, and wouldn't, stand for 'any more of this'. Apparently I was a liability every time I went out and she threatened to have me packed off somewhere if my transgressions continued.

Unfortunately they did continue and every time I had an accident Mother would shout and blast whilst Dad would try to help by offering practical advice which I tried to adopt. Dad's words finally began to sink in when I sustained further injuries from a fall whilst driving my bogie. Bogies, for those who don't know, are very simple home made box carts with two large wheels at the rear and two small wheels at the front. They were steered by a rope and stopped by a makeshift brake which, being home made, would not always do its job when you needed it. Therefore if you were going too fast for the brake to be of any use it was simply a case of having to bail out as you had lost control. After another accident caused by just such a scenario there came the final warning from 'she who mattered'. Dad, helpful as ever, suggested that I 'do away with the box and replace it with a seat' as it was easier to bail out. He also explained that the trick was not to have the wheels too large at the back as this made the contraption too fast. Me and my friends, Kelvin (1) and Peter, were always trying to improve on our current version of a bogie and following Dad's advice finally managed to build the best ever model which we named *JOKELPET* after the three of us. My friend, Kel remembers this marvellous piece of machinery as 'a few bits of wood fitted with four old pram wheels' but to us it was a Ferrari Daytona. Surprisingly Kel also remembers that I took my mother for a ride on it down Windsor Road. I can't believe she would have gone anywhere near the thing let alone sat on it. She was always so sensible and well aware of my propensity to accidents and she didn't escape this time as Kel tells me that as I turned the bogie to the right just before the main road my mother carried straight on! My dad was nowhere near as sensible as my mother and I remember a particularly daring escapade of his when building repairs were being carried out to the chimney at Glover's Mill which was next to Copster Reservoir. One night, when the workmen had left for the evening, Dad decided to climb to the top of the mill chimney (2) for a jaunt utilising the steeplejack's vacant ladders which were already in situ. Although I was only about fourteen at the time he said that I could accompany him so up we went, Dad first, fag in his mouth as usual, and me following. I feel that I coped reasonably well on the ascent but climbing vertically from the ladders onto the platform at the top of the chimney without the use of a handrail was something else. I felt like Spiderman scaling a building. With Dad's encouragement I managed to climb even further onto the overhanging, windy, working ledge which surrounded the very tip of the chimney. It was exhilarating and the view was breathtaking but in fact the view must have taken all my breath away for I cannot recollect being able to breathe at all on the descent which was a terribly tough assignment. Dad of course enjoyed himself thoroughly.

The epitome of a typical 1930's married couple, Dad went out to work whilst Mother stayed at home to look after me. She did not take kindly to women who did not devote all their time to their kids and my upbringing was therefore closely supervised. Unfortunately for me, Mother had some very Victorian ideas about child rearing; she was a very determined person and she had a strict routine which had to be followed to the letter. One of her rules was that I should always eat the food that was given to me and if I didn't then it would be served up at the next meal time when it would, of course, be cold and I would heave at the sight of it. To my profound relief Mother stopped this practise following a ticking off from Doctor Adler, the family doctor. All through my early years Dr Adler was a familiar figure, treating my childhood diseases and the bruises and stitches caused by my many misadventures. He was a very gentle, traditional, and much respected physician; in those days the family doctor was truly that, a person, almost always male, who treated the whole family and would make frequent calls to the house. Dr Adler was therefore fully aware of my mother's authoritarianism and determination and it was only because of his timely intervention and kindly advice that my mother gave in about the food. It would seem he knew how to handle her and actually Mother always said that Dr Adler was the man she fancied after Dad! What a pity he couldn't have given her some cookery lessons too; why did my mother make lumpy gravy and custard? Another culinary speciality of Mother's was boiled vegetables, and I mean boiled. They were cooked for hours; so long in fact that the water became the colour that the vegetables had originally been whilst the remaining mush was colourless. All vegetables looked and tasted the same. On a more positive note I can recall that Mother's roasted potatoes were good as were her hot pots, cheese and onion pies, home made potato cakes and rock buns. The rest of my childhood diet remains rather a blur.

My mother had no further children after having me. Maybe this was because of my predilection to accidents and the fact that I was, apparently, the cause of a very difficult breach birth. I'll never know but I'm sure she must have thought that one was enough! However this lack of siblings didn't really matter as I had lots of playmates living nearby and we would all play in the 'back' which was a large area beyond the rear gardens of the houses on our road. Thousands of hours with Kel and my other friends must have been spent on this spare ground playing games and climbing trees; we built dens and assault courses; we fought and made up and frequently stayed out there until it was pitch black and we were called in by our parents. Surrounding the back were wooden framed, asbestos clad garages, some of them smarter than others depending on the affluence of the owner. The older, more decrepit ones moved and swayed in the wind and it was great fun for us children as we dared one another to climb across the roofs of these creaking, groaning structures. As new cars grew in size over the years these old garages became a problem and many a hernia must have been caused by squeezing in and out of the car door in the restricted space caused by the ever decreasing walls. It was due to this lack of space that I witnessed at least two of the garages being partially demolished. In the winter time the cars would be started and left to warm up inside the garages. Once it was judged that the engine was ready to go the driver would prise himself back into his vehicle using the eighteen inch space

Me and Kelvin (Kel) Hall – we grew up next door to each other. Kel was the more academic one so I delegated my homework to him!

The gang on the 'back' where we played dawn till dusk. Here we are celebrating VJ day. Heather is the odd one out but we believed in equal rights for women!

Peter, Kel and me with our home built bogie – JOKELPET

Top row: Peter Whitworth, Colin Bracewell, Tony Stephenson, Peter Nield, Peter Rose.
Bottom row: Malcolm Williamson, Kelvin Hall, John Pellowe, John Freear, Heather Halliday

available between car and wall and it was then that calamity could strike. The space for manoeuvring was so tight it was very easy to catch the gear stick with a knee, accidentally engaging the engine which caused the car to move forwards at speed, crashing through the back wall of the garage and bringing the roof down. These episodes caused much hilarity amongst us children although I am sure the car and garage owners weren't amused. One of our neighbours, Frank Thompson, a small man who was a wholesale greengrocer and entrepreneur, always had a big posh car such as an American Chrysler or a Buick which were rare and expensive models in those days. He kept it in a garage which was situated at the top of a small incline and one day, as he got out of the car to shut the garage doors, his beautiful Chrysler rolled away down the hill. It quickly reached the bottom and proceeded to crash through two of old Mr Smith's felted, creosoted Mark II garages which remained standing despite their decrepit state!

When I was a little older we had a circuit around the houses and the back whereby you had to get round by climbing along roofs, fences, and trees, not touching the ground at all unless absolutely necessary. Most of the time you were a minimum of six feet above the ground and everyone's circuits were timed so that there was always a record to beat. In our garden we had an air raid shelter which was a good place for access to the washhouse roof. From there it was on to the kitchen, across the gutters of two bay windows onto a fence, from there a climb up to the roof of a garage and then a drop to the ground for a run to the opposite fence. In total there were about twelve garden fences to negotiate by either crawling along whilst straddling the top, or doing a tightrope act resulting in many broken fencing panels and loads of bum splinters! The circuit was exciting and worked amazingly well although some of the house owners would get fed up and chuck us off parts of their property. As a result our relations with the neighbours became tense and we would try to avoid being told off by waiting to run the circuit when they were out. There were some real rows but we did not stop. I have so many vivid and joyful memories of playing in the back with Kelvin and my other friends, then returning home tired out, filthy and very, very happy. One of these old friends, Jim Smith, has reminded me how my mother had to have bars put up at my bedroom window to stop me escaping once I had been sent to bed; but how difficult it is to lie in bed when there are exciting things going on just outside!

When you recollect your childhood the weather always seems to have been glorious but I can tell you it wasn't always so fine for there were harsh winters with freezing, snowy, and foggy conditions. The surrounding mill chimneys were constantly belching out smoke and this, mixed with the smoke from the adults' cigarettes (everyone smoked in those days) mingled with the cold air to produce a thick fog often so dense it was impossible to see beyond a car's length. Such was the pollution and the cold that there were considerable respiratory illnesses and I became a casualty at an early age as I suffered from recurrent bouts of bronchitis. As antibiotics were not available then I had to spend about a week in bed each time the illness struck, pure torture for a child who just wants to go out and play. My mother would apply the cure which always followed the same formula: the windows of my bedroom would be firmly closed at all times; a one bar electric fire that consumed all the available oxygen would be installed near my bed as we had no central heating; two tablespoons of goose grease and liberal amounts of cod liver oil would be administered frequently; prolific amounts of camphorated oil would be massaged onto my chest until my skin was burning; and for the finale a scalding hot kaolin poultice would be applied to the same place. I could offer no resistance. As the treatment took its toll, or as I became better in Mother's eyes, I was slowly weaned from my bed and moved downstairs. Later I would be allowed outside for ten minutes a day initially and this outdoor time would be stepped up gradually as the days went by. An incredibly pathetic routine. I can remember quite clearly how fantastic it was to breathe the sharp fresh air after the confines of the bedroom with the result being that I became a prolific window opener! (3)

When I wasn't ill there was no fire in my bedroom and during the winter it was rather a shock to the system to get out of bed and find thick frost on the inside of the windows; there being no such thing as double glazing. Upon scratching a hole in the frosty window I would peer outside and see that an extra few inches of snow had fallen during the night, adding to that which had fallen the day before and some of it would have drifted into piles which could be anywhere between six and sixteen feet deep. In really bad winters such as those between the mid 1940's and the early 1950's, the roads around Oldham were impassable and the outlying villages were often inaccessible for weeks rather than days. Blizzards were common, sheep died in the snow drifts, and the roads were not gritted. For the milkman and the coalman, who still used horse drawn transport, these were severely testing times. Some mornings it would take ages to dig your way out of the snowbound house and when you did eventually step outside the whole world seemed quiet and insulated; but for us children the snow was a big adventure. We loved to play in it: sliding, building snowmen, throwing snowballs and generally larking about. We loved it even more if it meant getting out of school early, or, even better, if the schools had to shut down. All too soon the snow would change colour from the purest white to a brownish, yellowish shade, caused by the smoke from all the local factory chimneys but we still played in it. The winters often lasted well into April in those days but eventually the thaw would come and, as the air grew warmer, the melting discoloured snow would come sliding off the roofs of the buildings with a great whooshing noise. Anyone passing at the time would be covered in it to the great amusement of us children. These days we rarely get such cold and snowy textbook winters like those experienced during my childhood but as there are many people now living in Oldham who work many miles away from where they live, it is perhaps just as well.

When I was a child there was no need to travel far for work or anything else as there was plenty of employment nearby and everything you needed could be obtained from local businesses and shops. Critchley's grocers shop was typical of its time, situated on the corner of a nearby street and run in the old fashioned way, Mr and Mrs Critchley, the proprietors, always wore long aprons starched to the purest white. The walls of their shop were stacked high with shelves containing tins and boxes; there were huge slabs of butter, cheese, and lard on the counter; hams were tastefully displayed and a large bacon slicing machine lived next to an equally large coffee grinder and a huge set of scales with lots of weights. Boxes of loose tea leaves together with sacks of flour, beans, rice, sugar, salt and large tins containing dried fruit, nestled in the sawdust that was sprinkled fresh and clean on the floor every day. The pungent aroma of all these foodstuffs mingled pleasantly with the smell of the sawdust. Nothing was pre packed in those days, everything had to be weighed out and then neatly wrapped in greaseproof or brown paper. The only items that did not have to be poured, cut or wrapped were the tinned goods. You can imagine the time it took to get served but that didn't really matter as the shop was the place for chin wagging and exchanging local gossip. Working in the grocers in those days was hard, heavy work which involved a lot of clambering up and down tall wooden steps in order to reach things on the topmost shelves. Mr and Mrs Critchley had a bonny daughter called Vivienne Mary, the same girl who was in my class at Werneth School and who would later become very significant in my life. During the winter Viv was sent to neighbours to get ready for school as it was bitterly cold in that shop when her parents were preparing to open up and taking in the early morning deliveries. Wrapped in a thick dressing gown Viv would run down the passage at the back of the shop to the Hilton's house which was only five or six doors away. Under her arm would be a bag containing her clothes and a box of cornflakes and she would wash, dress and breakfast in warmth before leaving for school. In the kitchen of these friendly neighbours was a large table with a bath tucked beneath it, a common occurrence as many houses did not have a bathroom. One day when Viv called in unexpectedly at teatime, she found Mr Hilton stark naked in the steaming bath which had been pulled out from under the table to aid in his ablutions! Scarring stuff!

As very young children we spent a lot of time together and Viv would often call at our house to see if I was coming out to play. One day she needed to go to the loo and Mother directed us to the outside toilet, the one inside being reserved for family only I suppose. The outside toilet was situated on the left hand side of the passage which led to the washhouse and it had a bright green tongue and grooved door. As Viv tugged down her knickers and sat on the scrubbed wooden seat, legs dangling, feet unable to touch the floor, she announced: 'You're my sweetheart and I'll marry you one day.' I quickly shut the door on her; I think I was very frightened. On another occasion she told me again that I was her sweetheart which I hastily and vehemently denied. Viv still remembers all this very clearly but nevertheless went on to plan her boy friends quite strategically in future years.

In our childhood we walked everywhere as there were very few buses and even less cars. We could play out safely after dark; no doors were locked, no one got attacked, and mugging was unheard of. People had few possessions but they were respectable and trustworthy and the law was upheld. It was therefore perfectly OK for us to visit neighbours freely and unaccompanied. Consequently during school holidays if the weather wasn't so good, Vivienne and I would visit the antique stacked home of Mrs Kidger, the Agatha Christie of Windsor Road. Mrs Kidger was a blast from the past of our glorious Empire Days; she would speak of India and her life there where she had servants galore. To have known both her and her house was an enlightening experience and there are certainly no such people left alive today, people whose lives were in their prime at the beginning of the twentieth century. For some reason, despite her friendliness, there was always an air of mystery surrounding both Mrs Kidger and the large house she lived in. She was housebound so she always occupied a huge chair which was angled towards the fireplace and to assist her she had a maid called Marie whose uniform had influenced that of our maid, Maude. Viv and I were always made very welcome on our visits and encouraged to pass the time doing unusual, creative activities such as putting on little shows or drawing. Sometimes we would be sent into the overgrown garden to gather twigs which we would then decorate with flowers that we made from melted coloured wax. On other occasions Mrs Kidger would read the stories of Rudyard Kipling and Enid Blyton to us, surprisingly expressing great feeling and imagination although she omitted to tell us that Enid Blyton used to play tennis in the nude! Visiting Mrs Kidger was fun and exciting; it was as though we crossed Windsor Road and reappeared in a Peter Pan world although the interior of the large house was dark with mahogany panelling and the kitchen was cold and dull with a Belfast sink and a lino floor. I remember finding it hard to imagine any good food ever emerging from there. The rest of the house was richly laden with trophies of Mrs Kidger's former life in India such as sumptuous rugs, pictures, and weaponry. Carved figures, both large and small were on display as were fine examples of swords and guns. I never saw Mr Kidger, he was probably dead, but I think he had been in the army in India for most of his life. Certainly there were many pictures on the walls which were all of a military nature. I do remember Mrs Kidger's son John. He was commissioned as an officer in the army and was also serving in India or in the Far East. When he returned home on leave he would bring exciting things such as a real .2 revolver of polished steel with a six bullet chamber which he gave to me. I cannot recollect if I knew which regiment he belonged to but he was probably in the same one as his father had been before him which was traditional in those days. John must have been involved in the war but I don't know any detail; he was Mrs Kidger's only child and thinking back I am sure she was a lonely woman. I believe she thought of herself as a godmother to Vivienne and me and that is why she made us feel so welcome. Marie, the maid, would bring drinks and cakes in at tea time and we would sit on the rug in front of the blazing fire. From that position it was impossible not to notice Mrs Kidger's huge, pink coloured bloomers as she sat in the chair above us with her immobile legs wide open. Strange how some things stick in your mind!

Starting Point: Notes

1) Kel – on childhood.................We really did have the golden years. Everyone showed concern for everyone else especially during the war. Food, clothes, sweets and toys were all rationed which made people more equal than they are today. In those days, even if you were rich, there was not a lot to spend your money on. There was so little traffic that we could play cricket in the streets and the height of naughtiness was playing knock and run.

And – on Bonfires................There was always a huge supper waiting in the Pellowe's double garage and I can still see JP's Uncle Joe lighting a thunder flash and putting it inside one of the Potato Pies – everyone got a bit! Old Mrs Easthope, whose rear windows overlooked the croft where we had our fire, didn't like us very much and used to watch us from her bedroom window until one night a rocket went through it! Uncle Lewis had to get the window repaired on our behalf.

JP - More on bonfires ....Actually it was the preparation for the bonfire that I recall most – we had a planned campaign which started several weeks before the event. We collected anything made from wood – if somebody had a rickety fence it disappeared! We nicked stuff off other gangs' collections whilst guarding our own as best we could from reciprocal raids but there was often a row when a rival group recognised some of their wood on our stash. We would take things thrown out from the mills; trees, anything we could drag back to add to our hoard, always operating under the cover of darkness. On the top of the finished pyre sat our 'guy' which had taken many hours to create and as the huge inferno burned brightly the nearby fences would have to be hosed down to prevent them catching fire. The embers of these huge bonfires would continue to simmer for weeks.

2) Chimneys and Fred Dibnah – watching Fred doing his stuff

Due to the revival and interest in our Industrial heritage one of life's real characters was suddenly thrust into the limelight. With the demise and decline of the mills many have been demolished but the mill chimneys required specialist attention. Enter Fred Dibnah who could drop a mill chimney on a sixpence. If you have not read his book do so. In it you will find in detail how he went about the felling of those massive chimneys – he certainly knew his stuff and enjoyed his work. I attended two of his performances and I will not forget how he ran around blowing on a klaxon, his face black and sooty whilst the chimney collapsed, breaking its back as it dropped within twenty feet of the centre target that Fred had set. What a sight and what a talented guy.

3) The legacy of all this barbaric childhood treatment is that I continually open windows. My dear wife of fifty years is rarely warm, but I remind her she is healthier. In my office at work the windows were always open and it was ages before I realised why people didn't hang around in there too long! However I am a great believer that fresh air keeps you alert and makes you healthy. Good air equals good performance.

The Way it Was

Have a good plan, execute it violently, do it today – General MacArthur

When I was a child in the 1930's people said that my dad, Lewis Pellowe, looked like Clark Gable. He had the same hair style as the actor and he sometimes wore a moustache. Around five feet ten inches tall, he was well built but had thin legs which I have unfortunately inherited. He bought his made to measure clothes from Goss's outfitters on Rhodes bank and also from Harold Cohen's, the Jewish tailor at the Market Place in Oldham. Dad liked his clothes. One of his favourites was a Harris Tweed jacket and sometimes he would wear plus fours which were half mast trousers worn with long socks; the type of trousers golfers used to wear although I never knew Dad to play golf except perhaps for once. Overall he dressed very well and was rather the dandy, only let down by the amount of things he would push into his pockets which were always bulging with paraphernalia. He would have fags in there, a cigarette case, a large penknife, a note book, ruler, pens, pencils, handkerchiefs, and, when he had a phase of making his own cigarettes, a tin of tobacco, silk papers and a roller. Although I take after him in so many other ways this odd habit of filling up my pockets is not one of them, probably because I remember how the gravity of his otherwise smart jacket shifted considerably! I have also managed to avoid another of his bad practices, that of leaving his socks on whilst in bed, something which my mother particularly could not stand.

Dad seemed like the scarlet pimpernel at times; he would come and go and didn't appear to have a set routine, the complete opposite of my rigidly organised mother. Because of their different personalities Dad's crazy ways drove my mother wild. He would return home late at night either from working or playing table tennis and, if he did not call at Sam Settle's Fish and Chip Shop on Lee Street, he would get out the frying pan and make what he called 'raw fry'. This consisted of a couple of chopped up potatoes fried in dripping and the smell as they were cooking was really strong. Reaching its zenith upstairs in the bedrooms, Mother would wake up and, realising Dad's absence from the bed, she would go downstairs to find him asleep on the floor, face down, with Whiskers, our black and white cat, purring comfortably on his back.

Another of his irritating habits was bathing at midnight when Dad would fall asleep with a Churchman cigarette in his mouth whilst still in the bath water. I witnessed this practise once when I got up in the night to pee. I threw half a cup of cold water over him in order to waken him up but I really wish I hadn't as he instinctively reached for the pottery soap holder hanging on the side of the bath and chucked it at me. I managed to duck but it hit the white tiled wall and made an incredible amount of noise. Mother leapt out of bed with a speed to be marvelled at whilst I rushed into mine as though forty thousand thieves were after me.

Because Dad was a night owl my mother had a lot of trouble trying to persuade him to get out of bed in the mornings and she would have to yell up the stairs to him. After several of her war cries had managed to rouse him, Dad would eventually wander into the bathroom which had a window that opened over the back door of the house. Being a prankster he couldn't help himself and on more than one occasion the first sucker to walk by the back door and under the bathroom window would get a tumbler full of cold water poured over them. Sometimes it was the milkman or Maude our maid, but other times it was Mother on her way to the wash house. She would storm upstairs, dripping wet, only to find that Dad had locked the bathroom door. Her rage was a sight to behold! Dad was a huge practical joker and my mother's lack of appreciation at his high jinks only encouraged him to add to his repertoire.

After the war when Dad visited London he would sometimes take me with him. Fortunately I was used to his eccentricities and nothing ever surprised me so when we stayed at the Turkish Baths in Russell Square instead of an hotel I felt quite relaxed. Strangers arrived in a constant stream from god knows where and the masseurs were seemingly overwhelmed at times but valiantly carried on all through the night. I didn't get much sleep with about fifteen snoring fellas in the same room but felt very clean as we left at 8.30 a.m. the next morning! Whilst at home

Dad spent a lot of time at the Liberal Club on Rhodes Bank where he was a strong party member; he was also a member of the Builders Federation and he played Table Tennis in the league. In essence he was a very busy restless fellow and he always had to be occupied; we are very alike in that respect. He had lots of friends but unfortunately my mother didn't like some of his 'cronies' as she called them and as a child this always bothered me as it appeared to cause a barrier between them and led to arguments. Rather than argue Dad would stay away from home for a few nights, bedding down in the Edinburgh Hotel at the top of Park Road although this could last for as long as a week depending on the severity of the disagreement. On reflection I suppose he could have been having an affair although as he loved his own company as much as he liked to be with a crowd I do not really think so. I believe it was just his way of handling things; he avoided confrontation at all costs just as I usually do. No, he just wanted his own space as they say these days, a cooling down period maybe.

Following my Grandfather Pellowe's death at the relatively young age of fifty, Dad and his brother, Arthur, ran the family building business between them. Dad was very good at his job and was well respected by his work force. If they were hesitant he would be there to help and, as he was very approachable, I often heard the men asking: 'can you manage a sub Mr Lewis?' Arthur was very different. The opposite of Dad, Arthur was pompous and rather affected; he was strictly nine to five whereas my father would work till all hours. Arthur was a better spokesperson for the company whilst Dad was the motivator and so each kept to their own areas of expertise, the ones in which they were the most successful. This was perhaps just as well as I do not think that they really got on too well together at times.

When in the office Dad would write his notes by hand but as a guide he would use the edge of a ruler for some reason ensuring that all his words were squared off at the bottom. It must have been a habit of his to write on lines as he often utilised the lined notepaper on the back of the Churchman cigarette packet when out on site visits. My 'old man' loved to smoke. He liked to puff away at a Churchman No1, a strong non filter cigarette which he only took out of his mouth when it burnt itself out. He could talk, cough, read, play table tennis, anything, with a cigarette in his mouth; the ash dropped on to his work but rarely did he succumb to removing it. Assuming he may smoke two or three packs of cigarettes a day, the empty packets were always being discarded and then a massive hunt for the missing notes they contained would ensue. Considering Dad's frequent movements in pursuit of his work the hunt could often involve rummaging through several job locations in the various mills and factories; roofs would have to be climbed and quite often most of the workforce of the premises being searched would join in the hunt. On one occasion the missing cigarette packet containing the vital notes was eventually found in the pit of a theatre, the place in front of a stage where musicians gather - it had fallen onto the drums!

My parents, Lewis and Mildred, were not the kind of couple to sit and hold hands at home but they embraced the 1930's ethos of marriage which was to keep up the appearance of love at all times. So, whilst both led rather different kinds of lives they loved each other, albeit with many make or break scenarios. Mum and Dad's relationship was a patchy one which could be compared to a ship at sea, consisting of many ups and downs. Just prior to Dad's untimely death they were having something of a renaissance but they had rather different personalities and Dad needed time alone, spent briefly away from the family. My stoical mother managed to tolerate their time together very well overall.

Lewis and Mildred lived at 307 Windsor Road in Coppice when they were married. In those days Coppice was regarded as one of the places where professional, comfortably off people lived. Shannon's, owners of the foremost grocers in Oldham, lived in a large detached house round the corner from us and there were also solicitors, doctors, accountants, undertakers, dentists and wholesalers. There were excellent local shops nearby and it was also a good central location for the OTS bus route into town although Dad would drive the short distance to his business, Arthur Pellowe and Sons Building Company (APAS), on Chamber Road. The house we lived in was a well built semi detached, one of several on Windsor Road that were built by my dad's company. In fact many of the houses which they constructed are still there today, mostly assembled in Accrington brick which is expensive and long lasting. Our house had three bedrooms and, at the top of a lovely, narrow, twisting stair case, an attic which I occasionally slept in because it was marvellous to lie in bed and gaze at the stars through the large casement window built out from the slope of the roof. The main staircase between the ground and first floor was constructed from gloriously carved solid mahogany. It had shaped spindles and a banister which was excellent to slide down so long as you remembered to stop before hitting the circular topped newel post at the bottom, an eye watering experience if misjudged. Opposite the bottom of the stairs was a small cloak room, telephone kiosk and meter cupboard. During the war there were five of us living in the house and so the cloakroom was always bustling with coats. You would have to fight your way through them to get to the phone which was fortunately not used very often; it was the type of phone you see in old films, like a candlestick with a mouthpiece on the end of a pipe. The dining room was super. My father and the shop joiners panelled it in mahogany and on one side of the chimney breast there was a fine bookcase with glass sliding doors, again built by Dad and his men. Between the lounge and dining room there was a folding panelled partition separating the rooms, another joinery masterpiece. In the lounge was a Royal Venton tiled fireplace from the potteries, very much in vogue at that time. It was impressively large and swirled to the right of the mantle shelf and up into a column. A Baxi under draught fire, when turned to full, seemed easily able to send the fire up the chimney whilst Whiskers, the cat, kept guard on the rug at a safe distance. The kitchen was not large but it managed to hold a solid table and a revolutionary stainless steel double drainer sink, an item which was not at all common when I was a child. There were no work tops in the kitchen; everything was prepared on the kitchen table. On the wall opposite the table there was an alcove housing the Siesta solid fuel stove whilst on the end wall were cupboards with hand grained, ply wood doors, which hid all the pots and pans. The kitchen door opened into a narrow hall where the scullery was set under the stairs. Inside the scullery there was a cupboard with a metal mesh door and all the fresh food was kept in there as it was relatively cool there being no fridges then. The surrounding shelves were stocked with lots of enamel tins of food which had the brand name and a picture painted onto them: Pears Soap; OXO; Heinz 57; Cadbury's biscuits; Jacob's Cream Crackers, are some that I remember. As the stairs declined above your head in the scullery it was necessary to bend lower and lower the further in you went until you were forced to kneel down. Mice liked that place and so did Whiskers.

The houses on our road that had been built by my dad's firm had flushing loos which were ultra modern then; we had one inside the house and one outside in the wash house. Also in the wash house was the washing system which consisted of a galvanised bin shaped thing which held the water and the clothes, a posser which was used to beat the washing with, a ribbed glass scrub board in a wooden frame, a Belfast vitreous sink, and a huge double roller mangle which was a green beast hungry for your fingers. Boiling water was poured into the bin and soap was added as there were no powders then although I do remember the arrival of Persil detergent. The laundry would be added and then it was in and out of the water; soap and elbow grease; wring out, change water, rinse, put through the mangle, steam everywhere, and then hang outside to dry. Traditionally Monday was always wash day, whatever the weather, just as Monday was always eating up day from the weekend's food as every day had its set meal. The house shared the smell of those far off times: dampness in unheated rooms, mothballs in every wardrobe, and San Izal in the downstairs wash areas. All this blended with the brisk smells of furniture polish and Brasso and was only overtaken on fish day, Friday, when the whole lot together smelt terrible!

WASH HOUSE.
High level flush lou. dolly board,.
posser, and tub, mangle green.
washing boiler, belfast sink.

AIR RAID CONCRETE
SHELTER.
small door.

The house was run and managed by my mother, Mildred Ena Pellowe who was very slim, of a wiry build and only about five foot tall. She walked very quickly and gave the impression of a no nonsense kind of woman. If she ever put on any weight this was soon corrected by the observance of a strict liquid diet as she was very self disciplined. My mother's hair was dark brown and well looked after; rollers were used to curl it and hair nets kept the ensuing style in place. I hated to see her in rollers and hairnets and have subsequently had a lifelong abhorrence to them. Welcome hairdryers! During the day, around the house, she wore a patterned, wrap around, cotton apron as did all the women in those days. However when she was going out, or had visitors, my mother was very well dressed in the fashions of the time and would wear make up. If the occasion demanded it then she would look very attractive and dress very smartly indeed.

Mother had two sisters, Joan and Verna. Mildred, my mother, was the eldest; Joan was the middle sister and Verna the youngest. They were very well brought up girls from a good family and I believe their grandfather had been an Oldham Councillor at one time. Mildred didn't always get on with her own mother and so at one time she went to live with her grandfather in his large impressive house in Waterhead. In her teens she attended a boarding school called Lowther College which was situated in Bodelwyddan Castle in North Wales and after her education had been completed she joined the family business which was John Heywood's Decorators, of Bridge Street, Oldham.

John Heywood's was a specialist firm which carried out fine, commercial quality work. They were top class decorators, *par excellence,* and the work in those days required a lot of true skill and craftsmanship in order to carry out such tasks as gold leaf graining and sign writing. These highly skilled procedures were in fact carried out by twin brothers, Ivan and Ian Rogers who were employed by Heywood's at the time and they would have worked on the ornate redecoration of many West End theatres and hotels in London such as The Windmill, The Savoy and The Ritz; all top names. Heavy wallpaper such as flock was the fashion then and that alone required a lot of skill to hang. Murals, stencilling, graining, tons of gold leaf on the decorative plasterwork; the expertise of the staff from John Heywood's Decorators was required across the country. During the time that my mother was a secretary in the firm, before her marriage, the business was run by Oscar Heywood, her father and my beloved grandfather, as John Heywood had passed on. Mother worked in the company office scheduling jobs, booking 'digs' for the travelling staff, keeping accounts, looking after the cat in the workshop whose job it was to catch mice, and generally making a nuisance of herself I heard! Grandfather Oscar was very much a

1.

2.

3.

1. Mum and her sisters with their parents
2. Mum in her yellow Austin 7
3. Dad and me on the sand dunes at St Annes – people said Dad looked like Clark Gable!
4. Viv on her first tricycle
5. Viv on holiday with her Mum – it was always Cleveleys
6. Later on in life Mum got Willie, an African Grey Parrot – 'now there's a nice girl'!
7. Me and Mum with Maude, our maid
8. And here the 'nice girl' is in Mrs Wild's class at Werneth School – front row second from right with a buttoned dress. I am demoted to the front row where I am sitting cross legged on the left.
9. Lovely captured shot. Viv and folks. Rhos, Dad pipe and paper, her with spade and sandals.

4.

5.

6.

7.

9.

8.

hands on boss; he was a stickler for good timekeeping and he was always the first to arrive at work in the morning. Every working day of his married life he put together a rice pudding and placed it in the oven before leaving for work so that it would be ready at lunch time. In his later years he did not retire but would leave the office in the early afternoon and go across the road to the Lyceum for a hand or two of bridge.

Several memories in particular remain with me of my grandfather Oscar. Bound to impress any young lad was the fact that he always had super, brand spanking new cars: Rovers, Daimlers, a Humber Super Snipe, or an Alvis. For his daughter Mildred, my mother, he purchased an Austin Seven in brightest yellow which was very unusual as all cars were black then. Oscar was a very generous man and his gifts were memorable and exciting. In those days of my youth presents were only given at Christmas and birthdays but on those two occasions I could be sure of receiving something wonderful from him. He bought my first pedal car; all the gear necessary for me to become a scout; a series of differently sized bicycles appropriate to my advancing height; and, best of all, a splendid, fully rigged, four foot high, model racing yacht with a solid mahogany hull, a lead keel, steering gear and sails. Together we would take it to Fleetwood where there was a famous large boating lake which boasted the most magnificent models of sail and steam. Another occasion I remember was when Oscar placed a bet on a horse on my behalf. As I recall it was a half a crown on the Derby and the horses name was Dante. Half a crown was two shillings and sixpence or 12.5 pence in today's money and the odds were around 33:1. When Dante won I had never seen so much money before as my grandfather placed four pounds and fifty pence in my hand. What a man! I was still in short trousers! One of his last gifts to me, before he sadly died, was a Raleigh bike with three speed gears and a large, shining head lamp powered by a friction driven dynamo on the front wheel. It had that lovely smell that only a brand new bike has and it was black of course as was everything else on the road in those days. He purchased it from a shop called Fenwick's at Mumps and to receive such a wonderful and expensive present was a huge event. The Raleigh bicycle was my pride and joy and added to my sense of rising confidence especially when I was allowed to ride from Preston, via Lytham St Anne's, to Blackpool tower; I was only about thirteen years old at the time. I have since entered the Manchester to Blackpool charity bicycle ride but it could not compare to that first real bike ride from Preston. Oscar should have written a book on how to be a good grandfather for he was the very best; but, if you adhere to his methods be ready to put your hand in your pocket. Overall the anticipation of a forthcoming present was part of the gift itself and this philosophy was the approach I would use in the distant future when buying for Housing Units – I would only buy when I had the money so there was a degree of excitement whilst waiting for that time. I appreciated my Grandfather's presents very much and still do for all the joyous memories I have of those times.

My mother also adored her father; however as I have already said there were times when she did not get on so well with her mother, nor was she always great friends with her youngest sister, Verna who was later to marry Harold Sanger, a really good architect. Amongst his commissions was the design of Oldham Crematorium which was considered to be revolutionary in its day and in later years my father was cremated there. Mother's other sister, Joan, married Joe Lees who was an accountant for a textile chain, and a good cricketer; Captain at Werneth Cricket Club in fact. Fortunately all three of the Heywood sisters were married to smart chaps who all became great friends and got on very well indeed. In fact I believe it was Joan's husband, Joe, who was responsible for introducing my parents to each other. Both my parents were good dancers and I think that is how they met, dancing, possibly at King Street Stores which I seem to remember them talking about. My mother was very sociable and her friends were mostly well off, middle class women with professional husbands, many of whom owned their own businesses. She was a member of numerous charities and committees such as Oldham Operatic Society, the Royal National Lifeboat Institute (RNLI), the NSPCC, and, when it was formed during the war, the Women's Voluntary Service (WVS), now called the WVRS. She used to stand in the town centre selling little flags for these various organisations, something which she was probably very good at due to her assertive personality. She was also a good bridge player and had a regular four with some of her pals. They all adored the jazz musician and cabaret star Hutch, or Leslie Hutchinson to give him his full name, who was a real lady killer. Periodically he would visit the Empire Theatre and have the ladies eating out of his hand even more than they had before. My mother's taste must have rubbed off onto me as I also like Leslie Hutchinson;

1.

2.

3..

1. What great lifetime friendships my parents had – we holidayed together year after year. This was taken in Saundersfoot, South Wales: Me, Billy H., Bea, her husband Reg in the cardi, Dad, Pat, Pam, Simon, Edna H., Peg, Simon, Mum, Edna P., Norman P., Jack L.

2. They were a game lot: Pam and her Mum, Bea, my mother, Peg, Edna and Dad – fantastic!

3. Early shot of eight of the fabulous 13 Keep Fit Club. Left to right: Elsie, Joan, Edna, Mum, Doris Chadwick, Doris Hibbert, Bea and Peg who very sadly was the first of that band to be called away.

4. The great Keep Fit Club again – 1940-1990

4.

I find his life story fascinating and adore his music, some of which has now been recorded by Rod Stewart.

As I have said, appearances meant a lot in the 1930's, and so, even though I don't think she particularly enjoyed it, my mother would smoke the odd Sobranie which was a small black cigarette in a gold holder. Also, owing to Mother's 'place in society', a throwback to her much respected family, we had a maid, even though our house was not very large. Her name was Maude and she was a Geordie. I think she had moved to Oldham to escape the heavy bombing of the shipyards in Sunderland during the war and she was typically down to earth as were all the other Geordies I met in later life when I was in the Army. Tall, with striking looks, she was kind and a very good friend to me. Due to the fact that we lived in a middle class area there were several maids employed in the houses nearby and again, to keep up appearances, my mother ensured that Maude was dressed similarly in the traditional uniform. Maude stayed with us for about six years after which she returned to the Sunderland area. We were all sad to see her go but it was time for her to meet someone and settle down and she did just that. After Maude left my mother still employed women to help around the house; I rather think she appreciated their attention and company and many of them would remain lifetime friends.

A group of thirteen ladies, including my mother, met up once a week in each others houses for the Keep Fit Club (1). Joan and Verna, Mother's sisters were among them and the group kept up these meetings without fail, every Thursday, from being in their late twenties right up into their eighties. In actual fact although it may have started out as a keep fit session the get together gave way at some time to more of a social evening although the name of the club stuck. No one ever missed the meeting unless they were ill, what an incredible way to share friendship, they stayed together until death. When Joan died, aged about eighty, it upset Mother very much as they had been very close and she would continually say, 'I miss her so much' for Joan was a star, full of life and humour. These thirteen women had a truly good and lasting friendship but my mother outlived them all. She did so much for them as one by one they lost their husbands or became ill, 'Send for Mick' was the call in such circumstances as her friends knew they could depend on her; 'Mick' was the nickname given to her by my mother's friends. Yes Mother was a toughie who could rise to any occasion; she willingly nursed dying people and was an example of power and strength when my dad died from cancer. She believed a spade was a spade and that there was a rule book for life. Sex was a taboo word and was never mentioned by her during my childhood, or indeed in my adult life. In fact with my mother around you could easily believe you would make a baby if you just kissed someone.

My mother lived until she was ninety nine. Now that is not a bad innings particularly as she often professed to have wanted to be shot at sixty! So that was a lot of years to live, a lifetime of stories, guidance and advice. Almost every single Sunday for forty years Mother, or 'Gran' as she became known after the birth of her first grandchild, was invited to lunch. Never one to hold back on her opinions and advice we had good Sundays and a few not so good Sundays. Gran would also join us on some of our annual holidays with many trips to Pendorlan, a family house we hired at Abersoch and later to our flat and then the house that we owned in Dartmouth. These could be difficult times as my mother could be a bit too advisory and direct to the point on occasions but overall we enjoyed an excellent relationship.

Ivor Novello, and that age of lush, romantic music is what Mother loved most of all and 'when a nightingale sang in Berkeley Square' she was there. In fact she was so perky in her later years that we did begin to wonder if she would ever fall off her perch but eventually, in March 2004, she succumbed and we lost her. She was a woman of the old school, a great person and she lived a long and mostly happy life (2).

The Way it Was: Notes

1)   Mum's Keep Fit Club consisted of thirteen ladies at its outset: Doris Hibbert, Edna Hoyland, Joan Lees (Mother's sister), Verna Sanger (also Mother's sister), Mary Eglin, Elsie Meller, Bea Cotterill, Peg Winfield (Lee), Doris Chadwick, Marion Chadwick, Edna Platt, and Dorothy Stranach.

2)   I'm sure Mum would enjoy this story. When she did eventually move on after her ninety nine years the funeral service was taken by Neil Chappal, friend and minister at Greenacres Church, before moving 'Gran' to the crematorium with just the male members of the family which had been her wish. Her ashes were to be buried beneath a tree in the Dovestones 'Life for Life' plantation so several days after the cremation service I got a phone call from Barlow's the undertaker's asking me to collect them. Strangely I felt a little unsure, a feeling that is rather hard to explain made me dither and it was a couple of days before I plucked up the enthusiasm to go to their office wondering what to expect. 'Good morning Mr P,' says a pleasant, gentle lady as she reaches down underneath the counter and places a decorative plastic urn in front of me. This really stopped me in my tracks and for a moment I was speechless but the bottom line was Mum was in there, in the plastic urn! She was placed inside a very discreetly coloured, quality carrier bag and as I mumbled my thanks whilst signing something or other I made my escape. When I reached my car I gently placed my mother's remains behind the driving seat and there she remained because for some reason I couldn't bring myself to display the urn in the house. So it was that my mother travelled around in the car with me until the tree at Dovestones had been planted. On my travels one day I happened to come across Graham Salter whose shoe shop in Oldham had supplied all my mother's shoes. Graham told me how sorry he was to hear of Mum's death and apologised as he hadn't been able to attend the funeral and see her off as he had been otherwise engaged at the time. As I began to thank him I couldn't resist adding: 'No problem Graham, in fact she's here so you can say goodbye now,' and I pulled the carrier bag from out of the car. The poor fellow was absolutely bowled over; he was stuttering and mumbling in disbelief whilst going very red in the face; a very sincere man he was genuinely shocked but my mother would have really loved that little episode! Actually I got quite used to driving round with her for company but eventually I get a call from Norman Armstrong Kirsch who manages the 'Life for Life' charity and its many tree

plantations. Norman tells me that the tree has been planted and gives me its location so in due course I quietly scatter the contents of the urn around 'Mum's' tree and return to my now empty car. On a later visit to the plot I found that the tree had been broken down and used as firewood by some campers so Norman planted a substitute tree in a more secure area of the compound and I carefully transferred the soil containing the ashes from the original site. However I had an idea and so this time I saved half of it so that it could be scattered in Dartmouth, our second home, in the Garden of Remembrance at St Petrox Church which had always been a favourite place of Mum's. Shortly afterwards Viv and I were loading the car for a trip to Dartmouth when she noticed the neatly packed bag of soil in the back of the car. 'What on earth is that and why is it there?' she asked, 'Oh, just some of Gran's ashes' I replied, 'I'm taking her to Dartmouth,' and Viv gives me the look that says: 'I give up,' a look she has perfected over fifty years of marriage to me! Now when I visit the two locations of Gran's ashes, which are three hundred miles apart, I always smile and as the old girl always liked to have her presence felt she is still achieving her ambition. I hope no one finds this unsettling but in life Gran rather put herself about at times but wouldn't quite have banked on this trip. She was, I assure you, a good sport with a sincere sense of humour.

The Cornish Connection

The only way to be sure of catching a train is to miss the one before it –
G K Chesterton

Our family name of Pellowe hails from Falmouth, the historic packet ship port and one of the leading resorts in Cornwall with a Riviera climate. How the Pellowe's came to settle in Oldham is rather a mystery to which I do not, unfortunately, have the full answer. It could be that my grandfather, Nicholas Arthur Pellowe, found it hard to get work in the shipyards at Falmouth where he worked as a shipwright, but whatever the reason he moved to Oldham with his wife, Margaretta, lock stock and barrel. Why Oldham and not somewhere else? Again I don't know. Maybe he had friends or contacts in the area but, anyway it was here that he settled on Plymouth Street in the St Paul's area. Once established in the north my grandfather must have worked very hard because he soon owned his own successful joinery and building business whilst still finding time to be a professional football referee. Later on my father and his brother, Arthur, worked alongside Grandfather Nicholas in the family business and therefore I was born in Oldham and am Lancashire born and bred. However I have always had a great affinity for Cornwall, home of my paternal ancestors, and, since my childhood, I have been a frequent visitor.

You are getting near the end of England down there, where the River Fal waters lead to Carrick Roads and the cathedral city of Truro. Falmouth is reputed to have the third deepest natural harbour in the world and, as you enter its waters from the sea you pass St Anthony's lighthouse whose duty it is to signal eternally to the shipping heading out, or returning from, the Atlantic passage. You will also pass by the Black Rock, where seals linger and doze in the sun at low tide. Guarding the entrance to Carrick Roads is Falmouth, my ancestral home, and, to the south of Falmouth, is the Helford River which has many secretive creeks and inlets and an atmosphere heavy with the promise of Cornish mystery.

It was in these rivers, in earlier centuries, that smugglers plied their cargo from across the channel. How fantastic to imagine the schooners and sloops navigating these creeks, sails billowing; there were no engines then! As I rowed and drifted in these sunny waters as a child on holiday from grey, old Oldham, it didn't take much imagination to conjure up the Cornish night time; a night with no moon to reflect in the creeks; a night when smugglers and wreckers were abroad; a night when cutters and other small craft would silently glide in under the cover of darkness to unload barrels of illegal brandy, continental wines and lace. Daphne du Maurier captured the magic and adventure of the bygone days of this coast in her novels, *Jamaica Inn* and *Frenchman's Creek* and the scenes of smuggling and wrecking contained within them are just as I had imagined them as a child. Apart from our Cornish connections, the main reason for my frequent childhood excursions to the south west was initially to visit my grandmother, Margaretta, who had returned to her home town of Falmouth following the death of my grandfather around 1923. We spent many of our family summer holidays visiting Grandma Pellowe and, in addition and when time allowed, Dad and I would go to visit her over a weekend. My mother never joined us on these weekend visits and I think there are a few possibilities why this may have been so. One irritating and apparently genetic trait of my father's was his erratic timekeeping. Dad lived on the edge of time and it drove my mother wild; he was always doing something else when it was time to go somewhere and he would say 'two minutes Mick' as she waited, her patience growing thin. Both myself and my son, Tim, are unfortunately the same; maybe it's the adrenalin rush of 'will we, can we, make it?' that appeals to us. However it has never been received well by the girls in the family and consequently our trips seldom get off to a good start!

Apart from Dad's terrible timekeeping, the other reason for my mother staying at home, I believe, is that she couldn't have stood the pace. What Dad and I managed to cram into those forty eight hour visits was incredible and obviously frenetic. It would not, overall, have improved my parent's relationship; in fact their marriage probably benefited from them having time away from each other. Possibly for Dad it was some different Cornish company that was the attraction for he had his routine when we were in Falmouth and he always used to visit old friends, one of these being a sister at the hospital which was right opposite to my grandmother's house.

Although times and details are a little hazy now after all these years I remember that many of our visits to Falmouth would be made by rail. On the Friday afternoon preceding one of our flying weekend visits, I would leave school and walk to Dad's office on Chamber Road from where we would be taken to London Road Station in Manchester, now called Piccadilly Station. From there we would embark on the LMS (London Midland Scottish) steam train service to Euston and, upon arrival in London, we would have to transfer to Paddington Station in order to catch the GWR (Great Western Railway), the overnight sleeper to Cornwall. Obviously in order to make our connections time keeping was of great importance, and, as I mentioned previously, that was Dad's greatest weakness and he seemingly thrived on the excitement of rushing around. So, although it wasn't Dad's fault, we would often be held up *en route* from Manchester and would then arrive in London with only minutes to spare for the dash from station to station in order to catch the train to Penzance. On several occasions it was a sheer miracle that we made the connection much to Dad's delight. We only had around forty minutes to get to Paddington from Euston and, if in addition to the Manchester-London train being late, the cab was held up in traffic, we had a massive problem. As we hurled ourselves into a taxi Dad would give the cabbie a generous tip thus ensuring a mad journey where the cabbie would tear through side streets and even mount the pavements on occasion. As we approached our destination Dad would be passing the fare to the still driving cabbie in order to save precious seconds and as the cab screeched to a halt at Paddington we would leap from the cab and sprint to the usual departure platform for Penzance praying that the station master hadn't changed things around as we had no time to check. Often, as we approached the train, breathless and sweaty, we would find that all the carriage doors were already shut and the guard would be at the end of the train with his green flag ready to set the train in motion. On a couple of occasions the train was actually moving as we boarded and one of our greatest performances was when we dived into the Guards van of the rapidly retreating train as the guard held the door open for us. Dad lost his trilby in the slipstream on that occasion but didn't seem to care as the kindly guard handed us a mug of tea each in congratulation. As we sip our tea with the guard, Dad winks at me and laughs, 'close shave, Will? and peacefully lights a Churchman as if nothing had happened. Dad used to call me 'Will' more often than he called me John and, to this day, I don't know why, I wish I had asked him.

Leaving the guard to his duties we work our way down the train to the First Class Sleeper Carriage to be met by the steward who was anxiously on the lookout for his two missing passengers. 'Tight timing this time sir,' he says, shaking his head in despair. He knows us of old as he has hosted this same nightly train service for ever. He is always immaculately turned out: black trousers, waistcoat, pill box hat and bow tie; a white shirt sporting cuff links and sparkling white gloves. 'Compartment number six tonight, sir,' he would say, as he led us to our quarters. Inside the compartment the woodwork is mahogany and the fittings are of chrome and brass. The light fittings are gorgeous, art nouveau or tiffany style, and their lights are welcoming and warming, giving off an amber glow. There are two generous bunks with starched sheets and pillow cases and luxury blankets emblazoned with the GWR logo. We soon get settled in as the train, rhythmically and romantically carries us on her nightly journey down to the West Country. Just before retiring there is a tap on the door and the steward gently places a silver tray on the table on which are set cocoa and biscuits: 'We will be arriving in Truro at 7 a.m. as usual sir,' he would say, often adding a weather forecast, 'it will be bright but blustery tomorrow, with unusually warm weather for this time of year.' Dad would always have the bottom bunk and I would lie above him, dreaming of Cornwall as the train rattled along. I always knew when Dad had finished reading his book and fallen asleep because his snoring would wake me up. Strangely though, it was very reassuring as it seemed to be in rhythm with the chuffing of the steam train, a steady heartbeat of comfort.

At six o'clock next morning there would be another tap on the door and the same steward, still immaculately attired, would bring our breakfast on another shiny, silver tray containing tea, toast and preserves. 'Blind, Sir?' he would query. 'Thank you steward,' my Dad would reply, indicating that yes indeed we did wish for the blind to be opened. Of course we did, for there, where there had been only darkness the night before, would be the wonderful sight of the River Exe estuary, and then the Devonshire town of Dawlish appearing out of the mist. Even now I can remember the sights from the train window and the feeling of excitement at the new day and the fresh scene. As I stare out at the calm estuary I can see early morning hunters: waders, herons and cormorants explore the incoming tide looking for their breakfast which will be served to them on silver sand rather than a silver tray. Sometimes the view outside the compartment window is not at all calm; there may be a gale blowing with the sea at high tide resulting in waves and spray breaking onto our jiggering train. As the sun rises the estuary is tipped by a distant golden skyline far away across the mud, and the lovely scene is reflected back through the train window.

As we look at the breathtaking view and consume our breakfast, the train clatters on towards Newton Abbot and eventually we cross the River Tamar from Devon into Cornwall via the Royal Albert Bridge at Saltash. As I look down at this wonderful bridge, built by Isambard Kingdom Brunel, I wonder and admire at this man, the fantastic Victorian engineer. He was not only famous for his feats of engineering but also as one of the main contributors to the creation of the Great Western Railway (GWR) on which we are travelling. I was, and still am, a great fan of Brunel and others like him; clever, talented men who have transformed people's lives in practical ways. Onwards from Brunel's bridge and we eventually arrive in Truro where we vacate our sanctuary of blissful travel before boarding the local train to Falmouth. The kindly steward gently places our bag on the platform, salutes, and shakes hands as Dad places a generous gratuity in his sparkling white, gloved hand. These trips, the steam train, and the welcoming morning view formed a magical time for me; a time which will always stay with me, the best of British journeys.

Grandma Pellowe looked forward to our visits, infrequent and hurried as they were. Her house was detached and pebble dashed and had a splendid garden in which she spent all her time. She would often be found moving in and out of the large, shingled, planked shed which always had a special aroma, redolent of grass cuttings, fertilisers, oil and creosote. Spiders webs, old and new were everywhere inside the shed and were never removed. It seemed to me, as a child, that these intricate webs held the shed together. The garden itself was overwhelmingly full of roses and their delicious scents, fragrances and colours, as Grandma Pellowe was a specialist in rose growing. From the bottom of her garden my Grandma could see the steam of our train heralding our arrival as it travelled through the valley below. Consequently we would always find a second breakfast waiting for us when we appeared at her house and, whilst eating, Dad would plan his day. He always seemed to have a lot of calls to make and a tight schedule to keep which left me free to do as I wished. He would drop me off at

Falmouth Town Quay before going about his business and I would meet up with my friend, the old peg legged, be-whiskered, salty sea dog whose name I am unable to remember, if indeed I ever knew it. He looked like Long John Silver with his crutch and he always had a small pipe in his mouth which gave off the wonderful smell of St Bruno tobacco. He sported the navy blue apparel of an ex seaman, his hair and beard were grey and he had a weather beaten face topped by his peaked, oil stained cap which was surely of ancient origin. He was a man of few words but I could just catch a glimpse of his tobacco stained teeth as he muttered: 'aw-right, n' aree? Ee be goin fur a row then 'e boy?' He sat on his capstan plying his wares which were in the form of two clinker built rowing boats, the traditional Cornish craft. The only way to tell the boats apart was by their size as they were both of an indiscernible colour although I often fancied that they may once have been painted white. I know them both well and I know their price: a shilling for half a day, two bob for the day. I usually opted for the smaller of the two boats as it was easier for a youngster to pull an eight footer rather than a twelve and in those days outboard engines were virtually undiscovered. So, as soon as Dad dropped me off I would rush down to the quay to see if the smaller of the two boats was available.

There was no messing about with life jackets and insurance forms in those days but fortunately I was already a reasonable swimmer and rowing around the harbour was sheer bliss, even more so because I was alone, free, and in charge of things. As I rowed around I passed warehouses balanced precariously on the harbour side, their foundations appearing to be rooted in the water. There were passages between the old buildings leading invitingly to who knows where? There were archways and doorways above which the carved and painted figureheads, salvaged from old sailing ships, stared longingly across the harbour and out to sea. The stone steps which frequented the harbour sides were solid and inset with heavy iron rings to provide secure moorings for the boats whilst I was surrounded by air fragrant with the smell of wooden barrels, tar and tallow, all mixed in with the salty sea tang.

It was here in the Town Quay in Falmouth that I learnt to love the water and anything to do with boats, for the harbour was a good place to learn the trade. I found that I soon began to know the tides and that it was better to move with the sea than against it. I began to be more adventurous and would pull out to the harbour entrance touching the sides of 20,000 ton BP tankers, and rowing on past the ocean tug *Turmoil* which looked enormous to me in my tiny rowing boat. *Turmoil* was always at her station, anchored and awaiting a call from a ship in distress, always with one eye on the salvage the tug masters may claim if things went wrong. Further out I would row over to St Mawes where the River Fal heads for Malpas at the river head before Truro, passing through King Harry passage. Moored opposite Falmouth off Flushing, was a magnificent racing yacht which belonged to Sir Thomas Lipton of Lipton's tea fame, who raced for England in the America Cup series. Dad was very interested in the story of his life and would tell me all about him. Inspired, I would get alongside and touch and admire the yacht which was called *Shamrock* and long for one of my own. It is therefore to Lipton that I owe my craving to sail; he was a great influence on yachting in his time and he was certainly a very interesting and fascinating character.

Although the trains had served us well my father soon got out his car once the war restrictions were lifted. Out of the garage, after six years of retirement, came our Morris 10 who had been jacked up on blocks to prevent her tyres from rotting and to relieve the springs from having to bear her weight. After she had been tidied up and serviced, Dad planned our road trip to Falmouth; he was really looking forward to this, the first long trip in our car since before the war. His excitement, however, was allied to apprehension, with good reason too as it turned out because the first trip was to be more of a nightmare than a pleasure. We left Oldham happily enough but, after travelling forty miles or so to Holmes Chapel, smoke began to trickle from under the dashboard. As if this wasn't bad enough, we also had one puncture after another. So much for jacking the Morris up off the floor during all those war years to protect her tyres! I'm not sure how, but we managed to make it to Taunton before the back axle broke and we had no choice but to stop and wait a full day for a replacement. What should have been a twelve hour trip ended up taking almost three days! When we did eventually get to Falmouth, Dad visited his good friends at Pollards Garage where Mr Pellowe, and Mr Pollard, did a quick deal, probably involving some petrol coupons, and the Morris was dumped for an Austin 12. Incidentally the Pollard's daughter, Elizabeth, was in my sights, albeit briefly, when I later visited Cornwall as a young man.

So, other than that setback on our first journey after the war, we would almost always motor down to Cornwall thereafter, usually without any further major mechanical failure! Our route would take us mostly down the A38 and through the industrial midlands: Newcastle under Lyme; Wolverhampton; Kidderminster, the home of real carpets; then on to Worcester; Tewkesbury and Gloucester; under the Clifton suspension bridge at Bristol and onwards to Bridgewater. Taunton and Exeter flew by and then it was Oakhampton where we would pick up a fish and chip supper. Refreshed and replenished we would drive on to Launceston and then through the wilds of Bodmin Moor; passing the infamous Jamaica Inn at Bolventor. It was usually at this darkest point of the journey I would realise that for the last hour we had seen no cars or lights apart from the eerie reflection of the eyes of the moorland ponies. Gradually we would pass through Indian Queens, carry on to Truro and finally drive up Dracaena Avenue into Falmouth stopping at the Dracaena Hotel. We could no longer stay with Grandma Pellowe who had sadly died at the end of the war but, as fortune would have it, the owner of the Dracaena Hotel, Daisy Boustow, was a distant relative of Dad's. There were not many places that would have accommodated us so readily at 2 a.m., this being the time of arrival if we came down the A30 on schedule, but whatever the time, Daisy would have a full English breakfast ready for us and she would provide it all over again when we rose from our beds at 8.30 a.m. After two hearty breakfasts within six hours, Dad and I would leave the car at Pollards Garage to have it checked over whilst we took a walk through Kimberley Park. After admiring the huge goldfish in the pond we would then proceed down on to the Moor in Falmouth, which was the name given to the town centre. We thrived on being back on Cornish soil. Later I would visit my peg legged friend at the Town Quay and row round the harbour whilst Dad would scrutinise the book shops and probably buy the latest Daphne du Maurier novel. He would also make his visits to relatives and friends, including, no doubt, the nursing sister! I would have to be back at the quay for 2.30 p.m. although it was not always easy to be on time as, edging thirteen, I found it very hard to row against a strong running spring tide and there was, of course, my inherited trait of bad timekeeping. When I did eventually meet Dad we would go to collect the car which had been checked over and given a clean bill of health, and we would set off to our next port of call.

This next stop would be at Treal Farm in Ruan Minor near Helston. John Johns, another distant relative of Dad's who may have been a second cousin, was a farmer there. He was a bachelor but he lived with his dear and rather old aunt, Alicia Boustow, who looked after him. Treal was reached via a narrow lane just off the road between Ruan Minor and Kennack Sands. The lane was about a quarter of a mile long and just before reaching the farm there was a ford which you had to pass through. If it had been raining heavily the water would be running fast and high and a couple of times the spark plugs in the car got a soaking causing the engine to cough and splutter as it made its way out. At the farm there was no electricity or running water, only a cast iron pump outside the back door. The toilet was a four foot square mobile shed with a wooden seat and no sewer; hence a hole was dug in the orchard for the shed to sit on top of. Once full, the hole was filled in, the shed moved, and the whole process repeated again. To prevent us having to go out scouting round the orchard for the mobile shed in the middle of the night, we had potties under the bed. In the morning the potties would have to be carefully carried downstairs to be ceremoniously deposited in a bucket, which was then taken to the latest orchard location. As you can imagine everything grew well in that orchard! The walls of the farmhouse were uneven and lime washed, the floorboards were dusty and creaking; there were spider's webs and a prevailing smell of the farmyard, but what a wonderfully warm and welcoming house Treal was. The heating came from a range in the kitchen although during the evening a fire was also lit in the sitting room which contained a hand pumped organ. John Johns would play a tune for us on this dated instrument whilst he puffed away at one of Dad's Will's Whiff cigars, his work cap still on his head. He usually chose hymns such as *Abide with Me,* or simple country tunes like *The Floral Dance* and when the organ ran out of wind it would moan its way through the decibels until it gradually came to a halt. Later, as I lay in my bed I would study the surprisingly comfortable surroundings. The tiny window panes of my bedroom window, and indeed the rest of the farmhouse, were held within wooden frames and to open them you just pushed one side across the other. Rickety and draughty yes, but I was never cold. The smallness of the windows made the whole house quite dark but this helped to keep it cool in summer and cosy in winter as the oil lamps were lit early and gave off their warm and friendly glow.

Hospitality at Treal was abundantly simple and benevolent; this rural hospitality had its origins in tradition as did the daily routine of the farm and when we arrived on one of our flying visits late on a Saturday afternoon, we were always made very welcome. John's Aunt Alicia seemed very old to me as a child. She always wore the same drab, old working clothes which were common on the farms and grey seemed to be the dominant colour. Even her hair, which was always tied up in a bun, was grey, and she never wore make up; I can't imagine she ever owned any! She probably only ever left the farm three or four times a year and even then it would only be to visit Helston on market day. Her whole life revolved around looking after John and helping him to keep the farm going. She was a very quiet, hard working, softly spoken, gentle soul and I have very fond memories of this lovely woman. After tea and a gossip John would take Dad and me down to the stream at the bottom of the field to fish for trout or eels. No fishing tackle was required, only a sack. As the evening settles John quietly leans over the water with his sleeve rolled up and feels very gently, with his hand, for any trout hiding under the bank. Finding none there he very slowly moves his hand up against the flow of the water and as soon as he makes contact with a fish he tenderly strokes its belly, slowly moving his fingers up to the gills, an action that makes the fish semi comatose and easy to lift out of the water. Having caught four or five trout John then turns his hand to eels. He puts two sticks across the mouth of the sack to hold it open, and places it into the water against the flow. Eels lie on the bottom of the stream so we gently poke through the weed and magically an eel slithers out of its hiding place and into the awaiting sack. John makes it look so easy that Dad has a go with no success and nor do I at first. After the fishing, around 9 p.m., Dad and John would drive or walk the mile or so to the fishing village of Cadgwith to have a drink with the fishermen. This was a great occasion for John who rarely left the farm and even then travelled no further than Helston. Whilst drinking with the fishermen Dad would organise a further treat for John by arranging a trip for Sunday morning on one of their boats. One such Sunday we found ourselves in a long pulling boat similar to the racing gigs which are very popular today. It was handled by four oarsmen and there was still plenty of room for the three of us as well. Chattering and laughing we rowed out from Cadgwith which boasts two coves, one for launching the fishing boats and one suitable for swimming. Between the two is the rocky headland called the Todden and it is just off this landmark, jutting out of the clear, calm water, that we spot the sharks' fin heading straight for the boat! The crew reassures us that it is only a harmless Basking shark but it is about sixteen to twenty foot in length, not much smaller than our boat! As it swims alongside us the beast begins to scratch its back on the hull, rocking the boat from side to side whilst its massive gaping mouth, some two foot in width, is only inches away from us. Upon our return to Cadgwith, Dad, John and I got out of the boat rather weak kneed; we were exhilarated but also quite chastened by the experience and to this day I have not forgotten being so young and how it felt to look into that gaping mouth which belonged to a creature almost as big as the boat we were sheltered by.

We return to Treal for a sound Sunday lunch which is a wonderful meal cooked on the wood burning range set in an alcove in the kitchen. As we tuck in we are watched closely by an audience of cats and hens who are allowed to wander freely in and out of the house. The food, although simple, was very good. Aunt Alicia would serve ham and goose, which had been cooked together, followed by fruit pie with clotted cream and all the ingredients of those tasty meals were either reared or grown on the farm. Full of good food and warm hospitality, Dad and I would regretfully clamber back into the car, around 2 p.m., and set off on the return journey to the north which would take about twelve hours. No matter how long and arduous the travelling had been we would always be looking forward to doing it all again in a few months time and I challenge anyone to fit more into sixty hours than we did on those trips.

When I was a bit older, in my early teens, I was left at Treal in the summer to enjoy some of the six week break from school. Treal was primarily a dairy farm although crops were also grown, and during my time there I assisted John with his work. I helped to hand milk the herd of thirty Friesian cows every morning and evening; I helped with the hay making and the heaving of the huge milk churns full of warm, fresh milk; and I was allowed to drive the small Ferguson tractor which was fortunately only a fraction of the size of today's monsters.

Apart from the dairy herd there were many other animals at the farm. There were several dogs; pigs who always seemed to have lots of piglets; a couple of large cart horses; some hissing geese; chickens who laid their eggs all over the place; and cats. These cats wandered around the farmyard as if they owned it. They came in all shapes, sizes and colours and some of them were quite wild. Their primary job was to catch the many rats which were abundant in the barn and yards, but sometimes John and I, together with the farm dogs, would help the cats by carrying out a bit of rat bashing.

When not working with John on the farm I was enjoying an existence like that experienced by Ratty, Mole and Badger in *The Wind in the Willows,* living and swimming on the riverbank. I would stand on Cadgwith beach begging a boat ride from the fishermen or I would fish with my hands as John had taught me. I also spent a lot of time collecting bird's eggs, an activity that ensured my climbing skills rapidly improved after enduring several falls from very large trees whilst in pursuit of the ultimate egg to add to my collection. I walked and ran everywhere all day long, out in the fresh air, until eventually I would fall into my dusty, comfortable bed at night, after removing a stray cat or two who had ventured in through the open window. As I blew out my oil lamp I would hear the owls outside calling to each other and it would only take about thirty seconds for me to fall soundly asleep. They say money can't buy everything and the fact is that all of this enjoyment was absolutely free; I never spent a penny except for the odd ice cream and the bus fare to Helston and these were some of the best days of my life.

The town of Helston held its weekly market on a Friday and I would travel there on the single decker Bedford buses of Western National which provided a daily service at morning and teatime. With a splendid livery of green and white, these round roofed vehicles were the main form of transport for the farming community in the late 1940's. I would board the bus at Treal crossroads and at each of the following designated collection points, which were usually at the top of a lane leading to a farm, we would come to a stop and David, the driver, would open the door and step outside to greet his passenger. 'Morn m'dear, howr' ze then?' As the country woman passed over her boxes she would reply: 'I be fine, I be, David. I have 'em chickens and they geese for 'e my son;' and so the two boxes of livestock would go into the boot and this scene would be replayed at each pick up. Once the boot was full any further packages would be piled up in the aisle whilst on the top of the bus there was a roof rack for items of furniture such as chairs, small tables and bedsteads, together with a variety of pots and pans. It took ages to get to Helston and even longer to load for the return journey. This rural bus service provided the farmers with a link to the outside world, and the driver, as well as being a carrier, porter and delivery man, was also the fount of all news and gossip, a human local newspaper. The country folk would spend their time in Helston meeting up with friends and family, transacting business, and buying and selling their produce and other necessary goods. When all business had been completed the farmers, their wives and workers would often take ale in the pub in readiness for the return trip when once again the bus is piled up with boxes of all kinds together with a small pig in a sack and a goose trussed up with only his long neck sticking out. The aisle is full of boxes from which a great variety of noises and scratches emanate whilst the pig is making a hell of a row; every seat is taken and the air is thick with the smells of pipe bacca, alcohol, the tang of cheeses, the warm, yeasty scent of fresh bread, and the earthy aroma of freshly dug vegetables. Amidst the smells, the crowds and the noise I am lost but the Cornish babble diminishes slightly every time David patiently stops and extracts people and their possessions. As they meet up with the fresh air upon disembarking from the bus some of the more inebriated folk fall over but everyone is happy. Finally at Ruan Minor crossroads I am one of the last to get off before this wonderful service continues on its way up the hill to Kennack Sands from where it will then travel onwards and over the downs to Falmouth.

John Johns used to always say he could never have a holiday: 'who would milk the cows?' In fact he never did have a proper holiday although he once went to Falmouth some fifteen miles away, the longest journey of his life! In that part of Cornwall, and indeed in many rural areas in those far off days, there were many people like John and Aunt Alicia, who lived in one place all their lives and were more like fixtures and fittings than individuals; in fact the countryside was built with such people. For John, going to Cadgwith for a drink in the fisherman's pub and boating with us on a Sunday morning were seriously big events in his life. It wasn't like today where we all rush around here there and everywhere and take for granted the fact that we can travel anywhere with relative ease. Another big difference between John's life and that of today is the money factor. It is hard to imagine now, but for John and the other country people money mattered only in as much as it was needed to run the farm; 'nowt' was spent elsewhere, frugal living made for happiness and contentment it seemed. John and Aunt Alicia were not financially well off but were hard working, happy and contented and had everything they needed. But everything comes to an end. Aunt Alicia slowly went to sleep at Treal. John Johns, the bachelor farmer with no other close family, eventually also passed on and that was the end of that. It is sad to feel that in just forty years the farming history of Treal, which had lasted for many, many decades, has disappeared but I feel very lucky to have been a part of that time. Now the fields do not yield crops as they used to, a bridge has been built over the ford and Treal farmhouse has been converted into a holiday lets. On a recent visit the only thing leftover from my childhood that I could see was the old cast iron pump that used to provide us with water.

1.

3..

4.

5.

6.

1.The Lane leading to Treal Farm – sadly the field no longer yields crops.

2.Treal Farm today – the only thing remaining from my childhood days is the water pump! A way of life that had lasted for about three hundred years has disappeared in my lifetime.

3.Cadwith Cove and the Todden

4. Sharkie the ex fisherman

5. Gig racing night – most of the coastal villages and ports compete.

6.The Lizard is famous for its pasties as well as being the most southern tip of Britain! 'Ann's Pasty Shop. Proper pasties boy!'

Treal Farm Today

Nowadays you see a converted building with running water, electricity, inside toilets, manicured gardens, converted outbuildings, stoned pathways, 4x4 and other assorted vehicles parked outside; security lights too, no doubt. Ugh!

Grandma Pellowe's House Today

Grandma Pellowe's house is still there on Kimberley Park Road opposite the hospital but it has now been split into two and the garden has given way to a parking area. There is a housing estate to the rear of the property which has consumed the farm that she used to walk to for milk.

Falmouth Town Quay And Harbour Today

I have often returned to explore the waters where I rowed as a boy, but the harbour has changed a lot and the new marinas stretch out their tentacles of berths and pontoons. With the easy availability and use of fibre glass there are now boats galore down there and as most of these craft have engines hanging over the bow there is rarely a need for the use of oars.

The Cornish Dream

.... is still alive. For the past few years I have sailed my twenty five foot yacht, One Day, from Dartmouth down the south west coast aiming for the Helford River and set to explore the creeks of the Carrick Roads. Then it's on to Malpas and the head of the river which is as far as you can go short of Truro. We also visit the harbours of Fowey, Mevagissey, Polperro, Falmouth and Helford, then sail on to the top of the Tamar and our own River Dart, nosing around the numerous smugglers creeks along the way where we sketch and paint some of Britain's loveliest coastline. However the county once known world wide for the supply of tin is no more. Derelict mine workings with their tall chimneys are being taken over by the advancing undergrowth, their neglected shafts leaking and damp beneath the ground. Nevertheless if you are quick and look hard enough you can still find the 'old' Cornwall.

On a visit there in July 2010 I came across an old salt in Cadgwith. His name was Sharkie and he had been a fisherman in the village when I used to visit as a boy. He was now eighty five years old and was still in the same cottage (which must have appreciated in value thousand fold!) overlooking the cove where he had lived all his life. He told me that in the old days the boats went out three times a day to fish whereas now many only launched once a day. He also muttered that 'crabbin' ain't proper fishin', as this is the main thing the boats go out for today, sending their resulting catch over to France. Sharkie started work aged fourteen when there were twenty four full time boats; today there are less than ten, and in his day each one had to be physically pushed down to the sea on rollers whereas now they take the easy option and use a tractor. To bring the boats back up to the beach an electric winch is used although this used to be a hand driven thing. It was a hard life and Sharkie had been a fisherman for fifty five years, which, based on three launches a day is over 20,000 trips up and down the beach often in terrible weather. He knew John Johns and Treal Farm and profoundly said: 'there be no animals in them fields no more.' Sadly he is quite right.

Great Grandparents

My grandfather, Nicholas Pellowe, died young at the age of fifty one but I have no idea how or from what he died. This has made me realise that it is helpful to leave a record of your own knowledge of family and friends before being taken by the great reaper. My father, Lewis, was also to die young, at the age of fifty two and once again we are left only with memories and many unanswered questions that we didn't think to ask when he was still with us, probably feeling safe in the knowledge that we had all the time in the world to ask him. Not so I am afraid.

Margaretta Pellowe returned to Falmouth after Grandfather's death where we understand she was happier than she had been in Oldham. Not hard to believe! Arthur and Lewis, her remaining two children (two had not survived much past a year: Lillian fourteen months and Eric thirteen months), carried on with their father's business and they were successful, but again, there is no record of how their success was achieved. Arthur Pellowe and Sons, or APAS, as it became known, employed qualified men and apprentices of all trades.

The Wonderful Age Of Steam

The 1930's and 40's was the age of true train spotters who would happily stand on the end of a platform in pouring rain, amidst clouds of steam, whilst taking numbers and ticking shunters off their lists. What they really wanted to see were the real 'namers', the dinosaurs of the days of steam such as the Flying Scotsman (Kings Cross – Edinburgh), the Royal Scot (Euston to Glasgow), and the Mallard which was the fastest steam locomotive in the world travelling at 126 mph. Trains were run by companies with enigmatic initials for a name - LMS was London Midland Scottish, whilst LNER was the London North Eastern Railway. GWR was the Great Western Railway on which we travelled from London to Cornwall and two of their most famous engines were 4079 Pendennis Castle and 7027 Thornbury Castle. Train Drivers in those days took great pride in these really impressive locomotives and prior to departure you would see them oiling and polishing their charges.

Into The War Years

We thought he was talking about our mess bills – 'so many owing so much' –
Squadron Leader Geoffrey Wellum, Battle of Britain Veteran, on
Churchill's famous speech

As I was born in 1934 that put me at the age of five when the Second
World War started. During the early 1930's Germany had been rebuilding
herself in the aftermath of the First World War and was putting together
another war machine. A slightly built chap, who resembled Charlie Chaplin,
had emerged as a powerful leader and this was of course, Adolf Hitler. His
charisma was such that his Nazi regime swept through Germany whilst the
rest of the world appeared to be sleeping. It seemed that the foremost
ideology of Nazism was concerned with crushing the Jewish race and this
they were about to do with an unprecedented violence. Although I was too
young to realise it at the time, the war would change my own and everyone
else's lives very quickly. Those long years are impregnated into my mind,
not so much for the major political and military issues but the local
movements, sounds and sights of war time Oldham.

One of the first things I remember noticing was the hanging of very
thick curtains at both the windows and doors. These were necessary, I was
told, as there was a compulsory blackout and no lights were allowed to
show at night time in order to deter German bombers from identifying
towns and targets. Police and ARP wardens patrolled the streets checking
for leaking lights; the streets were unlit and even the buses had only the
tiniest pinprick of a beam to see their way by. I can clearly recall the
mournful sound of the wailing air raid siren which was situated on the top
of the Lancashire Handbag Company not far from our house. Its sound
sent local people scurrying to mill basements, into air raid, or Anderson

shelters, or even under the kitchen table! Ears would be pricked and alert, listening to the German planes passing overhead and anxious for the all clear siren which told you when you could leave your place of refuge. Often you would have just got back into your house when the siren would wail once again and off you ran back to your place of shelter.

In order for the Allies to meet the German Army at full strength conscription was immediate for all fit men within a certain age range. The male workforce disappeared from the mills and the factories almost overnight but production had to continue and so women and retired men were brought in. It was at this time that we suddenly acquired our maid, Maude, and whilst the impending war may not have been of great significance to me at the age of five, Maude's arrival certainly was. Her appearance in our house may have had something to do with the evacuation of people from high risk areas as Maude came from the ship building area of Sunderland which was of great strategic importance and was a certain target for the *Luftwaffe*. Maude helped Mother around the house and did the shopping although as food rationing was introduced immediately there was not much shopping to do. It was because of the severe food shortages that Maude had to share her bedroom, throughout the war, with a huge galvanised bucket. Inside it were over two hundred hens eggs submerged in a preservative liquid called Isinglass and I took a real dislike to the container and the eggs and was very glad that it was Maude and not me who had to sleep next to them. Was this one of Mother's rationing campaigns? Did others store hundreds of eggs? Well yes they did. Although eggs were not actually rationed they were allocated which meant one egg per person per week except for pregnant women and children who were allowed more when available. As a child I couldn't understand all the fuss about the eggs as there seemed to be plenty of hens clucking around Oldham. Ah the innocence of youth.

Our meagre supply of eggs and other goods was about to be stretched even further. One evening in June, 1940, a large consignment of boys and their teachers arrived in Oldham. They had been evacuated form the Channel Island of Guernsey which the Germans were planning to occupy. The Guernsey boys were bewildered, tired and tearful as they were delivered to the Hill Street Stores around 7p.m. They stood in the large dance hall above the Stores with brown labels round their necks giving details of their name and age. The people who attended simply selected a boy who they thought would fit in with their family and took him home with them. My parents, my grandmother and my two aunts were all there and between them took on four of the evacuees. The whole process was over in under an hour and no one, least of all the Guernsey boys, knew how long they would have to stay in Oldham. At the age of six I thought the whole thing was very exciting but for Donald Falla, the evacuee who crossed the threshold of 307 Windsor Road that evening, the sheer speed of what had happened had left him rather shocked. Without warning he had been made to leave his home and his parents and the warm, sunny island surrounded by the sparkling sea where he lived. Torn from that virtual paradise he was rapidly transported to a grim, grey northern town and allocated a family of strangers to live with. It was a sudden and distressful upheaval for him.

Don was not very big in stature although he was about fourteen or fifteen years old at the time. He was not an outgoing person and was never really excited by anything as I recall, unlike me. In my eyes he never seemed to be very happy and overall he was quite a solitary chap. I think his mother was ill whilst he was with us and this was obviously upsetting for him particularly as he felt that my mother was too much of a disciplinarian. Many of the boys, not just Don, did not settle well, whilst others were lucky enough to feel very much at home. Of the boys who went to live with my aunts and grandmother I remember very little as they were so much older than me and we didn't hang around together. The only evacuees who were around my age were the children of the teachers who had accompanied the boys. One of these was Peter Rose and I remember that he was always very well wrapped up in coats and jumpers as he really felt the cold in our chilly town of Oldham! The Guernsey boys and their teachers were welcomed into Hulme Grammar School where they kept to their own classes whilst they became a very important part of the school and lasting bonds were made. Such was the camaraderie between Oldham Hulme Grammar and our guests that a school trip was made to Guernsey after the war. I remember going to visit the lovely island for a two week holiday with my friend, Kel, and about thirty other school mates and we stayed in the houses of the Guernsey folk. We were transported from Oldham's damp and dreary atmosphere amongst all the mills to a crystal clean island with magnificent bays and beaches. We had never seen anything like it and I am sure Don was equally, but not as pleasantly surprised, when he saw Oldham for the first time.

So now we had both Maude and Don living with us. Don was soon given his duties although to be fair Mother probably thought that having set chores would help him to settle in. He quickly commenced his daily tasks of cleaning the shoes and lighting the Siesta stove although he hated and resented these jobs. Don would be around fourteen when he arrived and nineteen when he left. These are difficult years for a young man and although Dad may have offered him some guidance it was not enough. Mother was in charge and her rules did not always comply with Don's views and as a consequence he tried to run away three times to seek other digs. However Don eventually settled and we shared the war years together.

In the back garden of 307 Windsor Road we were lucky enough to have our own concrete air raid shelter which mother had stocked up with everything required for a long stay. There was plenty of tinned food, a wireless, some blankets, a paraffin heater, a primus stove and access to water. Also, just for good measure, there were a couple of potties which I hated having to use when it was a full house! The shelter had been built by APAS, my Dad's firm and it was quite a fortification as I recall with a reinforced slab roof made of twelve inch thick concrete. I really enjoyed the excitement of the trips to the shelter. At the sound of the siren I would quickly grab Whiskers, the cat, and join the others as we all ran down the garden. As air raids were almost always at night we would all be in pyjamas and dressing gowns which seemed to add to the adventure and, I have to admit, that for us children at least it was thrilling to hear the planes passing over. Not so much fun for the anxious adults but overall it was a cosy and chummy time and I loved it. After a long stay the shelter got a bit stuffy so we would open the door to let in some fresh air being careful to extinguish the light first of course. With the door open the noises would be louder encouraging us to creep outside the shelter and look for an aerial dog fight between fighter planes. The German bombers were protected by a blanket of Messerschmitt 109 fighter's which were regularly attacked by British Spitfire and Hurricane planes and I clearly recall the noises of gunfire and plane engines passing overhead. Sometimes in the smoky light of morning pieces of shrapnel from shells would be found scattered about and we would collect them and later swap pieces with friends as if they were marbles or something equally innocuous. Although Oldham wasn't a particular target for the bombs several were inadvertently dropped and those which remained unexploded had to be dealt with by those brave guys from the Bomb Squad. A bomb was found on the local cricket pitch one morning resulting in play deferred, not due to the inclement northern weather for once!

Whilst we were huddled in the shelter Dad was out and about for he had joined the Home Guard and sported two pips as a Lieutenant. For some reason he was exempt from conscription but obviously wanted to do his bit. The members of the Home Guard, or 'Dad's Army' as they became known, were not provided with weapons initially but eventually Dad was issued with a Lee Enfield rifle. I could barely contain my excitement at having a real live rifle in the house although needless to say it was kept very securely away from me. I loved to watch Dad cleaning it and most surprisingly Mother liked the idea of having the rifle in the house in case a German knocked on the door! It is possible that it was partly due to his age and also the fact that his company was involved in war manufacturing that Dad was not called up for service. However he made frequent visits to London throughout the war which, with hindsight may have been to arrange M.O.D. contracts. My Uncle Arthur, Dad's older brother and partner in the business, was not called up into the regulars either so he too remained at the family firm. Unlike my Dad he did not join the Home Guard; he always said he was too busy as he was involved with some work for the BBC wireless programmes. Arthur was a romancer so this may or may not have been true but he did speak of it often.

Whether Arthur was involved with the BBC or not, the wireless was the most important item in any household or air raid shelter during the war. In fact it was vital as TV was not yet available. The old wirelesses worked from valves and were not remotely like the radios of today. Until the valves warmed up there was no sound at all and when you turned the dial to tune in the programmes there was often a whining noise if the station was not fully received. The news and the entertainment programmes always lifted our spirits during the dark days of the war and I particularly remember a programme at lunchtime called *Workers Playtime* on the Home Service. It was aimed at the workers in the factories but of course we all listened in. We sang along with Gracie Fields and Vera Lynn to the popular songs of the time and there was always a bevy of comedians to make you laugh. The wireless always seemed to be bashing out cheerfulness, humour and song, between the war news of course, but it was a real morale booster. Towards the end of the war the wireless was constantly warning us about V1 rocket propelled bombs which were unmanned, silent and sinister as they passed overhead tracking down their target in Liverpool or Manchester. On Christmas Eve 1944 our air raid shelter shook when a V1 dropped in nearby Abbeyhills. There was a hell of a bang and no wonder as a full row of houses had been demolished and twenty seven people had died. Dad and his colleagues in the Home Guard, together with many others, had to work hard that night digging at the rubble, amongst the huge and fearsome fires, trying to get people out alive. At noon the following day he finally returned home. He was very tired and black from head to foot; nevertheless he cleaned up and went straight down to the works. It was war and we could not and would not give up. Everyone was doing something for the war effort, even my mother who knitted hundreds of pairs of socks for the troops and worked tirelessly on many committees in between her voluntary driving for the WVS.

As I have mentioned, Dad's business had also turned all production over to the war effort. They had previously been builders, joiners and contractors, but now they made packing cases for the Arctic convoys, constructed wooden sections for the Mosquito Light Bomber and got involved in all sorts of other M.O.D. joinery requirements. On reflection I feel quite sure that Dad's company were also producing some very important and possibly secret items. I came to realise in later years that the curved mahogany claddings being manufactured in the workshop when I was a child were probably going to be used in the manufacture of the bouncing bombs which had been designed by Barnes Wallis in February 1943. These bombs were spherical in shape and had an outside surface of solid mahogany clad with high grade steel bands around the wooden surface. The items Dad and his workforce produced were definitely of a very unusual spherical shape, the exact shape of the bouncing bombs that were most famously used to destroy the dams of the Ruhr Valley in the famous Dam Buster's operation. I like to think that maybe some of Dad's claddings were on the very bombs used in this terrific venture. Of course the film about the Dam Busters had not yet been made but there were many other films to see and as no one had TV in those days the cinemas were very popular.

On Saturday nights during my childhood I would often be taken to the 'pictures' and we would queue outside The Odeon in the pouring rain; the inclement weather being part of the entertainment. Sometimes we would have to queue for ages if the folks inside did not want to vacate their seats at the end of the performance or the first show. Stalls cost around one shilling and sixpence whilst tickets for the front circle were two shillings and nine pence, about fifteen pence in today's money. It was really something to go in the most expensive seats in the front circle and I clearly recall one such visit which must have been in 1945 when I was twelve. In between the films was the newsreel, *Pathé News*, and on this occasion the audience were warned before it came on that footage would be shown of the Belsen Concentration Camp. It was suggested that some people may find the report disturbing and therefore anyone in the audience who wished to leave should do so. My parents had a brief word together and decided that we should stay. The memory and horror of that footage has remained with me. When Belsen was liberated by the British 11th Armoured Division they found sixty thousand prisoners alive, thirteen thousand corpses lying unburied around the camp whilst Typhus claimed another thirty five thousand in the first few months of 1945. Unlike Auschwitz there were no gas chambers but even so thousands died in that horrific camp. I have always remembered the appalling scenes I saw at the cinema that evening and am still unable to believe that human beings can inflict such shocking suffering on their fellows. Fortunately such atrocities were not going to continue for much longer. With the advance of the Allied armies across France following the Normandy invasion and the simultaneous Russian movement down through northern Europe, the German Armies were eventually beaten. On 8th May 1945 the German forces surrendered although Japan remained at war until the dropping of the atomic bombs on Hiroshima and Nagasaki.

And so on 8th May 1945 we celebrated VE (Victory in Europe) day by having a bonfire party on the 'back' near the double garage. Strangely I do not remember much about it although I would have been eleven but what I do recall was the almost tangible relief of Mother and Maude. The later Victory over Japan (VJ) day was celebrated on the 15th August 1945 and we held another bonfire party and burnt an effigy or 'guy' of the Japanese Emperor Hirohito. My friend Kel went to the celebrations being held at Ferranti's in Hollinwood where his Dad, Geoffrey Hall, managed the transformer department. Kel said that flags from all the allied nations were flying outside the massive works which had been so important to the war effort, for Ferranti's had been heavily involved with the early development of radar in the UK. There were huge crowds of people, fireworks, and a great party atmosphere. So with all the celebrations, street parties and lifting of some restrictions the latter months of 1945 proved to be a wonderful time. The whole world was at last free from bombing and uncertainty but I remember pondering on the fact that although the Germans had attempted to take over much of the world we, as victors, had no such ambition. This seemed strange to me as a child but now I am older and wiser I look back on the legacy of misery and lost lives the war caused and ask why? What was the point of it all?

The surviving troops returned home and the war torn countries attempted to get on with rebuilding. Those of my Dad's workforce who were fortunate enough to have survived the war uninjured returned after six years absence. The mills slowly rolled back into full production and things seemed to be returning to normal although food rationing continued long after the war, in fact for a period rather longer than the war itself. The shortages left a fear amongst people and just a few years ago, when clearing out my mother's cupboards following her death, we found a vast stock of tinned goods, some of them about ten or twenty years old. I believe this is a habit common in people who lived through the war, a legacy of the rationing and shortages they endured. Of course as a child in those years I had no such cares although it was truly wonderful to be given chewing gum by the American GI's when there were so few sweets about and the reappearance of bananas and Kellogg's cornflakes in the house was a sight to behold.

But with the arrival of bananas and cornflakes we had to say goodbye to two important people, for the end of the war signalled Maude and Donald's departure of course. It was time for Maude to return back to Geordie land with its battered shipyards whilst Donald would return to Guernsey. It must have been a worrying time for both of them as they wondered what to expect and once they were gone our house became very quiet. We all missed the pair of them. Maude settled in Sunderland and we stayed in contact for a while. She was quite old when she eventually married and she did not have any children. The last time she visited her hair had turned quite grey and we didn't see her again. Don was very glad to return home although he was thankful for the shelter we had provided during the war. I cannot recall any of the Guernsey lads leaving school and working whilst they were in Oldham although some, like Don, were nineteen by the end of the war. Being an adult, Don returned to St Peter Port in Guernsey and got a job at the 'Iron Stores', a large hardware store that sold almost everything the islanders could require. Many years later when I was married and had young children we returned to Guernsey for a family holiday. We met up with Don who now managed the 'Iron Stores' and had also married. We reminisced about the war years and old times in the 'regime' of Windsor Road and how Don hated his daily tasks of cleaning the shoes and lighting the stove. On his very last day with us before returning to Guernsey he had conscientiously cleaned the shoes, lit the stove, then put both shoes and polishing brushes into the blaze and burned the lot. Victory over my mother at last and no repercussions!

AIR RAID SHELTER 4 bunks. Chemical toilet, Valor parrafin heater mop bucket and mop. Wireless (vital) gas masks food. books. torch. two chairs. Whiskers the cat siren suit. water stock. kettle, tea pot. blankets Comics (beanoe, hotspur.) ... pottie!

Recently I have revisited France on several 'Battlefield Tours' with my pal, Richard. These trips have been very meaningful and have put my childhood war experience definitely into perspective. Time to reflect on the enormous wastage of lives.

1.

2.

3.

4.

5.

1. Below the dropping zone D2 of the 1st Airbourne comprising of 4 brigades led by Major General Urquhart parachute troops Glide Air Landing Brigade. The pathfinder group landed at 12.40pm September 1944.

2. Here is the Airbourne memorial to those who died in the battle – many were killed by intensive machine gun fire from the woods to the right.

3. There are many cemetaries in this area all immaculate by the wonderful work of the War Graves Commission. One such is Grossbeck Cemetary 1103 unnamed graves. On Remembrance Day one different child will place a flower on every grave. 4 V.C.s were gained at the Arnhem battle.

4. Arnhem Bridge taken and held by Lt Col. John Frost (Film 'A Bridge Too Far'). 740 men got cut off. Oosterbeck is nearby the centre of intense fighting on Sept 22 1944. It acted as a field ambulance for the 160 wounded.

There is a reunion lounge here – memorabilia lines the walls. The battle bought much death to the Dutch people but they thanked us for coming!

5. The grave of Private Corteil buried with his dog, who parachuted in with him. I believe his dog was chained to him when he died.

6.

7.

8.

9.

10.

6. If you go on a 'Leger Battlefield Tour, All Quiet on the Western Front' you will attend the 'Last Post Ceremony' at Ypres Menin Gate. On the walls are the names of some 55,000 men who were never found 1914–1918 WW1.

7. Eleven Victoria Crosses won in a short time. This was a terribly wasteful war – men were cannon fodder sent by insensitive Commanders of both armies. What have we learnt?

8. 'D' day landing beaches of Sword, Juno and Gold delegated to the British and Canadians

9. Omaha Beach which the Americans stormed, machine gunned from the cliff tops. If you saw the film Saving Private Ryan you have it – a massacre

10. This is Yeselstoyn German Cemetery. 24,000 graves, boys of 18/19, if you got to 25 you were a veteran! Many again unknown. What a waste.

With my friend, Richard Holden, on a visit to France in 2009, we found two graves in one of the British Cemeteries and noted the details:

L. BANKS 16 DURHAM LT/INFANTRY
He enrolled at 14 1/2
Cheerful, Smiling, always content
Loved and respected wherever he went.

PRIVATE E S CORTEIL PARACHUTE REGMT
6th JUNE age 19
'Had you known our boy, you
Would have loved him too'.

'Glen', a Paratroop dog, was killed alongside Pte. Corteil. They had parachuted into France together on D Day and so were buried together.

A Total Non-Academic

Grammar School – 'Academic Mill'

Things started to settle down after six long war years. Factories, mills, engineering businesses and entertainment returned to life gently and slowly. Vivienne's folks, Mr and Mrs Critchley, had sold the grocers shop to two old ladies, but Viv and I were still friends until we moved from Junior School to Grammar School. Vivienne was sent to a school for girls only whilst I was sent to Oldham Hulme Grammar School for Boys. Viv loved the girl's school but I was not quite so enthusiastic about my place of education.

Oldham Hulme Grammar School was founded in 1887. The presence of gothic arches gave the building something of a monastic feel and I particularly remember the impressive central hall with leaded light windows set amidst columns and pillars. The hall remains virtually the same today as do some of the classrooms although there have, of course, been many internal changes. In my day the smell of the waxed and polished floors percolated with the odour of boys, disinfectant, dust and school dinners. At one end of the school additional aromas were added because here were the Chemistry, Physics and Biology laboratories, each pumping out their own pollution. The Chemistry lab produced the best concoction of smells of course and this gave us much pleasure as we competed, in the best schoolboy fashion, by manufacturing odours from our very own bodies. The Biology lab, ruled by 'Squeak' Jones, was often enhanced by the appearance of creatures in various states of dissection and, depending on the season, copulating frogs. These frogs were always attempting to escape their fate by leaping around the place and provided us boys with lots of wasted class time as we tried to catch them.

Down in the basement was the woodwork department which had perhaps the friendliest smell in the school, a constant dry aroma of wood and sawdust. It was hot down there as it was rather near to the first pipes off the boilers which were always hotter than any others and so woodwork was a very popular subject. The teacher was a Scotsman called Nobby Clark, the apparent Laird of his department who always wore a brown lab coat. Further along the corridor was the gym which always reeked of sweaty pumps but it was preferable to some of the classrooms where I was a very mediocre student although it has to be said that even my abilities at team sports such as soccer and cricket were poor. I did better in individual sports though and, following some coaching and the encouragement of Pinky Green my House Master, I made the boxing finals in the main hall most years, only to be beaten by Theman, a lad of Caribbean origin who was very fast on his feet. Also at the school was a well run CCF (Combined Cadet Force) which had both an Army and RAF section. Now it shouldn't be hard for a lad to play soldiers but I really couldn't get into it which did not help my overall cause to improve my reputation at school. I was scruffy, hopeless on drill and found the whole set up a bore.

Academically I'm afraid I was not at all well positioned and was always to be found propping up the bottom half of the class. Maybe being dyslexic didn't help matters but I was collecting detentions and canings for fun, certainly well above the average number of punishments most other boys seemed to incur. The headmaster of Hulme Grammar School at the time was Harry Bamford Shaw, known more informally as H. B., and he had a tough, disciplined, Victorian attitude to education and the treatment of boys. If you were of an academic mind you would be assured a smooth passage through the school but, if you were not grooved into the Grammar way, life could be more difficult. Not painting too black a picture it must be said there were some good teachers at the school and it was my own actions that brought me into frequent conflict with the boss. Visits to his study became much too regular over the years and I would often be waiting outside his door for my punishment as the rest of the school left for the day. The rendezvous inevitably became equated with the cupboard on his wall which contained some half dozen canes of varying thicknesses and from which I was often invited to choose. You only went to H. B.'s study for one thing as he wasn't the kind of head who gave pep talks nor did he provide, as far as I could see, encouragement to underachievers.

Following the paternal family tradition of not being a good timekeeper I was often last into school at morning although I lived nearby. Each school day began with an assembly in the hall where all the pupils sat on benches whilst the masters, clothed in their black gowns, towered over us on the stage (1). When everyone was in place and there was absolute silence H.B. would come out of his study wearing the full scholarly regalia of black gown and mortar board. He was always loaded up with a mixture of hymn and prayer books, miscellaneous paperwork and the day's notices with the whole lot balanced precariously on top of his outstretched arms. He was a large guy, over six feet tall, and he would sweep majestically down the side of the hall and then up the steps and onto the stage. At this point the whole assembly were required to stand. One particular morning I was very late as usual and I was desperately wondering if I could possibly make it into the hall before my headmaster. Often when I was this late I would hide in the toilets until assembly was over, however if I was spotted it was double detention and then the cane if the offence was repeated. I had endured enough canings to not want any more and so, as I emerged from the basement cloakroom (2), I listened carefully to see if H. B. had made his appearance. All seemed to be clear so I dumped my coat on a hook in that disinfectant smelling room and tore up the stone stairs. As I rounded the bend at the top, opposite the headmaster's study, the door opened so I quickly tried to turn and make good my escape. Unfortunately the floor of the corridor was made from highly polished wooden blocks and of course I couldn't stop. I skidded onwards and hit H. B. mid region which caused him to fall, winded, onto the slippery floor. My brain was racing; his papers were everywhere and for a moment, red faced, I could not say anything. My lips pushed out the words eventually: 'So sorry Sir, are you all right? So sorry.' I picked up his mortar board, which had been flung from his head in the collision; together with his books and papers which were scattered all over the floor and handed the whole lot back to him. Once he had gathered himself and his dignity together he hissed three short words at me: 'my study 4.30.' Sliding into the back of the hall after him I contemplated my 4.30 p.m. venue before having to join in the singing of that bloody school hymn in Latin which we sang over three hundred times a year. Three hundred times a year for all those years and although I can remember the first two verses of it I cannot remember the name of the darned thing! The singing eventually ceased and the rest of the assembly passed by in an anxious blur until, right at the very end, after the notices were read, H.B. asked *me* to stand up. In front of the whole school. In the great hall. Now I knew he would go for the jugular and, as he explained to the school what a miserable object I was, the other boys quietly chuckled and nudged each other, glad it was me and not one of them. As he finished his tirade H.B. triumphantly rounded things off with a direct address across the hall into my red face: 'all you will be fit for in life John Pellowe will be emptying dustbins.' This was meant to be, and taken as, an insult; sadly dustbin men had a very low profile in those days. I felt wretched and after a miserable morning of lessons it was finally lunch time. In those days school dinners were so poor that even Jamie Oliver would have given up on trying to improve them and whilst I have already stated that my mother's culinary skills weren't anything to get excited about, it was actually the lesser of two evils to return home for my midday meal. Mother fussed as I ate even less than usual but I was pondering how I could protect myself from my forthcoming punishment. During my many previous visits for a caning H.B. had cottoned on to the insertion of a padding of newspaper or brown wrapping paper between two pairs of underpants and the discovery had led to an extra swipe so I had to find an alternative. Got it! This time I would wear three pairs of underpants!

As the school emptied that evening I stood outside H.B.'s door and was surprised and a little cheered as some of the departing lads, and indeed, some of the Masters, offered words of hope and encouragement to me. I waited and waited in the deserted corridor until the cleaners arrived, shattering the silence with their clattering metal buckets, a noise which matched my jangling nerves. Eventually the door opened, I entered the den and I received a lecture from my dear headmaster on school rules, timekeeping, standards, etcetera, etcetera. The cane was already placed diagonally across the desk; I didn't get to choose one this time. I was instructed to adopt the usual right angle degree bend with my hands resting on the chair cushion and off we go. Yes I had guessed correctly, six plus a bonus of three of the best. I held back the tears and upon release raced to the toilet block. Once there I locked myself in the loo and blubbered my heart out as I flushed the toilet to bathe my smarting bum in the cool water. No broken skin luckily. By now it was about 5.30 p.m. and my face was dreadfully puffed up; how would I explain the delay and my appearance to Mother? I bathed my face in loads of cold water and rehearsed a suitable explanation: 'sorry I'm late Mum, we've been on a run and I'm feeling a bit sore at the moment.' Luckily this excuse was accepted (white lies were absolutely essential in those days).

During my time at school we had monthly merit lists where you featured somewhere between top and bottom in the class depending on your performance. Together with Hubert Sowerbutts (3) of the well known market garden family, Harry Harling, and a couple of other regulars, we were often the foundation stone of that wretched merit list which formed part of the end of term report. When term finally ended we used to break up at lunch time and a brown oblong envelope containing your report would be handed to you. This was always a very sobering moment and I really dreaded that day knowing the anguish my report would cause for Mother. She would sit there in the dining room in her favourite tub chair with a handkerchief nearby; she liked to be prepared! The handover of the envelope took place, then there was silence and an obviously traumatised Mother would be speechless for a moment, but only a moment, for then would come the drama followed by a mild mental breakdown and floods of tears. After several of these end of term scenarios it was imperative for both our well beings that I sort something out as genuine improvement seemed a real long shot. I had a friend in a similar situation to myself who had made an amazing discovery and so I purchased a type of bleach which came in a small bottle with a suction rubber stopper. The two things Mother always looked at first on my report were conduct and punctuality and both of these were always signed 'unsatisfactory'. The next end of term my plan was put into action. After receiving the report at school I quickly went into a quiet corner in the toilets where I steamed the envelope open via the hot water geyser and gently applied the touches of bleach. Just by removing the 'un' from unsatisfactory my report was changed for the better but I also altered my form position in certain subjects where I was a poor student so that instead of being 28/30 I would remove the 2 and become eighth out of thirty pupils. There was a small problem in that the Masters remarks next to the form position did not seem to tie up with my result so I had to be a bit careful. Where the comment said something on the lines of: 'he is trying hard,' or, 'has improved this term,' I would have a really good stab at improving my place. As I got more confident I managed to acquire a selection of various pens used by the staff and I became a master forger. I had no problem with History, Geography and Art, good marks, great comments normally, but crumbs: Maths, English, Latin, Languages and Physics needed serious attention and required careful manipulation. By and large my ploy worked very well but what I could not disguise would be the Headmaster's summary, often written in red ink: 'unless this boy improves....' Unfortunately the comments made by the Head of the School mattered more than anything else to Mother and so these final words would be like a red rag to a bull; it didn't much matter about the good marks and observations I had helped to appear earlier in my report, if H. B. didn't think much of me then Mother was very unhappy. Upon Dad's arrival from work he would be implored to tackle me but he was a shrewd cookie with a completely different attitude to life than my mother. It was likely that his most serious comment would be: 'come on Will, you can do better than this.' Somehow he only ever seemed to be on the fringe of my education except for when my mother attempted to have me packed me off to boarding school which he definitely did not agree to. However with hindsight I can see how such a move would have benefited me. As Dad was reading my report he would say: 'doesn't read quite right this Will, bit of adjustment gone on here do you think? Now you know it upsets Mum so just try to do something about it.' Of course this would not be said within Mother's earshot and I knew that I had been rumbled but as Dad read through some of the hazed bleach he gently passed it off with a nod and a wink. He was a good guy, light hearted and lots of fun; no, he never came down heavy on my pathetic school work.

Unfortunately, in addition to my end of term report problems, there was often another slight predicament to cope with. To add salt to the wound already inflicted on my mother I would have to return to school in the afternoon although the term had officially ended at lunchtime. This was due to the fact that my detentions had piled up so much they could not be cleared before the end of term and so would have to be worked off after the school closed. To have to return for detention the very afternoon following the report saga, and possibly the following day as well, in order to clear my backlog was just too much for poor old Mum. I dejectedly returned to the empty school for the afternoon detention session and reported to Fred the groundsman as all the teaching staff had now finished for the holidays. There were usually two or three other pupils in a likewise situation to me and our detention task would be to roll the grass of the 'Big Side' pitch. We pushed the huge, heavy roller back and forth over 'Big Side' until we were well and truly tired. The next morning I would reappear at the school following a stony exit from home: 'Morning Fred, how many hours are left?' 'Not too bad this time lad, five and a half hours,' he replies. There is now only one other detentionee there besides me and he is free after two hours not having been as bad as me the previous term. In fact it seemed I was the worst boy in the school, no wonder Mother despaired. After my partner in punishment had served his hours and departed there was just Fred and me to push the roller which was, of course, now much heavier. Good old Fred, he lets me go at 1.30 p.m. instead of 3.30 p.m. All in all, that roller got pushed thousands of miles in the normal course of its life, and many of those miles were covered by detentionees such as me!

Eventually my schoolboy antics got Mother into such a state that every time she saw me she started weeping. This was unforgivable and sobering and I promised myself I really must buck up. So in order to placate Mother I tried really hard to pull myself together in the late fourth form and to not always be the bearer of bad news. In fact, in some JP friendly subjects, substantial progress was being made by genuinely getting into the top six; I even managed a couple of firsts in Geography and Art! Other fields of study were not so hot although I was managing a middle form position on the whole. My reports started to improve without any extra help and it was good indeed not to have to witness Mother going into a mental breakdown every time she received one. I felt reprieved and rather chuffed. At last I was able to leave the school at lunch time at end of term and be free to join all my mates for a trip to Hathershaw baths where we stayed for the whole afternoon until we were chucked out.

My rebellious progress through the school was tedious and not, I have to say, the happiest time of my life. Maybe I did not see any reason to be clever as I only aspired to do well in subjects that I found interesting. My concentration levels were not good as I was always thinking about more appealing things than geometry or verbs, an escapism for which I now apologise to the folks who expected more. The teaching methods in my school at this time probably didn't help either; many were amusing, some bordered on corporal punishment, and others were of a really bizarre nature. One particular French teacher had a unique way of commanding your attention in class. At the beginning of the lesson he would open his large and tatty case, place a register of class names on the desk, and, without looking down, he would place his finger anywhere on the list and then call out the name of the lucky pupil. As soon as his victim had been selected he would also take from his case a wooden mallet and an old fashioned motorcycle helmet and clutching both items he would stand next to the unfortunate one who had 'copped out' and command: 'repeat after me: *Marcel et Denise prennent leur chien plus bas dans la rue au magasin.*' If the poor wretch stumbled over the words the motorcycle helmet was fitted on his head and down came the mallet in time with the words of the French sentence as he demanded once again: 'repeat after me.' The rest of us would quite enjoy the entertainment having missed selection this time, but beware, this is just the start; eventually all of us would get a turn. There was definitely no *dormir* in this class!

Spanish lessons brought a much more painful solution to a mistake or lack of attention believe it or not. The Spanish teacher would drag you at full speed across the classroom by your hair and whilst you would be left with a red face and a very sore head he would usually be clutching a considerable handful of your hair. This guy could seriously be rather sinister and there was not much laughing in his class. However being bright chaps we quickly worked out an antidote to his punishment. The application of plenty of Brylcreem just before his class, although it made us look like toffs, did the trick as the Spanish master could not get quite the same grip on your hair. On a lighter note there was the flying blackboard duster teacher. This man would chuck the chalky duster into the class hitting his target eight times out of ten and covering the unfortunate victim in a cloud of white dust. If the launcher of the missile was in a good mood we would applaud by gently banging our desk lids down in unison. As with the mallet and hair treatment this punishment was often used to drive home a point but unlike the other two this method was well received.

Not all of our teachers were men; in fact during the war we had about three lady teachers. It may have been difficult for them working in such a male dominated area but for one, at least, our male presence seemed to add excitement to her day. In the classroom where this particular teacher held lessons her desk was on a raised platform about eighteen inches or so above us boys. She was a very attractive young woman and we were adolescent boys eager to make discoveries and so there would be a rush to get a desk in the front two rows so that the lesson could be spent gazing up at a lovely pair of legs. The teacher was perfectly aware of what was going on, there is no doubt about that, and she gave us an added bonus when she came to your desk to check your work. As she bent over you her body smell and perfume were overpowering and exciting.

As well as the women we also had some different male teachers during the war, probably because some of the regulars had been called up. One of these unfortunate supply teachers always came to work on a bike and one morning he arrived at the school black and blue with both eyes nearly shut. Apparently he had cycled into the back of a bus and as he walked through the school you could hear our cheers. The poor man. Ernie Bullock was his name and he will be well remembered by my aging classmates. He could not maintain control in the class at all. He was only a small man and, as he pleaded for our silence, we would see that he was getting close to the point of breakdown so we would let him have it by bombarding him with soft missiles together with his own blackboard duster which we had taken from him. In desperation he would leave the class, who were by now in high vocal acclaim, and the teacher in the next classroom would have to come in to settle us. Two or three of the ringleaders would be selected for the whack but it didn't stop us and consequently Ernie did not last long. We were utterly cruel to him as only school children can be.

Of course some of the teachers were different, I remember their help and encouragement and I remain obliged to them to this day. The school was divided into four houses and I belonged to Assheton House of which Pinky Green was master. He was one of the more encouraging teachers and I would bust a gut to win the cross country races to gain the house points he so cherished. Other good guys were Cyril Ashton of Platt House, Bill Whitworth of Hulme and Budge McCann, the master of Lees House and teacher of Latin. How Budge found the time to talk to me after my Latin exam seems a miracle; I had only managed to spell my name correctly and write the first and last lines of the school hymn with the final result of 13/100. I remember feeling quite sickened as I sat there unable to put pen to paper during the exam whilst the other boys were writing their hearts out right up until the deadline.

Many years after leaving school, well about twenty five or so actually, when I was the owner of my own business, I was obliged to attend a dinner at the Union Club in Oldham. It was a men only black tie job, probably a Rotary or Masonic occasion, I'm not quite sure which. Chatting and networking as you do I caught a glimpse of my old head teacher, H.B. or Harry Bamford Shaw MBE as he was now titled. He was on the landing half way up the elegant staircase of this handsome Victorian building. He still appeared big to me, after all he was over six foot, but I knew I was as big as him on this particular night. Moving away from the gin and tonic people I headed towards him. They say an elephant never forgets and now I just had to get something off my chest. As I approached him he looked impressive in his 'black tie' outfit with titles on his chest but I was not put off at all, I had waited a long time for this: 'Good evening Sir, could I get you a drink?' I had broken the ice and as he accepted my offer I returned to the crush around the bar. Eventually I rejoined him, gave him his G and T and small talk ensued. At last he gave me the opening I had been waiting for: 'I believe you are doing well in your business John,' he said (yes first name now). Go on do it, I urged myself and calmly replied: 'Yes, thankfully we are and we have a hardware department. Could I remind you Sir of an address you made to the whole school at assembly one day on my behalf?' I then quoted back to him his very own words: 'Pellowe, all you will be fit for in life will be to empty dustbins.' As the recollection hit him I continued: 'well Sir, I do not empty them but I do sell them.' It hit the spot; his reply carried little weight this time, and we were saved by the bell as dinner was announced. I made a mental note to have a brand new dustbin delivered to his home on Broomhurst Avenue, a mischievous gift from me but I didn't actually do it. At the end of the evening H. B. came to say goodbye and he wished me well for the future. Somehow I felt sorry for him and wished we could have continued our conversation. On reflection H.B. was probably just a product of his time but experience has taught me that if he had related more to his pupils and practiced a little more equanimity throughout his distinguished career he would have had more general success with underachievers. Thirty four years is a long headship so maybe he did something right and certainly if you were an academic student all would be well between you and H. B. Maybe it was some of the 'academic' Old Boys who thought up the wording for the commemorative plaque which is currently in the school's main hall attributing H.B. as striving to do his duty 'honestly and fearlessly, without favour or malice.'_

Sadly my first few years at Oldham Hulme Grammar were not the happiest chapter of my life and having a disciplinarian Victorian headmaster in charge did not help. Obviously I never became a prefect although a good friend of ours, Austin Hall, became head boy at one time; besides I left before I was old enough. No, I was a breakaway and I wanted things to stay that way. It was only because of my mother that I bucked up at all. I rebelled against H.B.'s authority and have few regrets. Education has now changed thankfully, and, in complete contrast to my schooling, today's kids are encouraged and not punished. All four of my grandchildren currently attend Oldham Hulme Grammar School where I like to think that they are happy and treated with respect. What my schooling experience did give me however, was resolve, and I vowed to myself that when I finally got away from this school I would one day deliver; that was my secret promise.

A Total Non-Academic: Notes

(1) In complete contrast to my school assemblies were the ones at my son, Tim's boarding school, Rossall, where he went at the age of thirteen. The church at the school is beautiful and attending an assembly service there whilst on our Sunday visits was something to look forward to. We loved the atmosphere of the place as the robed Masters took their seats in the cloistered back row followed by the youngest boys then the top gun lads. Before the start of the service you could hear a pin drop as there was utter silence but suddenly the organ interrupts like a tempest hitting the gothic ceiling of the huge hall. The lads shuffle and square up to sing the first hymn although it is obvious that they haven't quite the same enthusiasm as the organist. Nevertheless they belt out hymns such as *O Worship the King*, *Praise my Soul the King of Heaven*, *Abide with Me*, and *All People that on Earth do Dwell*. The huge sound vibrates round the hall and from where we are seated it is easy to study the spectrum of mixed boy's faces, from the very young to the seventeen year olds. I feel quite sure the boys were not as impressed with the occasion as we were and probably couldn't wait to escape but it did demonstrate the gentle discipline that prevailed in the school.

(2) The cloakroom was an airless place with cream and green gloss painted walls and hundreds of those cast steel double coat hooks. There were many odd items residing there: discarded pieces of kit, scarves, socks, hats, bags, and sportswear. Periodically the cleaners would have a round up of all the debris and off it would go into the popular lost property office. Each afternoon as classes finished there was a great rush as everyone tried to be the first to get down to the cloakroom, grab their coats and get out. Thinking about it now we must have been rather like rats abandoning ship. All this rushing around and competing always had the inevitable effect of causing a scrap as some of the lads would be swept back by the main escapees on the stairs. Once outside only very few boys had cars waiting for them, if any, and there were hardly any buses; mostly it was Shanks' pony everywhere and that is why we were always fit.

(3) Hubert Sowerbutts went on to become very successful as he moved the family horticultural business into architectural artefacts salvaged from the many mills being demolished at the time when the market place was all about nostalgia, tradition and atmosphere. All the pubs and restaurants demanded this theme with mahogany, brass and period lighting very much in demand. Hubert had the foresight to create and move with the time – he wasn't such a dunce after all then!

Motoring On Through the Years

The only sure way to avoid making mistakes is to have no new ideas –
Albert Einstein

As I have said before, my father loved cars and driving. LP, as he was known, was in some ways ahead of the times; inventive and carefree, he had a very unique way of overcoming restricted travel just after the war. In fact he became a coffee trader!

As the family business picked up, Dad and his brother, Arthur, eventually found themselves in the fortunate position of being able to purchase a brand new Austin 16 each. I clearly remember these cars. The registration number of ours was HND862 and it was a lovely car with a real walnut dashboard and a wonderful smell of leather. The roof opened and there were lots of other extras but no built in radio as yet! It was a revelation. It would cruise steadily at 60 mph, a speed previously unknown, and it had a top speed of around 85 mph flat out, not that we had a lot of opportunity to experience this as petrol was scarce and usually only available if your occupation warranted it. Consequently driving for pleasure was initially very limited indeed but my father had always had a yen to drive to Normandy on the north coast of France and from there to the borders of Brittany should the opportunity arise. Now that he had a car suitable for the trip he was raring to go but, having somehow secured a basic petrol supply, there was the additional problem of currency. Travelling abroad was very difficult at this time because of post war restrictions; you were only allowed to take a small amount of sterling out of Britain and it was not enough to finance a holiday. As usual when faced with a problem, Dad's brilliance came to the fore and he devised an ingenious plan to alleviate the holiday money shortage and he ordered a huge quantity of fresh ground coffee in quarter and half pound bags from a specialist shop on George Street in Oldham. Once ready the packages were collected, neatly stacked into the boot of the Austin 16 and off we went on our way to France for a ten day trip financed by selling the coffee to the impoverished French hoteliers and restaurateurs. Upon our eventual arrival in Boulogne we began our journey down the coast to the Brittany border, as far as Mont St. Michel. Dad was intent on finding a hotel or café to stay at which had a table tennis table and I wondered about this until he explained how he wished to take on a French man at the game to extract a few francs from him to supplement our holiday kitty. He was a great table tennis player and actually played for the local league so I felt sure he could deliver. We eventually found ourselves somewhere appropriate to stay and when it came to settling the hotel bill with the proprietor the payment was made in coffee and the francs from the table tennis winnings. As well as a table tennis table he was also always on the look out for fish tanks which they had in the entrances of the more refined hostelries. Again I pondered the reason and wondered what possible money or petrol making scheme he could have in mind. It soon became clear, however, that the fish tank fetish was only due to his liking for trout and lobster which were always displayed alive to be chosen by a prospective diner. Out of the tank and into the pan, he liked that!

Following that first trip we made about two or three more and on one occasion took Mother. It wasn't a success. For one thing I developed pleurisy after a stay in a seedy hotel where the bed linen was dirty and despite complaining and getting fresh sheets and towels my condition deteriorated. As well as my illness she found the language a problem and didn't really enjoy the food; but the final straw came when we drove over a bumpy French railway crossing far too fast causing Mother, who sat in the back of the car surrounded by the luggage, to disappear under the lot! I still think Dad had probably caught sight of a train bearing down on us and had had to put his foot down; he always enjoyed a close shave. Nevertheless we continued our trips, obviously without Mother, our mission being to supposedly help with my schoolboy French but it didn't work too well and both of us were totally useless with the lingo. Nevertheless upon our arrival in Boulogne we would set off full of good intentions to speak more French but would soon forget once we were on the way. We always took the same route to Mont St Michel, firstly passing through Le Touquet which was once the Ritz of the Normandy coast with its hotels and casino's and its Ascot air of grandeur. Then it was onwards to Abbeville which was terribly damaged from the war as was also the major port of Dieppe. Keeping the sea on our right we would travel via Le Havre and cross the bridge to pretty Honfleur, the home of many artists; then onwards to fashionable Trouville and the high class resort of Deauville. From there we would go to Ouistreham and past Pegasus Bridge which was heroically taken by Major John Howard of the Airborne Forces during the war. The next town we would travel through would be Arromanches where the remains of the D Day Mulberry Harbour can still be seen even today. We would avoid Caen which was also still war torn and move on to the likewise damaged areas of Granville and Avranches. As we travelled through France I experienced first hand the overwhelming destruction brought about by the bombs and battles of the Second World War and it really brought the consequences of the conflict home to me.

What few cars we saw as we travelled were French Renaults and Citroens, most of them bangers dragged back into use after the war. There was very little else in the way of traffic and this was probably the reason that our car always caused such interest as it was British and rare over there. As we journeyed we frequently got lost but wherever we ended up we were always well accepted and were often asked to share food and drinks. In fact we would often feel most embarrassed by the exceedingly generous hospitality we received, which I believe was due to the fact we were noticeably British and it was, after all, the allied troops that had liberated the French. They had not forgotten this and as we drove around from town to village we were heralded with great accord and enthusiasm everywhere. It was a wonderful time.

With the resources at our disposal Mont St Michel was usually as far as we could go and without coffee power we would have been hard pressed to travel at all. At low tide we would drive across the sand and causeway to the island which is much larger and more impressive than our equivalent in Cornwall. Untouched by the war, the impressive stone fortifications, walls, towers and mini chateaux were wonderful to see. We would leave the car and walk amongst the old stone buildings which flanked the narrow cobbled streets. The smell of Gauloises cigarettes combined with real French cooking drifted around each corner and in the basements of the restaurants which lined a steep hill there were chefs in their number one dress complete with traditional headgear. We were in serious omelette country and so they would be cracking twenty or thirty eggs into a huge burnt pan whilst a fellow chef would be in the more advanced stages of omelette making; chucking the mixture up in the air and cleverly catching it as it descended. The tradition of omelette making was obviously unchanged by time or war and the sight of the chef's skill was always very impressive. In a stone walled, wooden beamed and splendid room, with subdued amber coloured reflections and tables covered in white linen, we would eat these wonderful French omelette's served to us amidst the blue flashes of flaming brandy; absolute magic. As we relaxed on the bench seats, stomachs full of omelettes and bread, we would study the other patrons and take in the electric atmosphere. This was France, the home of cuisine and we adored it.

Other than his motoring trips to France, masquerading as a coffee merchant, Dad would drive around in Britain as much as time allowed; driving was in his blood and this tendency appears to have been passed on to me. The British car industry was blossoming at that time and we were lucky enough to be able to change the family car quite often and we had some real beauties. One company were producing an unusual horizontally opposed engine which they put into a stunning creation called the Jowett

Jupiter and we had the first model in Oldham, a two seater sports car in British Racing Green, registration number HBU 144. Although he was a first class driver with a clean record, my father had a very bad accident whilst driving this car. Travelling along a narrow switchback road he met with a stationery waggon on the blind side of a hump. Coming the other way and approaching fast was another car so there was only a split second to decide whether to carry on or to brake thus allowing the other car through first. He decided to brake but as soon as the other car had passed he had to swing round the back of the waggon at speed or crash into its rear. Although the front of the Jowett made it the rear end did not. Dad was very badly shaken but fortunately had no serious injuries and, being as good natured as he was, he had no axe to grind with the truck driver who was definitely at fault parking as he did. In fact it came to light that he had actually left his cab in order to relieve himself at the side of the road; what a stupid place to choose to stop his vehicle! When our car eventually arrived at home on the back of a breakdown trailer Mother and I were extremely shocked at the severity of the damage and it seemed a miracle that our family was still intact. Over the next few weeks the wreck was totally rebuilt at the Jowett's factory and thereafter continued to be the family car until it was replaced. In later years Mother often wondered if this accident had in any way contributed to Dad's cancer as it really unsettled him. Obviously there is no scientific evidence of such a thing but sometimes you know people so well that you have intuitive thoughts about them. Anyway that's what she believed.

Following the disastrous Jowett (1), our next car was a Sunbeam Talbot (2). My father was already a member of the Lancashire and Cheshire Car Club and was competing in their rallies, road trials, and driving tests but he often came unstuck on the navigation. Although I was only fourteen I was taken along to tackle the map reading for him but in fact I was never very good at it and we would often fall out over my mistakes. On one such sortie I had made a pig's ear of the route finding and we were arguing our way through the higher parts of Derbyshire, trying to make up time for my navigational errors. Cigarette in his mouth as usual, Dad quickly rounded a corner only to be confronted with a baby elephant walking up the road towards us! As we screeched to a halt we noticed another much, much larger elephant trailing in its wake. Out of the car we hopped to size up our position. The baby had stopped and looked at us curiously; 'come on Will,' said my father as he noticed the huge elephant approaching as well. With his Churchman's cig still in his mouth he attempted to stop the big beast and when this did not work he took hold of its trunk and walked the elephant round. Unbelievably after a couple of turns the big elephant settled down. I was not surprised really at his coping with such a situation, such was his nature. We had no idea at all why we would find two elephants walking along a quiet moorland road in the middle of the day but Dad intended to find out. 'Look after the elephants Will,' he said moving away down the road looking for clues. Now I was not in a comfort zone and stood shaking and petrified wondering what would happen to me if the elephants made a move. Recalling this event now I do not think I would have left my own son to look after two stray elephants – although yes, perhaps I would! The whole scenario was typical of my father's unflustered and casual approach to most situations; health and safety were not an issue then and I have to say life was probably more exciting as a result. Fortunately for me the elephants just stood still, sniffing interestedly with their trunks at the warm car bonnet and whilst I was relieved I still looked for Dad's return with a lot of anxiety. The larger elephant, which turned out to be the baby's mother, was now surveying a wound on her leg and cleaning it with her trunk. The mighty beast seemed like a block of flats as it towered above me, throwing out lots of body heat. Her feet were so large that if she had decided to stand on the bonnet of the car the engine and suspension would have been pasted onto the road. My imagination was working overtime as she looked straight at me but fortunately at that very moment Dad returned. It was probably only about five minutes since he had departed although it felt like hours. Accompanying him was a shaken looking chap with a wound on his head; he was the elephant trainer and had been found just round the corner where a van and a loaded trailer from Billy Smart's circus had gone over the edge of the road and rolled partway down into a field. It was not good. Llamas and horses were lying there badly injured and later the sound of a gun would be heard as some of these poor animals had to be destroyed. We stayed with the trainer and the stricken animals for a while until more help came in the form of Police, one or two ambulances and the Fire Service. As we left to resume the rally we realised that this delay would have cost us a placement and we were, of course, well and truly late as we returned to the finish. Not, this time at least, solely due to my poor navigation.

Dad and I had a lot of fun driving together and in later years he would be of great and generous assistance to me with my various cars and my interest in rallying. He maintained his own interest for all of his short life and his daredevil streak made for some great escapades; typical behaviour for this much adored man who lived on the edge of time.

Motoring on through the Years: Notes

(1) Between the Jowett and the Sunbeam Talbot, Dad had a brief time with a Triumph TR2 rebuilt by Jim Smith at Borough Garage. It was fast and manoeuvrable and it was one of these models that won the Great Britain Rally at that time. I used it myself briefly and it was a cracking sports car.

(2) The Sunbeam Talbot was bought from Hartley Schofield's garage. Julie Schofield, Hartley's daughter, is a car enthusiast and still runs her Hillman car circa 1950. Together with her partner John she has actually bought and restored a Rothwell car which was built by her grandfather and she now has a fully working model. She has also published a book about it.

The Turning Point

Everyone knows they are going to die but no one really believes it –
Spalding Gray

As I have mentioned previously my mother had two younger sisters, Joan and Verna. Joan was married to Joe Lees and they had three children: Bob, Anne and Joyce. Verna's husband was Harold Sanger and they had only one child, a son called Michael. As my cousins were all much younger than me we didn't spend an awful lot of time together although on one occasion Michael and his parents joined us for a holiday. I would be almost sixteen when it was arranged for us all to go and spend the festive season in Llandudno; Michael was eight years old and he attended the Preparatory School at Oldham Hulme Grammar whilst I was in the seniors. Unlike me, he was a very bright lad and he wore glasses which made him look even more studious. Although he was only small in stature he had a fiery temperament to go with his red hair but overall he was a very likeable boy.

Christmas Eve arrived and we all settled into the County Hotel on the sea front. We were looking forward to the evening's entertainment when the hotel owner, Fred Davis, and his equally famous brother, Joe, were to give one of their famous snooker displays. The Davis brothers were both very well known stars in the snooker world and we were not disappointed as we watched them swerve the ball and jump the white over a line of reds to pocket the last one. Watching these professionals perform was a Christmas present all of its own but Michael and I were still more than happy to receive all our other gifts and we had a wonderful family time in the hotel on Christmas day. On Boxing Day Michael was keen to go onto the beach for a game of football and urged me to join him, so we got well wrapped up and went out into the strong wind which was whistling noisily. We had a great time on the firm sand in the fresh, bracing air as we kicked the ball around whilst being buffeted by the gusts of wind and listening to the noise of the sea as it angrily pounded upon the shore. Eventually it was time for us to return to the hotel for lunch so Michael picked up his football and started to run exuberantly across the windswept beach towards the wide promenade. He was very excited and happy as I followed him, running and calling and asking him to wait for me. He did not stop. Perhaps he couldn't hear me because of the wind, I was trying to catch up to him, shouting for him to wait as he headed for the marked zebra crossing he had been trained to use. On Boxing Day in Llandudno in 1949 there were very few people around and in fact, as I chased after Michael, I noticed that there did not appear to be anyone at all on the whole of the promenade as far as the eye could see. However, in the distance I noticed a silver Standard Vanguard car racing towards us, it was the only car in sight and it was travelling very fast. By now I was about thirty yards behind Michael and I shouted and shouted for him to wait. He turned round laughing; did he think we were in a race? The car and Michael were in line to meet at the crossing. Surely the people in the car had seen him for nothing inhibited their view? Surely he would stop anyway? Neither the car nor Michael stopped. The noise of the wind was drowning my screams when the worst possible thing happened; the car hit the little fella as he stepped onto the crossing and launched him spinning into the air before his slight body landed sixty feet from the point of impact. He was killed instantly.

I tore into the hotel and remember very little after that.

Many lives were changed that day. The terrible shock of losing their only child put Verna and Harold in bed for days and they had to be very heavily sedated. All the other hotel guests also shared in our grief as Michael had been a very popular and engaging young boy; everyone was fond of him. As soon as possible we all returned home where, full of remorse and anguish, I soon became very ill with shingles and although they were ill themselves, Verna and Harold could not have been kinder to me and I was very grateful for their compassion. As a result of the tragic accident there was a court inquest a few weeks later which I apparently attended; I have no recollection of it and was only reminded by the recent unearthing of a newspaper report which quoted something I had said whilst appearing there. As I remember, the car that hit Michael did not actually belong to the woman who was driving it, she had volunteered to chauffeur a group of holiday makers who were taking part in a treasure hunt and the car belonged to one of them. Working to a limited time the group had to solve a clue and then get to the next location as quickly as possible and at the time of the accident they were hurrying towards the paddling pool at the end of the promenade. Visibility on that fine, windy day was one hundred per cent, there was no way the driver could not have seen Michael but the speed of the car was not adjusted. Perhaps the driver anticipated passing Michael before he set foot on the crossing? We will never know but it must have been a thousand to one chance that both Michael and the car arrived at exactly the same spot at the same moment when there was the whole of the empty road and promenade surrounding them. The pressure of the timed treasure hunt, the car being strange to the driver, surely it was a recipe for disaster? The inquest established that the speed of the car as it hit the poor lad must have been in excess of sixty miles per hour and initially the charge against the driver was manslaughter. However a good defence team ensured that the charge was reduced to dangerous driving, at least that is what was always believed within our family. Now, all these years later when reading the newspaper report on the inquest it seems that the verdict of Michael's death was misadventure which I suppose was the end of the matter unless a separate case was brought to court. I understood that the lady driver was greatly upset and made unwell by the accident, as indeed was everyone else; this bright young lad was lost to the world for ever and nothing would bring him back.

Following Michael's death the family life that Verna and Harold had previously enjoyed was no more. They became frequenters of the social scene surrounding the cricket at Old Trafford where they became friendly with a few of the well known players, such as Ken Grieves, Jack Dyson, and Geoff Pullar. Some of their new friends were Jim and Hilda Hilton, the same people who used to allow Viv to get ready for school in their house on those cold winter mornings when her parents owned the shop. They now ran the Falconers pub opposite Copster Park and Jim was a fine county cricketer playing for Somerset whilst his brother, Malcolm, who played for Lancashire, had twice bowled Don Bradman, the greatest Australian batsman, in a test series. Verna and Harold focussed their changed lives around this sporting fraternity and spent a lot of time with their friends in the Falconers which must have been a welcome distraction from the pain of the death of their son. For additional comfort they also got a Pekingese dog which Verna carried everywhere, even to the pub where it would sit upon her knee as she gazed at Michael's school cap which was hung behind the bar, a sad but cherished memento of the son she had lost. However both Verna and Harold were living in a false world and things never really got better for either of them; they both died at a comparatively early age never having managed to totally recover from their grief which, in turn, very sadly affected their health and well being.

As for me, when I eventually recovered from shingles I returned to Hulme Grammar where I received a lot of sympathy and understanding; everyone was very sad and Michael was mentioned in prayers at the daily assembly. A trophy with an engraving of a young boy on it was donated to the school in his memory, it is a beautiful piece of work and to this day the Michael Sanger Trophy is awarded annually to a boy at the end of year six who is considered to have been outstanding. I tried very hard as school life continued but I could not settle and although I had started to shape up and had got good results in the pre Christmas mock exams, I was now even less happy than I had been before. Something had to be done and so the family conferred and a complete change for me was suggested as Dad came up with the idea that I leave school and take on a joinery apprenticeship with the family firm. My education would not suffer as I had to attend the local technical college on day release whilst at the same time learning a trade and I was pleased at the thought of leaving school and working at something I could enjoy and succeed at. Also the new beginning would hopefully help me to come to terms with Michael's death.

The decision being made it was now time to face my headmaster, H. B. Shaw, and so my mother requested an audience with him and asked for me to be released from school mid term. Surprisingly H. B. appeared to have great sympathy and feeling on this occasion, even going so far as to comment that I would probably have got some good marks in the School Certificate exams if I had been able to stay on. Wishful thinking on his part surely? So, having got the required permission I left school early, ready to join the world of work as the lowest apprentice. My childhood had ended abruptly when Michael died and I was now a much chastened and sadder person than I had been previously; I had, after all, been in charge of Michael on that fateful day. The guilt was truly overwhelming at the time but I knew that I had to work through my grief and turn the most horrific of experiences into something positive in memory of the untimely death of my young cousin. I hope I have managed to do just that somewhere along the way.

Everyone Needs an Apprenticeship

Dedication to Derek Brierley
Culture is the ability to describe Jane Russell without moving your hands –
Bob Hope

'Nowt like havin' a 'prenticeship, better than't Bank or't mines.' Such were the words commonly spoken in Oldham families as children approached school leaving age when I was a lad. A university education was rarely a consideration unless you were at the very high end of the academic scale which of course I was not. So 'get a trade' was really the thing to do. Apprenticeships in the early 1950's were not hard to come by as many tradesmen had tragically lost their lives during the war and needed replacing so that we could rebuild Great Britain. I was therefore well placed to join the family firm, Arthur Pellowe and Sons Ltd (APAS), and become one of over a hundred staff employed there. Each tradesman at APAS (1) had at least one apprentice attached to him who was able to learn a skill over a five or six year period and the trades on offer included: bricklaying, plumbing, roofing, drain laying and joinery. It was joinery that was of particular interest to me at that time although with such a variety of skilled workers APAS could offer all kinds of experience from clearing drains to building a site of sixty houses. They laid floors, put new roofs on factories, relined mill boilers, built tournament tennis tables, and produced sawn planks as well as fine cabinets. The whole enterprise was situated at the bottom of Chamber Road and was comprised of offices and showrooms; a joiners shop, a machine shop, glass department and stores. There was also a massive basement where the timber was stored and where the mighty circular saws were kept busy cutting tree trunks into planks. This wood storage and cutting area also contained a kiln for drying the sawn timber whilst outside was the huge builders yard containing several handcarts, lots of concrete mixers and a five ton Bedford tipper which was always kept in immaculate condition by the driver, Humphrey Childs.

Entering the works on my first day I was soon made aware that in the world of an apprentice the last in starts at the bottom and prays for another trainee to join the company soon. This was because my job mainly consisted of brewing up, going for the lunches and sweeping up. Until another lad joined I was unable to move on and, depending on how soon another apprentice started after you, it could be a full year before you got a chance to hold a hammer! Menial jobs apart, each apprentice was sent on day release to the local technical college to take a course in City and Guilds or National Certificate for the building trade. This course lasted for three or four years and as well as the full day's attendance there were three compulsory evening classes plus homework. However what the course didn't teach you was how to have the ability to face a national crisis in the canteen if you messed up on the sandwich orders! After six months spent as the lowest esteemed object around, a new recruit arrived. I impressed on him the importance of getting the twenty five brews in the enamel brew cans just right, whilst also dealing with orders for sandwiches, fish and chips or pies, and left him to it. At last I could step onto the second rung of the apprentice's career ladder where I would spend three months in the machine shop on the belt sanding machine or backing off from a huge circular saw.

After my initiation in the machine shop I gradually progressed to general domestic repair work. Each morning I was assigned to a joinery tradesman for that day and we would be handed a green job sheet by Cliff Wrench, the outside foreman. Cliff was lucky enough to be allocated budget mechanical transport in the form of the not too young 250cc Royal Enfield Motor Cycle which I also used to cut my teeth on. For work purposes it was used for site visits but unfortunately Cliff was not cut out to be a motorcyclist and parted company with it frequently! Because he was the foreman he wore a trilby instead of the usual flat cap and somehow he managed to tie it onto his head before mounting the bike as crash helmets were not compulsory then. Later, probably tired of his time spent on the tarmac, he got the works to provide him with a brand new Ford 10 open pick up truck – hurrah! The job allocated to us by Cliff could be for anything from the fitting of a new door to the repair or renewal of gutters;

replacing rotten window frames or strengthening someone's floor. As an apprentice it was my job to load up the handcart with all the equipment necessary but the most important task was to ensure I chose a good cart, one with solid wheels that wouldn't fall off en route to the job. Of equal importance was paying close attention to ensure that everything we needed was on board, otherwise the apprentice, me, would have to walk back to the yard from the job no matter how many miles away from the works we were. The appropriate materials and tools, which probably included ladders, were loaded and then off we would go, with me quietly hoping the job would be close by and not in Royton or Summit which would mean about five miles of pushing the heavy thing. As we departed from the yard two white enamel brew tins, complete with chipped edges, would be swinging on the shaft of the handcart and these were the most essential items in the eyes of my master, the tradesman to whom I was apprenticed that day. We always had a large torch in the tool bag as we used to get terrible fog and smog which often reduced visibility to a car length. Should this happen one or the other of us had to walk in front of the cart to ensure that our twenty foot extending ladder, which was balanced precariously, didn't cause any damage to things looming up out of the pea souper (2). Actually it was best if we both walked in front of the cart, pulling rather than pushing, as a car could easily loom up out of the fog and hit you in the trousers should you be stood at the back! The handcart had two large wheels and no brake system and as there were a lot of hills where we operated the only way to handle it downhill was to ram the wheels against the kerb when we needed to slow down. In contrast the only way to get the heavy cart uphill was to generate some muscle! Depending on the location of the job our journey may take two or three hours whilst the work itself would possibly take only an hour or so to complete. Such were the transportation circumstances in those days. The Transport Manager employed by APAS was Mr Wilson, a large man with nicotine stained moustache and fingers. As the firm only possessed one five ton truck, Cliff's pick up and the handcarts I'm not sure if he deserved his title and he must certainly have had other work to do besides managing the 'transport'.

The daily handcart pushing could be gruelling but it was something an apprentice had to do whilst working his way up the ladder. I worked on general maintenance jobs for quite some time whilst keeping an eye open for the larger jobs and at last, I was allocated to a big job re-roofing the Ivor

Mill at Shaw. It was a real treat to be on a job like this for many months, something to really get stuck into. Plus there was the bonus of not having to push a hand cart as all the materials were delivered by the truck. Ivor Mill employed mainly female workers and the rich humour of the mill girls brightened up our day as did their attire, for they wore very little apart from a head scarf, a wrap around overall and some oversized knickers which seemed to be the only type available in 1950's Oldham! They were constantly covered in cotton fluff which adhered easily to their damply attractive and clingy attire as it was always very humid in the mill in order to keep the cotton from splitting. The work that the girls did was mostly on the ring machines where the cotton was wound onto bobbins (3). They were required to quickly tie any broken cotton thread and their nimble girlish fingers were good for this type of work. The winding equipment clattered away as the smells of oil and cotton rose to meet us as we worked on the roof above. Special care had to be taken whilst up there as it was only in extreme circumstances that the machines would be closed down which they would have to be if we dislodged a shower of dust and spiders whilst removing the ancient and heavy stone roofing slates. Once the slates were removed, we merrily cut into the replacement asbestos roofing sheets using a special bladed Bosch circular saw causing asbestos dust to fly everywhere with no protection at all; we didn't know any different then and there were no rigid Health and Safety regulations.

When the whistle went at the end of a shift, the machinery clattered to a standstill and if we were not still busy on the roof we would be in grave danger of being trampled to death by the departing lasses. Talk about 'Girls Aloud'; these mill girls were a traditional breed of Northern Hardware and they could seem quite formidable to a nice lad like me! However one of my fellow apprentices, Derek Brierley (4), was more than capable of dealing with them. As well as being a champion dancer he also seemed to be a champion womaniser. He could not date these girls quick enough, even shooting off at brew time if he got a chance. He was a stocky well built stallion and spent all his time sizing up his next conquest as we worked on the roof above the girls. Apparently old habits do indeed die hard and when I recently attended Derek's funeral his brother, Alan, told me that Derek had been married four times. There were a lot of grandchildren at that funeral!

When they weren't out courting with Derek Brierley the girls lived on the doorstep of the Mill in rows of stone or Accrington brick houses which had yards at the rear. Beyond the yard and between the rows of houses were passageways providing access for the rag and bone man, the coalman and the dustbin man. Often in these passages you would find a couple of bricks stacked against a wall on which a smaller lass could get more in touch with her young man as this area was also used for courting. These Lancashire lasses, whilst full of fun in the mill, were actually quite well behaved socially, especially when compared to the skimpily dressed, confident brigade to be found today on Friday and Saturday evenings in Yorkshire Street, Oldham! They did not go into pubs on their own and only rarely did they go to a pub with a guy. Courting was carried out on the back row of the cinema in the 1/9d seats or at the dance hall although later in the evening the lucky couple may progress to the back alley and the bricks if necessary. Tights had not yet arrived; stockings were held up by suspenders and proved to be an interesting challenge in the dark; enough said but in fact sex was rather more discreet in those days and if a lass got herself in the club then it was frowned upon by all. It was very, very different from today where single mothers are accepted; the girls in my day found a boy friend, went courting for a while and eventually he would be asked to the girl's house for tea on Sunday when he would be signed up to marriage! It was a wonderful world of simplicity and order, totally void of materialistic paraphernalia, selfishness, rushing around and greed – well mostly!

When we had finished the roof at Ivor Mill I moved to another long term job, this time in a cinema. These jobs were as sought after as the mill jobs and this particular one was for the renewal of a dance hall floor at The Odeon in Manchester. Most cinemas in those days had a dance area, as well as a restaurant or café and I am sure that in any old cinemas that remain today you would find the gorgeous wooden dance floors under the carpets somewhere. This particular flooring job had to be carried out over several nights to avoid disruption in the cinema so we would arrive as the last customers were leaving, the five tonner truck dropping us off with the necessary materials. Up come the old boards, down with the new, which were three inch wide, knot free maple, lovely stuff. A job like this would take a minimum of five nights and it was important to have the dance floor up and running for the weekend. At 2 a.m. its time for the night shift's lunch and as apprentice I am obliged to sort things out. Cinemas in those days usually had a big restaurant open to the public and I eventually located it and the adjoining kitchen which was a huge place with walls of aluminium and ugly cooking units. It is pitch black and bugger, the light switch is right at the other end of the room. Feeling my way through the space in the stuffy warmth I hear scratching and scurrying whilst treading and slipping on god knows what underfoot. I also notice a peculiar smell. Eventually I locate the lights. Click, they are on and as I turn around the sight is amazing. Thousands of cockroaches are swarming over the floor and on the unit tops, in fact on every surface. Within half a minute of the light going on they all disappear except for the trail of squashed casualties which indicate my route across the room. The following night I made sure to take a torch but trying to shift the horrid swarm with a tiny torch beam was really spooky. Understandably I was never very keen after that experience to eat cinema food. As the lowest hour of 4.30 a.m. approached, we would all be feeling whacked and by the time the lorry picked us up at 8 a.m. we would be falling asleep on the journey home. Eventually our work at the cinema was completed and another splendid maple dance floor had been laid of which we were rightfully very proud. We know that folks will trip the light fantastic on the warm boards to the melodies of Billy Cotton and Victor Silvester; real dancing folks, strictly come dancing style, feeling, touching, and sensing the dance, on our perfect floor.

The next job is at Hunt and Mosscroft's engineering works in Middleton where we were required to fix a suspended insulation system to the whole roof. Again it is night work when the thousands of megawatts of overhead crane cables are switched off. We manipulate our way between them, not daring to get within a foot of these still lethal forces of power. This job takes quite a few weeks to complete but at the end we look upwards and see a fantastic suspended system, white and clean and saving huge heat loss from the factory. Following such a major job completion, there would be a celebration and the workforce would meet on a Friday night at The Mare and Foal Pub, across the road from the business. Another occasion to celebrate was the awarding of the yearly pay rise. Wages were basic for apprentices and minute though the pay award was, the esteem that came with that extra couple of quid was like Christmas and birthday in one. To make up for our low pay the opportunity to work overtime on Saturday morning at time and a half rate was very attractive even though this was the time traditionally set aside for the local miserable jobs such as the clearing of blocked tippler toilets. Many houses had one of these contraptions housed in its own four foot square building at the bottom of the yard. The very nature of the toilet's mechanism meant that they were always becoming blocked so Saturday overtime may consist of several local calls. Without getting over technical and not being too clever it is as it says – the toilet tipples as and when the tippler plate is loaded. The resulting sewage is then flushed away by the water draining from the sink in the nearby house. 'Three jobs this morning, all local, all tipplers and Mrs Sidebottom at number six had lost her bulky knickers before her toilet packed up,' says Cliff handing out the work sheets. Sparing a lot of gory detail it has to be said that the Saturday handcart run produced some real shocks. Normally it was possible to free up the blocked tippler by tinkering about and peering down through the scrubbed wooden toilet seat. If the initial tinkering did not get things moving then some low level pot holing was required. This exploration often revealed some amazing things wedged under the tippler, items often found were underwear, rats, and shoes. What really fascinated me was how someone could lose a shoe down there unless you stood up on the job!

One Saturday I arrive at a house not too far away from the works. I park the handcart at the rear of the house and knock on the door: 'Morning Mrs H. Believe you have a problem with the toilet?' 'E lad am glad t'see thee, been that way for a few days now, wen't cat disappeared.' Her comment gives me a clue and it is a fact that horrible kids have been known to put all sorts down the tippler, dead or alive. I carry out an initial inspection. The toilet is well blocked. Nothing is visible so it's a pot holing job. Fortunately, although there was very little in the way of equipment, I did have a boiler suit and cap to wear for such trips plus various angled tools for working in the bowels of tippler technology. After rummaging about in the not very fresh air I find it; yes a dead cat. This is going to be upsetting. Fish the thing out, wash it down in a bucket of water, knock on the door holding the dead cat: 'Sorry Mrs H. I've found your cat.' I thought she would be upset but no, she was puzzled: 'Eh lad that in't my cat, I dunna know where it can be then.' I wrap the orphan animal in a sack to give it a state burial in the rubbish bin back at the yard. You win 'em you lose 'em!

As the yard closed at midday on a Saturday it was always a mad rush to get through the allocation of jobs and return the hand cart in time. This often left little time to clean up before meeting the team bus at the Star Inn for the weekly Saturday afternoon fixture of rugby. Although I was pretty hopeless at team sports such as soccer and cricket I joined Keb Lane Rugby Club as hooker when I was about sixteen or seventeen. This was mostly due to the fact that I relished the idea of travelling, having scraps and being in the thick of a training club atmosphere. As I boarded the coach accompanied by the remaining aroma of my morning's adventures I would be promptly demoted to the back seat but once the game was over and I had been disinfected in the team bath I was accepted once more and allowed to mix freely.

The rugby afternoons continued, my experience and knowledge as a joiner increased and the time eventually arrived when I was allowed to team up with the house building squad, initially at St. Anne's Crescent and North Close, Lydgate and later followed by Merton and Harrow Avenue off Frederick Street. APAS purchased plots of land for their ongoing house building programme, each site usually on the scale of around sixty semi detached buildings. In those days the only luxury by way of building machinery was a concrete mixer, so all digging was completed by hand and this work usually fell to the navvies who came from Ireland. The initial drainage work leading into the houses was laid by Frank Whitehead, a supreme foreman, who handled a spade like a teaspoon and he would follow in the wake of the legion of Irish navvies. Joe Hales was in command of the whole house building show and his team of bricklayers was led by Ernie Dagnall and Jack McFarlane of that well known local family of brickies. Tug Wilson was in charge of the hod carriers and he was a bull of a man, an ex war marine commando and a professional drinker. On site I was in company with some of the other apprentices: Derek Brierley, the lothario from the mill, David Johnson, Keith Palmer, and Jack Jones. We were a good crew. The plumbers on the building site were led by 'small in size high in output' Freddie Clarkson and his apprentices. They installed all the pipe work, heating systems, and sanitary ware. They would also glaze the windows after we joiners had put in the frames. Plumbers and joiners usually worked well together except for when we nailed into the plumbers pipes whilst laying the floor boards after which it would be difficult to find any joiners on the scene of the crime for quite some time!

The floor boards together with everything else were made in the joiners shop at the back of the APAS yard before being shipped to site; whatever the item we made it, nothing was bought in. The firm had made a huge investment in machines which were required for many tasks such as sawing through mighty tree trunks or shaping wood via the lethal spindle machine. We had Wadkin saws, planers, belt sanders, and tenon machines to name but a few. The man in charge of the machinery and the bench joiners was Granville Bradley, a towering man of about six foot three who always wore a brown buttoned coat and a cap. In his corner of the workshop there was a desk, a bench and a huge array of cutters, blades, sharpeners, and micrometers. Granville was feared by many because of his authoritative manner but he was brilliant at his work. He would allocate the jobs to the men, passing the most difficult and technical to the chief machinist, Neville Kershaw. Neville's assistant was Jim Goldthorpe who I remember well and we would team up again later when I set up the Housing Units business and he came to run the timber and building sales. Frank Hounsell was the boss of the bench joiners, an incredibly skilled man. Others included Sid Wagstaffe, Alan Warburton, and Sidney Redfern, a lovely guy who lived at home with his mother and would now be called gay. There was also Ron Jackson, another colleague who worked at Housing Units when I arrived there. Many of these bench joiners had incurred injuries on the machinery and were missing fingers or thumbs, or indeed both together. When Jock Simpson lost bits of himself on the spindle he never felt a thing and wasn't aware of having had an accident until he saw the blood. Not having the close attention to detail required by a bench joiner and being naturally accident prone it was just as well that I found my forte with the site joiners. The skills of a site joiner include the building of floor joists, roof timbers, partitions and frames, which are known as first fixings, whilst second fixings consisted of the finishing touches: laying the floors, fitting doors, fixing skirting boards, installing built in kitchens and wardrobes, and all other joinery work. First and second site fixings soon became routine to us and following the initial excitement of working on a house building site the work soon became repetitive. Some of the men were good at both bench and site joinery and Frank Lees was one of them; there was also a strong band of Polish joiners and a real grafter with a short fuse, Eric Ibbotson. Eric later emigrated to Canada where he established a business and built his own wooden house and when I was hitch hiking over there in 1957 I called in to see him.

Back at the yard the works office was run by Harry Howard who was deputy to my dad, Lewis, and his brother, Arthur, the owners of APAS. Harry was in charge of supplies, accounts, and the staff wages. Also in the office were Terry Munday, Derek Lomas (5), and Derek Delhide, the office junior who, a few years later, I was to join at Housing Units (6). Next to the office was the stores and Bill Pass, an ex army Warrant Officer, was in command there. Bill would assemble all the requirements for a particular job and pass both them and the green job sheet to Ernie Berry who was in charge of the yard. Ernie would allocate a handcart if we hadn't already picked our own, and any necessary yard materials. If it was plumbing you needed the King of the Plumbers was Harold Slater who always wore collar and tie and pressed blue bib overalls with immaculately polished brown shoes. Frank Druggitt (7) was another excellent plumber; in his earlier days he had volunteered as a parachutist when Churchill required an airborne force for World War Two. He trained at Manchester Ringway which was then just a shed and airstrip, not the multi runway, world class airport it is today. His brother, Arnold also worked at APAS as a decorator. Other fine plumbers were the ever cheerful Danny Costello, Jimmy Palmer, Tommy Gowers, Jack Percival, Jack Ridings, and Roy Hobson, to name but a few. Roofing was handled by a charismatic Welsh wizard called Tommy Owens and a small chap called Freddie who was his mate. These two were masters of their craft, seasoned roofers well used to dodging very extreme weather. The pair of them always seemed to be more in tune and at home when off the ground; it was almost as though the roof was their stage. Also at the Chamber Road site was a very large fireplace showroom and offices together with a smaller kitchen and bathroom section which was run by Harold Berry (8). Fireplace sales were big business pre war and right up until 1960 and we had about a hundred different items on show with all the latest in heating appliances, stoves, and all night burning fire grates. Once a fireplace had been sold instructions for fitting would be given to Freddie Wolstonecroft and 'Little' George who were the fireplace fitters. They were very efficient and professional although Freddie resembled a gallant Quasimodo as he had a stoop and a shuffle due to all the heavy work lugging monstrous slab fireplaces about! The waggon would drop the pair of them off at the site at 8.30 a.m. together with the fireplace and they would have the job cleared by 5 p.m. There were many others guys of course but their names and faces have become blurred over time, it feels good, however, to go back and recall some of the people from my long ago days as apprentice, every one of them dedicated to his role, a combined and coordinated work force of tradesmen and apprentices, the likes of which is not seen today.

After five years of attending night school and day release I finally obtained a National Building Certificate at the Oldham Technical College. Completing the course meant that I had something to show for my time, unlike the Grammar School experience. At last, the oldest apprentice could now go onto tradesman's pay, and my promotion was of course celebrated with a boozy do at the Mare and Foal pub together with the obligatory butties and beer. Paul Bowers, the youngest apprentice, handed over my indentures, known locally as a 'ticket'; he was just starting out and was on the bottom rung but he did very well and eventually went on to run his own joinery business in the tax haven of Jersey. Meanwhile, as a newly fledged tradesman, I continued to have a great time, both in and outside of work.

1.

2.

3.

4.

1. Arthur Pellowe and Sons in the 1930s, left hand side of the photograph. It was situated on the corner of Chamber Road and Ashton Road and there is now a church on the site.

2. Arthur Pellowe and Sons circa 1930. This is the only photo of my Grandfather that I have been able to trace. Here he is with his staff

3. One of very few shots of my father – at work with Jim Powndall the book keeper. In the background is Dad's Austin 16 – the car we did all the trips to France in after the war.

4. Joe Hales, Site Manager and my boss when I was an apprentice at APAS – we are in the Mare and Foal celebrating the end of my apprenticeship

5. The same occasion – left to right: Bill Pass, stores; Arnold Druggitt, decorator; Frank Lees, Master joiner; Dad; me; George the yardman; Joe Hales; Jack Sykes, plasterer; Sam Grisham; and at the front Little George the roofer and Owen Proctor the new apprentice with his first cig!

6. And there's more! Left to right: Bryn Schofield; Tom Fielding; Kevin Hilton; Jack Barnes; Mel Warburton; me; Ronnie Moores; Sid Redfern; Jimmy Goldthorpe; Paul Bowers and an unidentified person.

5.

6.

Everyone Needs an Apprenticeship: Notes

(1) APAS – Dramatis Personae

Harold Berry – manager fireplace, kitchen, bathroom and plumbing showroom

Freddie Wolstonecroft and Little George – fireplace fitters

Harold Slater, Frank Druggitt, Danny Costello, Jimmy Palmer, Tommy Gowers, Jack Percival, Jack Ridings, Roy Hobson, Freddie Clarkson, Bert Harding - plumbers

Arnold Druggitt - decorator

Tommy Owens and Freddie – roofers

Cliff Wrench – outside foreman

Mr Wilson – transport manager

Jack Jones, Derek Brierley, David Johnson, Keith Palmer, Paul Bowers – some of the apprentices

Frank Whitehead – drainage supremo

Joe Hales – house building chief (my boss)

Ernie Dagnall, Jack McFarlane, Tom Bealby, Joe Bamford – bricklayers

Tug Wilson – hod carrier

Harry Howard – office manager

Derek Delhide – office junior and later a director at HU

Terry Munday and Derek Lomas – office staff

Irene Delaney – office morale (big boobs!)

Bill Pass – stores

Ernie Berry – yard manager

Frank Lees – bench and site joiner

Eric Ibbotson, Frank Kure – site joiners

Frank Hounsell, Sid Wagstaffe, Alan Warburton, Sidney Redfern, Jock Simpson – Bench joiners

Granville Bradley – machine shop manager

Neville Kershaw – chief machinist

Jim Goldthorpe – assistant to Neville Kershaw and HU

Humphrey Childs - driver

And many more fine craftsmen whose names are in my head somewhere but I can't find them!!!

(2) One snowy winter afternoon after completing a job we were returning to the works with our handcart when we came across an appalling scene on Wellington Road which is a very steep hill. At that time coal was delivered on the back of a cart; the heavy, sooty, black bags stacked on top of each other and the whole lot pulled by two horses. Unfortunately on this occasion the horses had lost their precarious grip on the snow and ice covered road and were unable to hold the weight resulting in both cart and horses being pushed down the hill. They were only stopped by crashing into a stone wall which had caused both animals to suffer terrible injuries; they were about to be destroyed. As we passed the scene the whole area was awash with coal, snow and blood and the screaming of the horses rang in our ears as we quietly toiled to get that handcart home. Such were the conditions then, harsh work, and hard winters.

(3) The mill machinery, over which we worked, was built by Platt's who had started making machines for the woollen industry as early as the eighteenth century in very small premises on Nicker Brow in the nearby village of Dobcross. From those humble beginnings Platt's became world class machinery manufacturers exporting looms and such items to mills all over the world.

(4) Derek Brierley, the infamous lothario to the mill girls, was also a champion jive and rock dancer. All the young apprentices were well into the new music scene; Cliff Richard was starting his career, Elvis Presley was on the way to becoming a king and, really importantly, rock n roll had arrived with Bill Haley and the Comets. It was a great time to be young and carefree. At brew times on site we would assemble in one room of a new build whilst Derek put us through our paces. He would demonstrate the latest moves: over the top and under the leg, full body swivel, up in the air, and we would do our best to copy him. This truly was the stuff for the young, well outside the waltz and quickstep era. As well as trying to imitate his dance moves when we were out at night, some of us would also dress accordingly: long jackets with padded shoulders; drain pipe trousers; huge black suede, crepe soled, brothel creepers; and a mop of hair all brushed smooth and greased to form a V down the back of the head. Fortunately, apart from maybe the hair, I personally did not adhere to this dress code. It was an exciting era but even so at chucking out time from the pubs and dance halls the worst the boys in blue could expect was a scrap over walking a girl home or a mild drunken brawl. If a girl had no date she would walk herself home quite safely even at well turned midnight, as indeed Viv tells me she did. Whilst walking home with my pals we would be listening out for a party at someone's house for these events usually finished up with the lights out and, if you were lucky, a snog with a girl behind the settee!

(5) Derek Lomas, Terry Munday and I all played rugby at Keb Lane. Derek went on to

greater things whilst Terry, as well as being a friend, was also a trainee quantity surveyor at APAS. Later he became Company Secretary at Holdsworthy Stockbrokers then moved on to become full time executive at Pall Mall Property where the artist Lowry had worked as a rent collector. In fact one of his pictures adorned the office wall but it was of little importance then. Later Terry and his wife, Francis, went big time – to work in the City of London for UK Land and they settled in Kensington. Amongst Terry's other credits was the fact that he was one of many blokes in Oldham who fancied my wife! Once he was settled in London I would meet up with him when I was down there on business and we would have champagne in his lovely apartment before going on to a show and dinner. Work the following day was always a blur! At one time Terry and Francis visited Guernsey for a holiday and whilst having a casual drink in a bar they got talking to the guy next to them who only turned out to be Donald Falla, our evacuee in the war. What a coincidence. Since settling in London dining at the Savoy has become one of Terry and Francis' habits but they haven't quite mastered the skill of booking a table overlooking the river yet!

(6) I'm sure that Derek Delhide had no idea then how our paths would cross in the future with the ultimate result being that he was later a director at Housing Units.

(7) Frank Druggitt was a master plumber and very well respected by Lewis, my father. In later years Frank nominated me into the Oldham Round Table. During the war he was in the Airborne and was a trained signaller; in fact he took the signal that Wingate, leader of the Chindits in Burma, had been killed when his plane crashed. Following demob in 1946 he was given immediate leave which, according to his son, Steve, he must have made the most of: 'as I was born exactly nine months later.' Frank's brother, Arnold, had been in the Navy during the war and his claim to fame was being involved in the liberation of the Channel Islands. One of their colleagues at APAS, Bert Harding, would join up with the Druggitt brothers when they left APAS in 1950 to set up their own business. Bert also had war experience and had been one of the first into the Belsen camp when it was liberated. Out of the three it is Frank I remember very well. He had started work at APAS when I was born and when I joined the firm as an apprentice he was just about to leave.

(8) Harold Berry ran the fireplace and plumbing division at APAS – he was a good colleague of my father. I believe it was Harold who first went over to start the Housing Units business before Derek Delhide moved there. Harold's brother, Ernest, ran the yard and was often to be found driving my mother around. There was a definite family atmosphere and loyalty at APAS – very much so in fact.

Freedom Years

Life is like a sewer – what you get out of it depends on what you put into it –
Tom Lehrer

As I settled into my apprenticeship I found that life also opened up a few more doors. My interests grew and I was soon involved in training, boxing, rugby, rock climbing and getting into, or on to, anything on wheels that moved. To fit this in as well as three evenings a week at night school made life very busy but manageable. Overall, though, it was motor sports that took up any spare time.

As soon as I was old enough to get a pair of L plates the 250cc Royal

Enfield motorbike which belonged to Dad's works and was used by the foreman became my plaything. By today's standards it was a clapped out bike but boy don't you remember your first wheels. As the works closed around 5.30 p.m., I would be standing there, L plates in my hand ready to spend the evening out and about on the unpredictable machine. As the bike wasn't used at work on a Sunday I would take the opportunity to sometimes venture further afield and would splutter my way over to Blackpool, usually having several minor breakdowns on the way. The Enfield was not a very reliable form of transport but it was a start. My interest in motorbikes grew and in September a few of us bike enthusiasts would catch the overnight ferry from Liverpool to the Isle of Man to watch the Senior Manx Grand Prix. This autumn race was for amateur riders, the main TT races being held earlier in the year (1). We would have a few beers on the boat as we sailed across and morning would find us at a good spot somewhere along the course where we would watch the entrants practice until the actual racing began at midday. The Manx Island course covers thirty one miles but this is not Silverstone or Goodwood, it is run over normal roads, pot holes and all, making for an exciting race and on the return ferry in the evening a party mood usually dominated as we talked over the day's events.

I wanted a motorbike of my own. A lad I had known whilst growing up called Gordon Clark was a keen motorcycle enthusiast; he owned a Trials BSA Bantam and he was a truly competent biker (2). How I envied him as he tinkered about with the bike in his back yard; I was desperate for one of my own so that I could do trials work as well as pleasure riding but there was a problem. Dad had been a biker until he had a bad accident on the Snake Pass between Glossop and Buxton whilst riding his Vincent Black Shadow and he had suffered a leg injury. Nevertheless he was OK about me riding a motorbike whilst the font of all power, Mother, was not. Bearing in mind my catalogue of injuries and propensity to being accident prone over the years her words were: 'he won't last five minutes;' too true actually. So, unbeknown to Mother as well as smuggling rides on the shop bike I became the proud owner of a DOT trials bike (3) which I kept carefully stashed away. Her prophecy came true though as I cracked a collar bone whilst somersaulting over the DOT's handlebars into the river at Parbold during a trials section. Obviously none of this was admissible as proof of my expertise and despite my pestering an 'official' motorbike was banned and deadlock ensued until salvation finally arrived in the form of an unusual contraption called a Bond Minicar which was being built successfully at Preston.

The Bond was a three wheeled vehicle with two seats and a pull over hood and it was categorised as being somewhat similar to a motor cycle whilst having the appearance of a car, a situation which satisfied both Mother and me. The body of the Bond resembled a large wheelbarrow and was made from light aluminium. It had a basic rear suspension and attached to the front wheel was a 125cc Villiers Motorcycle engine which was later upgraded to 197cc. In the cockpit was a pull ratchet handle you had to heave to start the engine, rather like the kick start on a motorcycle. The Bond was a fun car and didn't cost very much, and so I went to the factory to take delivery of the latest model which now had a glass windscreen instead of perspex. One of the Bond's characteristics was a tendency to flip over due to its insubstantial bodywork and this meant care had to be taken whilst turning a corner quickly or you would find yourself scraping your hand along the road as you tried to push the car back into an upright position. The use of a thick leather gauntlet glove sorted that one out! Having been driving the Bond around for a few months on my car licence it came to light that the vehicle was actually classed as a motor cycle which presented a problem because I had ridden my previous bikes on L plates. The solution was incredibly simple, or so I felt, and I started to keep the L plates inside the car in case of emergency, not wanting to damage my street cred by having them on display.

Of course one such eventual emergency soon arrived. Gordon and I drove the midget three wheeler down to Cornwall one Easter to view the classic Lands End Trial, an event he actually competed in later as a representative of the Army in a three man team from the Royal Signals. (I would also compete in these trials many years later together with my son, Tim). Back in the 1950's Gordon and I headed for Blue Hills mine on the coast near Penzance where there are two good sections of the course, both tricky and rough. After spending an enjoyable day watching the field go through we left for Treal Farm where we were to stay for a couple of nights with my vintage relations, the farmer John Johns and the seemingly eternal Aunt Alicia. After the usual fantastic Treal supper which had not changed over the years, Gordon and I piled into the Bond to drive the mile or so down the lane to Cadgwith for a drink. The fishing village consists of a small cove with lots of tiny cottages tumbling down the hillside on to the stony boat cluttered beach below. To one side of the beach was the three hundred year old Cadgwith Cove Inn which was our destination so we hurtled the Bond Minicar down the steep hill which was wet from a recent downpour, skidded round the right hand hairpin bend and aimed for the pub doorway. But pride comes before a fall they say and the tiny wheels of our vehicle offered little resistance on the diesel impregnated tarmac of the bend resulting in us sliding uncontrollably and making a hell of a noise as we crashed into the piles of bins, rubbish, fishing tackle, crab pots and the other flotsam and jetsam of a harbour. To add insult to injury as we came to a stop the debris rained down on top of us but Gordon and I extracted ourselves, cleared the debris and lifted the car back on to the road. As we gazed round it seemed that people had appeared from nowhere to witness the scene but the person who really took our eye was the local bobby who was putting his helmet on as he walked out of the pub. Remembering my absent L plates I muttered to Gordon, 'keep him talking,' as I searched for them in the car. As soon as I had hold of the plates I threw one into the junk surrounding the car and kicked the other underneath the wheels, hoping that the policeman wouldn't notice my actions as it was fortunately dark by now. In a scenario reminiscent of 'Dixon of Dock Green' the Cornish Copper asked: 'What be your name boy?' as he took his notebook out of his breast pocket where it had been resting, untouched, for months or even years as nothing ever happens here. My provisional licence was produced upon request together with Gordon's full one but unfortunately for me the bobby hadn't failed to notice the lack of the obligatory L plates. 'Strange,' I said as I searched around with a puzzled look, trying not to make it too obvious. Eventually I 'found' them, the bobby was satisfied and I relaxed. We checked over the car and, finding only minor damage fixed the L plates to the car as the policeman looked on before joining him in the pub for a little late night drinking with the locals. Of course drink driving laws did not exist at that time so we had no worries about getting back to Treal, racing along the pitch black country lanes, the L plates flapping in the wind.

As well as providing pleasure the Bond was also useful at work when it illegally assisted with towing the occasional long handcart haul to save our legs. Frank Kure, the joiner who always had a tang of garlic about him and spoke interesting English with a Czech accent, became quite adept at leaning over the back of the Bond to hold the end of the ladders steady on the handcart as we negotiated the bends of the Oldham roads on our way to various jobs. In the middle of Oldham was the Star Inn and you would always see a copper or two there as they met up at the Victorian tiled basement public toilets, always on foot of course. Whenever we had to pass by this high risk spot Frank would hop out of the car, detach the hand cart and push the load past the police whilst I drove by. Once out of sight Frank and I would meet up again and reattach the cart to the car. On one occasion as we climbed a steep hill on our way to a job Frank disappeared over the back of the car as he could no longer hold on to the heavily loaded cart but nor could he allow it to become loose and charge down the hill. Poor chap; he was badly grazed but he did not let go of the ladder or the cart. All this was huge fun of course, health and safety being unknown in those days and although we tried to keep our exploits a secret from the management at APAS we were eventually found out because of the speed with which we cleared our jobs! The Bond was great fun; it was only some 15 inches above road level and it ran for ever on a couple of gallons of fuel; however it soon became time for a replacement. Great cars were being made in Britain in the 1950's and 60's whilst in Alvechurch near Birmingham a sports trial car was designed and built by Delingpole and Lowe; it was called a Dellow. The Dellow had a light body on a strong tubular chassis with a 1172cc Ford Popular engine hotted up with a couple of SU carburettors or a supercharger. Unlike the Bond it had a high ground clearance, suitable for off road trialling, but it was also of dual purpose and set to compete with the MG Marque as an 'on the road' sports car with the option of entering as a trials car. So £375 changed hands and I was thrilled to become the proud owner of a second hand Dellow, one year old. She was black with an open top, long flared front wings and red wheels. By the time I had finished with her she also had two indentations in the floor where my passengers would attempt to brake for me whilst I was having 'fun' (4). The registration number was LEL35 and she was named *Waltzing Matilda*.

Having previously competed in rallies with Dad as his navigator I fancied having a go myself and now that I had the Dellow I could get into some serious motoring. The key to my future success was my good friend Jim Smith (5). He and his father ran the Gainsborough Garage in Oldham which later became the impressive Borough Garage, a main BMC (British Motor Corporation) agent. Jim was a good mechanic, and this was very useful as together we would prepare *Waltzing Matilda* during weekday evenings ready for any weekend events. There were many National Rallies to enter: Lakeland, Morecambe, Plymouth (6), Scottish and Welsh, all leading up to the big one, the Great British Rally (GB) and Jim and I competed up and down the country. The Welsh Rally was run in wintry conditions through mountains and passes covered in snow. On a cold and sparklingly clear night the competing cars were bombing on, trying to make up time in the tricky conditions and as we raced along we could see the headlights of the cars in front reflecting the whiteness and purity of the pristine snow. Strangely, as we progressed, the snow covering the road began to gradually turn into a sea of red and as we looked closely we could see dead and dying rabbits all over the place. The answer to this mystery was sad. Britain was at the peak of a

1.

2.

3.

5.

4.

1. Me and Dad in the Jowett Jupiter on the Lakeland Rally
2. The Great Britain Rally with Jim Smith. We are clocking in
before the test on the Promenade at Blackpool.
3. Putting our 'girl' through her paces whilst Prince Frederick
of Prussia tries to do the same in his toppled Porsche
4. Jim rebuilds a written off TR2 – similar to the red one only
ours was green.
5. Aren't they gorgeous?! – Maserati's
6. And so is she! Goodwood Revival meeting 2009

6.

7. Johnny Oscar never believed me but one day I surprised him. Aston Martin for the weekend.

8. Tim and I early dawn climb – one of the Classic Trials

9. Tim airborne – Beggars Roost, Lands End Trial

10. With Gordon Clark, section 2 Blue Hills, Lands End – nearly lost her on the bend

myxomatosis epidemic which had been purposely introduced to reduce the rabbit population and this horrible disease causes the rabbits to become almost blind and unable to see anything much. The intensity and brightness of the car's spotlights reflected by the white snow drew the rabbits to the road and there was no chance for us drivers to avoid them. What an utterly miserable disease to inflict on any animal. It was successful in eradicating the rabbit population though; it wiped them out and walking the Saddleworth moors with the dogs we see very few rabbit even now all these years later.

One day my Old Man announced: 'I've entered you two lads in the RAC GB Rally,' (7) and Jim and I actually went on to compete in three of them over the years. The circumstances of this national event called for us to virtually live in the cockpit of the Dellow for the duration of the four day rally and it was also necessary to drive through two nights. Obviously this kind of action requires a lot of adrenaline and understanding with your co-driver, as well as several doses of Benzedrine and fortunately Jim and I got on very well. One of many bizarre experiences we shared involved an incident when we had been driving all day and all night, taking it in turns to sleep curled up on the floor of the Dellow. It was my turn to drive and Jim was being bounced around on the floor of the car, semi sleeping when in front of us I spotted Anne Hall, a Yorkshire lass and excellent driver who was competing strongly against the famous Sheila von Damm for the ladies prize. It was about 6 a.m. and we were in the Newmarket area where the dew was rising to form a hanging mist; God it's hard to concentrate as dawn is just breaking and you are so desperately tired. As we hurtled round the corner after her I realised that Anne's red Jaguar XK120 had stopped on the verge and in front of her car was a push bike with a bent front wheel surrounded by loads of newspapers which had also scattered across the road. Out of the corner of my eye I noticed Anne consoling a young lad and even though we were running tight on time to get to the finish in Hastings I pulled over as it seemed Anne may need help. As I slid to a halt Jim woke up and muttered bewilderedly: 'What's up?' 'Dunna know,' I replied, 'get back in your hole and rest.' I wandered over to Anne and the boy who, it turned out, had innocently been delivering his newspapers unaware that the competition cars partaking in the main rally to be held in Britain were about to disturb him. Unfortunately he had been in line with her car and had come a cropper but after checking that he wasn't injured Anne quickly thrust a £5 note in his hand for repairs to his bicycle and the newspaper boy was ecstatic; his bike was only worth ten bob! I helped to pick up and fold the papers whilst Anne dusted the lad down as she murmured: 'Are you sure you're OK, we really have to leave we are late.' 'Thanks missus, I'll be OK and thanks very much.' Can you imagine today's headlines if there was such an incident now? Jim has reminded me of another incident on a Welsh mountain section in the early hours. We were on a narrow road which took us over a humpback bridge followed by an immediate left hand bend. Apparently the Dellow became airborne as it hit the bridge and the whole scene was illuminated by the headlights of car behind us. Jim says he remembers seeing me turning the wheel whilst still in the air and as the car landed we managed the left hand bend perfectly! Times change of course; the GBR was originally two thousand miles and was known as the 'Rally of the Tests' but it is now competed with works teams sponsored by car manufacturers and is a world event. There are off road and forest sections to race through at one minute intervals, omitting the use of public roads, and it is a completely different ball game with no overnight driving so everyone gets a full night's sleep. In our day it was still possible for the amateur to pull off a great win as a chap called Doc Hardman did in the Daily Express Redex Rally. Doc was the king of all Dellow drivers and, together with his wife and co driver Mollie, they were an ace team. His car ran on Wyresole tyres and as we followed him through the night we would see the sparks from them taking off the tarmac whilst on another occasion he drove his Dellow up the front steps of the Grand Hotel in Brighton to receive a winning cup! Doc was not just a nickname as this man was actually a GP from Blackpool who used his trials car to do his medical rounds; together with him and Mollie, Jim and I carried the flag for Dellow in the early Great Britain Rallies.

Eventually we were driving *Waltzing Matilda* accurately and fast and would periodically drive for the North West Driving Competition team. She was a kind car although quite often airborne. She always looked after us so that we arrived home in one piece and we shared some exciting experiences; things you could never get away with nowadays. All the competitors spent a lot of their time crawling around their machinery, 'fettling' it to give the driver the edge, cursing, patching, repairing, burning hands, emerging in the early hours of the morning after an all night engine change, or replacing back axles mid competition. It was all good fun. Jim and I changed the front wheels from the standard seventeen inch to non standard sixteen inch ones and fitted a three inch diameter pipe into an air intake box to get more cool air to the carburettors. These modifications greatly improved the performance of the car and we had a distinctly fast Dellow, we even got to the stage where we could beat Doc Hardman to fastest time of the day on some driving tests although admittedly not many. But despite the modifications we were driving her right to the edge of her limits and eventually we came to the end of our rallying career (8). Jim had been a great mechanic and co driver, whilst Dad had been very supportive all the way through and had in fact helped out financially by sponsoring us which we really appreciated.

Although most of my freedom years were taken up with driving I still had other interests to squeeze in and so when the Dellow was not in action the weekends were still full. Occasionally I would revisit the climbing crags of Saddleworth and of course I still played rugby. On a Saturday evening some of my friends would meet in a house come off licence called The Hole in the Wall. After getting well oiled there the lads would take the floor at Froggat's dance hall where couples would meet, swap partners, and generally size up the talent, some eventually teaming up for the long term. Maybe it was the memory of the children's dance classes at Billington's that I had at one time endured but dancing was not for me in my teens although I enjoy something which resembles dancing these days and get itchy feet when I hear the beat. No, for me it was preferable to have a game of rugby then make regular stops at pubs on the way home in the team bus. By the time we got back to Oldham most of us were well beyond steering a lass round the dance hall floor anyway. However I may occasionally have been spotted skulking around other venues such as King Street Stores or the Savoy ballroom. It was around then that I established my convenient friendship with Margaret who happened to live next door and this did in fact curtail some of the after game boozing. Margaret decided to train to be a physiotherapist and went to live and study at Oswestry Hospital. If I was not eventing in the car on the Sunday then after Saturday's rugby game

I would drive down to Oswestry in the Dellow to spend some great weekends with her, staying at the pub by the railway crossing in Gobowen. On the Sunday we would have dinner at the pub and much, much later I would drive Margaret back to the hospital. The following morning saw my early dawn departure as I rushed back to work in Oldham and as I had to be back on site by 8 a.m. I had a few hairy trips. One icy Sunday evening I parked my car in the pub's garage after dropping Margaret off. Now I may have had a drink or two but I remembered that I must cover the car radiator to stop it from freezing and so I looked round the garage for something suitable to use and grabbed an old sack. I remember thinking that it felt very bottom heavy but I plonked it on the car anyway, supported by the number plate bracket and thus covering the radiator. The following morning saw my usual hasty, last minute departure to make it back to Oldham in time for work; the roads were full of snow, it was very cold and as I belted up to Mere crossroads the car spun on the ice; round and round it went until eventually stopping of its own accord. I couldn't believe my eyes. Surrounding my car and scattered all over the road was half a hundredweight of potatoes and a large sack; passing cars, already having difficulty in the snow, now had to negotiate a load of spuds as well. I had to chuckle though as I thought about the pub landlord back in Oswestry who would be looking for his sack full of provisions, scratching his head and wondering where they could have gone. I'm sure he didn't think for one moment that they had hitched a lift and were now scattered all over a main road many miles away!

Looking back I question whether I always got life's priorities right and Viv assures me I didn't. She says that whilst I was doing all my messing around with bikes and cars I was missing out on courting – and she was right. Nevertheless I was very appreciative of having the opportunity with the Dellow. Eventually *Waltzing Matilda* and her history of good performances would be sold; she had indeed been a true, safe friend to Jim and I in some very touch and go situations. Even to this day I remain great friends with Jim Smith and am indebted to him for his mechanical brilliance and belief in keeping our wheels on the road. Many years after my Dellow was sold I was fortunate enough to find her again and buy her back (9); in fact she was bought through the company and put through the books as a circular saw! She now stands proud and polished in my son, Tim's, garage, semi retired like me.

So, whilst completing my apprenticeship I had also enjoyed a good and busy period with hardly any spare time, but now I was twenty one there was something else I had to do; National Service.

Freedom Years: Notes

(1) Remember at this time British bikes were king; Norton dominated and the rider's were great guys such as Geoff Duke, John Surtees, and Derek Minter. Each year these lads were smashing the TT (Tourist Trophy) lap records. The Manx course is demanding with a long mountain road where you can hit 130 mph followed by the hairpins of Creg-ny-Baa where you need to slow down to 15 mph. After the experience of watching a race like this the smell of burning Castrol R oil stays with you forever.

(2) Gordon worked as a dental technician but later on left dentistry and joined Geoff Coop at Fairfield Motors in Shaw before going on to start up his own body shop. Many years after that he joined me at Housing Units where he ran the customer service van; we still remain friends now after all these years and although Gordon has now turned seventy he remains a good rider and still has a motorcycle hidden away in an outbuilding!

(3) A DOT trials bike was being ridden about by a local lad, Eric Adcock, and he represented the DOT works team in National and International trials. He was a splendid rider, much encouraged by his Dad and out competing every weekend. His house was full of cups and awards and it was Eric's influence that spurred me on to buy my own model but I was better on four wheels!

(4) One of the fun features of the Dellow was a toggle brake which was situated on the outside of the car on the driver's side. This, together with the necessary practice, enabled me to become adept at spinning the car round in its own length, amidst much burning of tyres of course. However if you got it wrong the car could turn over.

(5) My Mum assisted Nina, Jim's wife, with the birth of two of their children who were born at home as was usual in those days and it was certainly not the done thing for the father to be present at the birth then. Jim was hovering outside the bedroom door at the crucial time asking if he could be of any help and my Mother, not one to mince words, replied: 'You've done enough damage; get away, we'll call you when we need you.' To this day Jim and Nina tell me how glad they are that they met the Pellowe family. They were both very good to my mother in her later years and even took her along with them to their holiday home abroad. When my Dad died Jim felt a great loss.

(6) At one stage I decided to enter the Plymouth Rally but as Jim wasn't available I had to borrow Dad's navigator, Tom Martin. The event turned out to be an 'edge of the wall' experience for him as in the middle of the night, somewhere on Exmoor, the gear lever broke off. Tom and I frantically attempted a temporary repair using barbed wire of all things from a nearby field. Following this 'tweet' when it came to some hard driving or speed tests Tom had to hold the barbed wire link as firmly as possible to prevent the car jumping out of gear. On Plymouth Hoe, during the final tests, we hurled the car through her paces even though she twice slipped out of gear and we were convinced that we would not be placed very high and so didn't wait for the results but drove home. The next day we got a call to say we were runners up; we had missed a win by only 2.5 seconds despite the difficulties we had encountered. Tom was elated, a premier rally, almost won with the help of a piece of barbed wire which just goes to show - never give up!

(7) Winner of the GB rally more than once was Ian Appleyard in his white Jaguar XK120 whilst Johnny Wallwork, a great exponent of the Triumph TR2, was also a winner. Stirling Moss and Mike Hawthorn were the big names in racing driving in those days using works cars in the GBR. Mike actually made a brief appearance driving a couple of numbers in front of us in an Austin Healey and he later went on to win the World Championship from Stirling Moss by one point 42:41 in the final race of the season in Morocco. Ironically Mike was killed on the Guildford by pass (then the A3) in his own 3.4 Jaguar saloon. He had just passed Rob Walker, another well known racing driver who was driving a Mercedes Benz 300SL and the speed was approaching 100 mph. Were they having a dice? It was a wet and very windy day on 22nd January 1959 and he was only a few miles from home on a road he travelled constantly.

(8) In 1964 Paddy Hopkirk won the Monte Carlo Rally in a BMC Mini. Jim and I had been invited to co-drive a Riley Pathfinder in the same event with Hugh Gault but declined.

(9) Only around three hundred Dellow's were produced. Two hundred and fifteen have been traced (as at 2006) and there is a Dellow register. *Waltzing Matilda*, the old girl that we competed in is retired and stored in Tim's garage as mentioned where she is longing for the wake up call for her to compete in Classic trials. Perhaps when Tim gets more time and Sam, his son, is older, LEL35 will get back to competing which is what she likes best. My money is on it anyway.

Two Year Holiday

You know, I'd buy you a parachute if I knew it wouldn't open - Groucho Marx

Surprisingly I was absolutely comfortable at the prospect of joining up when the letter arrived ordering me to attend a medical prior to being conscripted. This was the time when all young men had to join one of the Armed Services and there were very few exceptions, so I ambled along to a Manchester venue to be checked out for fitness prior to my scheduled two year holiday. I had received vibes from those who had gone before me about the two year time warp that was called National Service and I had my own ideas about this which I would play out in due course. The venue for the mass medical was a large drill hall which contained a real mixed bag of guys: office workers, farmers, steelworkers, professionals, butchers, bakers; there may even have been a candle stick maker! There were guys in drain pipe trousers with mops of hair swept up in the popular DA style; gents in city dress; even the odd overall clad manual worker but mostly there was an air of uncertainty about the place. At one stage we were asked to give a urine sample and those who could not get their plumbing going had the sink tap turned on to encourage them but once underway found they could not stop. This maybe had something to do with the fact that they had bladders full of beer following a lunchtime trip to the nearby pub! One of the leakers was mopping up in a cubicle under the supervision of a female nurse's disdainful eye when a sergeant in the RAMC (Royal Army Medical Corps) popped his head in, saw the mess, and shouted something unprintable at the embarrassed recruit. Loads of guys were spluttering and limping, putting on well rehearsed acts of disability, but even they had to eventually line up bollock naked whilst they were visited by white coated people including female nurses. Some of the lads covered their tackle with a sheet of paper whilst those with rugs of hair on their chests participated enthusiastically in their exposure. During this physical examination any men getting too excited by the occasion were given a flick with a slim form of baton which seemed to do the trick. Clothed once again it was time to sit the so called 'IQ' test which could have been handled by a twelve year old but still gave the duckers an opportunity. As well as fumbling the test, some of the lads made a play of having poor eyesight assisted by the wearing of bottle bottom glasses. However, regardless of the fact that some of the 'would be' recruits had damp trousers whilst others were bruised and battered from bumping blindly around, it was inevitable that everyone would eventually be passed as fit one way or another. And so it was that the bed wetters and 'blind' people were devastated to know the army would take even them, and those who had worked so hard to fail were astonished to find they were fit enough to join. Personally I was quite happy to be passed as fit and enquired about joining the Marines but I would have had to sign up for three years so, remembering my old mate Ian Platt's impressive appearance as a Military Policeman with a motor bike thrown in, I thought I would go for that. And so I was sent to the South Lancashire Regiment, located in Warrington, for basic training.

Warrington was absolutely freezing in January 1955. I had already anticipated a culture shock but it soon became obvious that a lot of the others hadn't expected what they got at all; however we all recoiled at the power mad corporal bursting into the bunkhouse at 5.30 a.m., throwing anything that came to hand and bellowing at us. It would have been the wish of many to demonstrate we were here to kill starting with this noisy b*****d. Nevertheless we put our heads down and pressed on as thousands of others had already done; it's the army's way of welcoming a crumby, uncoordinated mob of individuals and you are treated as the scum of society. Actually they may have had a point. With the basic training out of the way it was down to the Royal Military Police (RMP) depot based at Inkerman Barracks in Woking for sixteen weeks training. Initially this consisted of intensive drill which made sure you stood taller when finishing the course than you had at the beginning. The weather was cold, miserable and gloomy and, towards the end of my time there, I picked up a chest infection which inevitably led to a bad dose of the bronchitis to which I was prone. Stuck in the sick bay for a few days I found I was sharing a room with a lunatic who was seriously trying to get himself discharged. Apart from plenty of other odd behaviour he would consistently wet his bed and his ultimate party piece was to trash the room in the middle of the night. I really wasn't feeling up to this and had no sympathy for him and so tried to restrain him. He retaliated by threatening to kill me and so we both set about trying to kill each other at every opportunity and after three nights of battle we both looked the worse for wear. Meanwhile the Doctor actually asked me for my opinion on whether the guy was really crackers or just acting and I replied that I believed he was faking it all, but they must not have taken much notice of my view for he got his wish and was discharged from the Army. Three nights of a self survival course whilst spluttering my way through a dose of bronchitis was hell and sick parade was to be avoided at all costs in the future.

In due course we passed out from Woking after making a hash of a drill movement at the passing out parade, even after the hours and hours of practice we had put in. Just before completing the course we had found out that if you went on to train for the Airborne you would get an extra quid or so in your pay. This seemed a really good idea and fun as well so a couple of us signed up for it and as soon as the police course finished we were sent to Aldershot. The pre Para course is hard going and the drop out rate can be very high but once that was out of the way we were sent to RAF Abingdon where we learnt to fall out of aeroplanes. Our first jump was made out of a balloon rather than a plane. Once in the basket of the balloon everyone sits round a hole in the floor looking pensive and keeping quiet whilst rising to about one thousand feet. I remember thinking that it didn't seem natural to just slide your bottom over the edge of the hole and out into space but as it meant extra pay I forced myself and, as it turned out, it was a stimulating experience. Attached to a metal rail above your head is a stake line from the parachute pack. The dispatcher stands in front of you and when he says 'go' you just slip over the edge with a whoosh; your body speed hurtles to the maximum and your stomach hits your brain. After three seconds there is a crack like the sound of several sheets being torn and your rapid descent is arrested as your harness grabs your body. You will open your eyes, wondering what the hell has happened whilst above you is a wonderful white mushroom canopy suspending you as you stand on air. It is a fantastic moment and absolutely the quietest place I have ever been; I felt like I had actually arrived in heaven. Looking around the 360 degree vista I wanted to stay up there for hours, semi comatose, whilst holding the canopy straps and tilting or spilling air from the canopy. Wonderful and they were paying me extra to do this! As the ground loomed nearer I had to quickly pull myself together, a rude interruption in a moment of oblivion.

However it was not always to be so good. The next seven jumps will be out of aircraft and we will have to carry heavy canisters; also one of the drops will be at night and although a water drop into Poole Harbour is cancelled the night jump is still on. With a small degree of apprehension we bundle into a crowded Hastings and fly off into the darkness, heavy canisters containing about eighty five pounds of tackle in them attached to our harnesses. The trick is to pull the pin and release the canister away from your body on a thirty foot line when you are approaching the ground but unfortunately I didn't mange to do this; I was one of the last out of the plane and the wind had shifted slightly taking me away from the dropping zone. I misjudged my height and release and all I could see was blackness as I dropped downwards eventually landing in a heap on a tarmac road together with my heavy container. I eventually came to in an ambulance as the canister had knocked me out when it hit me; my ankle was fractured due to the impact with the road and although it was subsequently strapped up this damaged ankle still comes back to haunt me. Thanks Margaret and Beverley at Oldham Hospital Orthotics department for all your help with my converted boots over the years! I was fed up to say the least as the rest of the qualifiers attended their 'wings' parade whilst I was languishing in hospital. Needless to say it was a bit of a downer after all that training, having to receive my wings from a hospital bed!

At last we were moved to our first posting with the Para Provost 16th Independent Parachute Brigade. The unit was made up of: I/C Captain (Captain in charge), RSM (Regimental Sergeant Major), two sergeants, three corporals and between twelve and eighteen lance corporals. Our MP red top peaked hats were now substituted for red berets although of course the police cap badge was still on board. Late summer saw us back in Aldershot with the Army where sport was greatly encouraged so, not wanting to be left out, I latched onto the boxing team. In the morning we would do a little sparring and in the afternoon we were expected to do road work i.e. jogging. This turned out to be an incredible skive. Simply donning a maroon army issue track suit I would jog past the various drilling activities, out of the gate and down into Aldershot where I would evaporate into the cinema. As you can imagine I was well abreast of the film releases in 1955! After the show I would go into the gents to give myself a good dowsing with water ensuring I made an impressive and exhausted looking entrance back at the barracks for tea. It was a routine that worked very well for me for the few months we were in the UK although just now and again you were expected to box in competitions which was completed with great enthusiasm although we seemed to have only limited success. General police duties around Aldershot were actually quite boring and only broken up by the odd military exercise but Christmas was approaching and we were to get a good period of leave as we were going to Cyprus in the New Year.

It was good to be home although I had to be careful what I said as Mother had somehow been under the impression that I was being trained in PT (Physical Training); something Dad and I had allowed her to think to keep her quiet. Whilst home on leave I joined up with my pal, Ian Platt, the ex MP. Ian had been living in India whilst learning the tea trade but after eighteen months he had been obliged to make a hasty departure when there was trouble and some plantation owners were shot; Ian was not the type to hang around with that kind of thing going on. I had received a telegram from him asking me to meet the ship he was returning on which was due to arrive in Liverpool the next morning. He gave me the dock number and asked me to be there at 6 a.m. sharp which was not a problem as fortunately I had access to a lovely green TR2, rebuilt after becoming a write off by my old co driver Jim Smith. As I arrived on the dock alongside the ship there was not a soul to be seen, no security, nothing. I pondered over the situation but at 6.10 a.m. I saw a figure loaded up with suitcases and carrying a bag of golf clubs on his back leaving the ship. Dressed in a smart black gabardine coat, black cap and white polo neck sweater, Ian, looking suave as ever, gestured for me to keep quiet and as he got into the car he said: 'quick Johnny let's get out of here.' The TR2 ghosted out of the dock area, hood down, Ian's gear spilling out as he explained: 'I'm dead broke and wasn't able to leave a tip for the crew.' He goes on to tell me how he was travelling steerage but after chatting up an attractive Indian doctor he had moved in to her first class accommodation for the remainder of the journey. Nice one and very typical of Ian, nothing had changed. We teamed up together throughout that Christmas leave period, both of us just back from 'somewhere'. On New Year's Eve we went to a dance and I was dressed in my Number One Blues dress uniform, a real bloody show off but it didn't cut any ice with the girls. Part way through the evening I saw an old friend across the dance floor, Vivienne. Vivienne was the girl I had met on my first day in primary school and been friends with throughout our junior years. Of course we had seen each other around since those early days but not too much. She was with her fiancée, Geoff Shore; just shows how people forget but I remembered the time when Viv sat on the outside loo at my house, aged five, telling me she was my sweetheart and how she would marry me one day. Ian had his eye on Jackie Walker that evening; a most attractive blonde girl (and still is) she had with her an equally stunning brunette called Margaret Shaw (not the student physiotherapist from Oswestry) and although our paths crossed I regret that I did not date her. No excuse even though I was due to return to the Army in a few short days to be kitted out for a tour in Cyprus which was a good posting I believed.

1.

2.

3.

4.

5.

1. Dad's Army – Dad with his fellow officers of the Home Guard – he is the one in the bottom right hand corner– smoking!
2. My unit, 16th Indp Para Provost Company ready to go on patrol in Nicosia, Cyprus
3. Clean exit
4. A patrol in the Troodos Mountains, Cyprus
5. The unit football team – rubbish at football but some really good guys

Two Year Holiday Part Two

This is great. When does it start? – Groucho Marx after watching a cricket match for one hour

In 1957 the Greek Cypriots were getting really uppity about British presence on the island whilst we needed to maintain our bases there which were of strategic importance for defending that area of the Mediterranean. The political situation was very complex but suffice to say the Greek Cypriots formed a resistance movement and dealing with them would be our lot for the year ahead. The Brigade and Regiments to which I belonged slowly made their way out there and for some reason three of us flew out ahead in an old Dakota via Ta'Qali airfield in Malta (1) where we landed for refuelling. We were met by a tall red cap MP in a smart Land Rover: 'We heard you were coming bugger,' he said as I recognised Gordon Ryder, an ex Oldhamer who had passed out a few intakes ahead of me at the Woking training depot. Small world. Our stay in Malta would be brief as we were due to fly on to Cyprus the following afternoon but we later heard that there was a problem with our plane and we would be delayed so we slipped into our civvies and enjoyed a couple of days break. Few servicemen will visit Valetta without visiting the 'Gut', the B and B of Malta, brothels and bars from top to bottom. Not a trip for the faint hearted and it would be unwise to attempt to quote what is on offer in that narrow street. So much to say as you sit at a bar a young woman will sidle up to you, take your hand and pass it under her skirt where you find she has no underwear. 'Johnny it is all for you,' she whispers and if you haven't already choked on your drink with shock the shopping list is offered and you become more and more astounded. Previously the Army attempted to show us a film about 'what could be picked up for free in the red light districts'. It had seemed like a huge joke at the time but that evening there was no rush towards the curtained off alcoves across the room.

All too soon our plane was repaired and we pressed on to Nicosia in Cyprus where the Parachute Brigade settled into the job of policing and protecting our assets on the island although it was immediately very clear to me that we were not welcome. The Greek Cypriots wanted to get rid of British rule and had formed a resistance movement, EOKA, to deal with this and, whilst many of the island's inhabitants were still friendly towards us, it was apparent that there was a dangerous undercurrent. Ledra Street in the old town was a crossing line between the Greek and Turkish communities and there was so much trouble there that it became known amongst the troops as the Murder Mile. Later this crossing became the barricaded border between the Greek Cypriot and Turkish parts of the island which remained in place until 2008. As MP's we patrolled the streets (2) or spent time searching out EOKA encampments in the Troodos mountains where the resistance were entrenched in the thick forests. There were terrorists all over the island and they were supported by the Greek population who sheltered, hid and fed them. How do you deal with that? It was a difficult and confusing time not helped by the abundance of underground information we were given, which was often duff. If intelligence told us that terrorists were sheltering or working out of a certain village very often a dawn raid would ensue. Troops from one of the Regiments would surround the suspect village well before dawn then gradually they would move in and conduct house to house searches. An interrogation compound would be set up and all this would be completed before the sun had barely risen. Any suspects found in the village were brought into the compound whilst the Intelligence Corps (lovely title) set themselves up in a large tent where the 'chat show' would commence. We, as police, ran the compound but what went on in that interrogation tent I could not say; however, if a detainee was suspected of being an EOKA member or helper but had not confessed, he would be handed to us to supervise as he dug a deep hole in which he would have to spend the night. The hole would be filled once he was in it leaving only his head exposed and periodically throughout the night water was gently poured into the soil surrounding him ensuring a shivering person was extracted the next morning ready to go into the tent for another chat. I honestly doubt if much was achieved by all this but it kept us busy and maintained a presence. Never, to my knowledge, were the prisoners seriously mishandled other than maybe on the odd cold night. In fact in the compound there was usually a party atmosphere as the various detainees met up and their wives brought fresh bread, cheese and olives which we passed to them.

When not out on exercise the troops come back to barracks and our work would take on a different role. Certain areas in Nicosia were out of bounds as they were considered to be vulnerable to EOKA (3) attacks and we had to police these places together with the MP's of the RAF. One such place was Tanzimat Street, the place of the ladies of the night, and it was strictly out of bounds but not to the determined trooper in need of company. As the MP vehicle rumbled through the red light area the girls would wave and shout: 'no Johnnies here.' As we passed they would disappear back into their lairs believing us to be gone but we would double back and surprise a soldier in situ, boots and rifle butt sticking out from under the bed! The EOKA fighters were smart and knew that a soldier visiting a brothel would probably be armed and in order to go about his business he would have to put his gun down. They recruited lithe young boys who were able to ghost in and pinch the discarded weapon whilst the soldier was otherwise engaged; even the girls themselves would work together on this one as there was good payment for weapons, probably a lot more than they charged for their own services! Losing your gun was a serious offence and so a Court Marshall often ensued but even this did not deter the woman hungry blokes. There were lots of other incidents mostly of a humorous nature and we always practised a little bit of give and take if one of our own had strayed as long as he had been sensible enough. However, if booze had taken over brain it could be a completely different matter. One night we got a call from the RMP police station in the old walled town, asking us to collect a Para they had arrested. We found him out cold on the floor of the police station looking in a very poor state. 'He's been busy throwing things through windows,' we were told. 'You haven't hurt him have you?' I asked looking at his bruises. 'No, he did that himself,' is the debatable reply. That particular night I am in company with Brian Hadfield, also known as Stan; a six foot plus Yorkshire lad from over Grimethorpe way. We pick the unconscious guy up from the floor and heave him onto my shoulder in a fireman's lift whilst Stan carries my gun together with his own. The cool night air hits us as we approach our vehicle and I feel a movement, the unconscious guy is coming round: 'Nothing serious, soon be there,' I tell him but then I stop dead and freeze. His head is on my shoulder facing into my neck and as he stirs he opens his mouth and bites down hard on my ear. I have no time to speak but quickly spin round; in a flash Stan has sensed what is happening and throws one of the Sten (4) guns at the guy's head resulting in him relaxing his bite but my ear is badly cut and subsequently needs stitches. One more second and he would have bitten it off completely.

Another of our duties was the miserable job of checking all the civilians as they came through the gate to work in our camp. One Cypriot always played us up: 'Hi Johnny I have a bomb in my bag,' or some such troublesome remark. I would then have to search him which was a pain and I got so fed up that I decided to catch him out. The next time he came through the check point I slipped two bullets from the magazine of my gun into his basket as I frisked him. As he passed through he gave his usual insolent wave but this time I called him back and ordered him to: 'tip out your basket.' Lo and behold there were two bullets being 'smuggled' into the barracks! He rapidly changed colour as he was read the riot act and desperately pleaded his innocence, he was in a real state as he broke down spluttering whilst peeing in his pants but I was getting a lot of value from his discomfort after all the trouble he had repeatedly caused me. Pulling him to one side I told him that in future he must not play us up and that this had being a warning. He wobbled off, sweating profusely and assuring me 'no problems in future Johnny.' That afternoon the RSM marched me into the CO's office where I was asked to explain what had happened earlier at the gate. My case was put forward, how the Greek needed a lesson and how he was a nuisance and a worry to us, but it was all in vain and I got a severe warning. The little bastard had shopped me but I had had my monies worth and he did conform thereafter when he passed through the gate.

For their own safety, lots of soldiers were more or less confined to barracks but quite often they would be treated to an escorted trip to the beach at Kyrenia or to a safe venue for some recreation. Some great stars came over to Cyprus to entertain us and there were many superb shows. It was on such a show night that it was my turn to act as escort for the Brigadier, Tubby Butler, who was commander of the whole Parachute force, a good and popular man. The concert hall would have been security checked before the evenings entertainment but even so there were armed troops swarming all over the place. I escorted Tubby to his seat on the second row and retired to the back to view the show. Jimmy Edwards had been billed as the star and was to appear with two girls one of whom was Joy Shelton I recall. Whoever they were they really inspired the lads! The band struck up a merry tune and up went the curtain but the stage was completely empty. The initial clapping died away as the stage remained empty and still no one appeared. The first three rows containing the top brass were getting restless and edgy as they chatted to each other wondering what was happening, then, right out of their midst, on the second row, a guy in uniform stood up and walked on to the stage. I had noticed this fellow earlier, seated quite near to Tubby with his head buried in an apparently very interesting, full sized newspaper. As he stood on the stage I realised it was him, the star of the show, Jimmy Edwards. His large handlebar moustache bristling he proceeded to bring the house down as he addressed the moaning whingers in the audience. He had waited until the very last moment when the patience of the men was severely tried and many of them were about to stand up and complain vociferously. He had built the momentum to a perfect pitch and his timing was just right; he had taken them to the edge, he was absolutely great, a true star. Jimmy was dressed in something like a Lieutenant General's Mess uniform and he went through his repertoire and played his trombone. He was at his peak and must have gone on for at least an hour before he brought the girls onto the stage when the entire hall erupted with clapping, whistling, cheering and foot stamping. It was brilliantly awesome stuff. At the end of the show encore followed encore and there were a few damp eyes in even the hardest of men but eventually everyone left the hall and I went to look for Tubby.

Now Tubby Butler was a very charismatic and sociable chap and he was found back stage with some of the other Brass drinking bubbly and chatting to the tired but jubilant stars. 'Be out shortly,' he told me as he noticed me waiting in the wings so I went outside where the staff cars and escorts were thinning out leaving our large Mercedes in centre stage. Eventually, after a long wait, Tubby appeared with the female stars, one on each arm and they proceeded to spend the rest of the evening in a smart nightclub in one of the hotels in Nicosia. As I waited for Tubby with his driver we deployed ourselves strategically outside the hotel, feeling quite uneasy at the unnecessary risk he seemed to be taking. It was perfectly silent and there was no hint of trouble but nevertheless we were in the middle of a violent episode of unrest on the island and Tubby was a real scalp. We waited in the cool evening air; 1 a.m., 2 a.m., 2.30 a.m. It's so bloody quiet out here, 'come on guvnor, enough's enough'. Just before 3 a.m. the boss and his friends at long last appear in a blast of light, hot air and merriment. He takes the girls to their hotel and says his good nights as they wave us off. Wow it has been a long night for all of us but as we drop him off at his accommodation in the camp Tubby turns to me and says: 'Corporal, could you collect me at 0500 hours, just us, no escort, see you then.' By now it is only a couple of hours until 5 a.m. and so no time to ponder much about what he wants. Uniform off and pressed, webbing blancoed, boots polished, then back into the car and the driver and I are there on the dot. Now what? 'Drive down to Archbishop Makarios' place,' was the order and as we arrive at the entrance the car pulls up, the boss slides the glass partition aside and informs me: 'morning prayers will just have finished; would you knock on the door and ask that Archbishop Makarios and the Bishop of Kyrenia come out to the car?' We have made calls here before but this time it is different. I walk up the path and knock on the large posh door. A young dark skinned service boy appears and behind him a servant lingers: 'Compliments of Brigadier Butler who has requested the two Bishops join him in his car,' I say and the servant seems to understand. There is a pause and it is so quiet and tense that the seconds seem like minutes but eventually, to my great surprise and almost as if orchestrated, out of the dark interior of the palace there emerge two men wearing full black robes with huge chains and crosses hanging on their chests, their black box hats adding to their height and impressiveness. I am unsure what to say: 'Good morning, how do?' or a more formal 'your Highness, would you kindly join my Brigadier in the car.' There is a sense of expectancy as they walk to the parked car where the rear door is already open. Two good sized folding seats have been dropped to accommodate them and as the door shuts a conversation ensues. As the driver and I are in the front of the car behind the sliding glass window we cannot hear what is being said but following the conversation in the back we were to make one more journey before returning to the barracks. Once back the boss thanks us and tells us to get some rest as it's been a long night. I will never forget his words. History was being written in those early unassuming hours of 9th March 1956 as the events of the day would reveal. Suffice to say that later that day, at 1630 hours to be precise, Archbishop Makarios, Bishop Kyprianos and two close associates received a deportation order to say they were to be exiled at the Governor's pleasure. All hell let loose when the Cypriots realised that Makarios and his pals had gone, security was stepped up and a lot of trouble followed. I often think back to that day; good old Tubby would be written off after a night out like that one but it's not so and he knew it; whatever actually went on that early morning of 9th March 1956 remains unwritten.

With Makarios out of the way Georgios Grivas, the EOKA leader, took on the political and military leadership of the resistance and launched a new offensive designed to transform the whole island into a battlefield. Grivas was a very experienced operator and was always one step ahead; in his memoirs he said he believed that the Governor General of Cyprus, Sir John Harding, had made a great mistake by getting rid of Makarios and that he was more than ready to take advantage of the error. He went on to explain how the British Army missed many opportunities to catch both him and his men; on one occasion he and his band dressed as shepherds and actually saluted to a British patrol as they walked by! Another time he was hidden so well that our troops nearly stood on top of him. The guerrilla war was being conducted mainly in the Troodos Mountains where patrols from the Marines, Gordon Highlanders and ourselves made concentrated efforts to locate EOKA camps and capture a long list of wanted men. Kykkos monastery was a well known harbouring post for terrorists and resembled a bed and breakfast run by the priesthood for EOKA. Spot checks were frequent here and signs of the terrorist's visits were often quite evident. Patrol exercises lasted a week or longer before we handed over to the next group and a dusk to dawn curfew was imposed. Anything that moved in the morass of forest during that time would be shot although the main casualties were goats who moved so stealthily and some soldiers, it was said, who were sadly shot by their colleagues whilst out on ablutions! On one of our patrols a guy with a camera accompanied us although we didn't take much notice of him at the time but when I was home on leave a few months later I had cause to remember him. I was at the Odeon Cinema with a friend when the Pathé news came on with its fast rolling commentary and there on the silver screen, right out of the blue, was our patrol in action being led to a terrorist camp in Troodos by a collaborator.

Pathé continued to show us arriving at the empty camp where fire embers were still warm; doubtless the EOKA members had been warned about our visit. At the time I found it very hard to believe that I was seeing our patrol on the news reel of our local Oldham cinema.

Back in Cyprus we continued to search for terrorists in the mountains but a major operation was being formulated and on the 10th June 1956 'Lucky Alphonse' was launched. The cordon lasted for days and it was finally understood that we had Grivas and his men surrounded. As the loop tightened a fire started in the Paphos forest. A strong wind made things much worse and when it suddenly changed direction the following day there were many casualties. Although numbers are often disputed it seems that at least thirteen Gordon Highlanders perished, together with some other soldiers from 3 Para and the Norfolk Regiment, all of them killed whilst trying to fight or escape from the fire. At the time Grivas was blamed for starting the blaze in order to cause confusion and divert the encircling troops away from his hideout but that theory was later disputed and the British Army appear to have been the likely instigators. Possibly the mortar bombs of the Marines were responsible or other army firepower, for the forest was very dry and even a small spark could have started the inferno. Personally I think this theory is the most likely but whatever caused the fire the outcome involved heavy casualties and the escape of Grivas who went into hiding.

Following the tragedy of Lucky Alphonse, army activity in Troodos was curtailed to a degree although EOKA kept the pressure on. However something else was brewing. Our training was stepped up and we had to undertake extra long route marches with full kit. These training sessions commenced well before dawn and we would trudge from Nicosia prior to the heat of the day, until early afternoon would see us descending into Kyrenia. As well as the increase in the tempo of training there was a great build up of vehicles and many more planes buzzing about. Together with extra equipment there was also a massive influx of extra personnel, about twenty thousand guys from the two year reserves. It would only be a matter of time before we knew our fate. Apparently General Gamal Nasser, President of Egypt, had nationalised the Suez Canal thus upsetting Anthony Eden's British government and the French. Together with the Israelis a plot was launched to take back the canal and on Guy Fawke's night, November

5th 1956 the fireworks really went up as British and French troops invaded Port Said and took control of the Suez Canal. The first waive of troops to depart from Cyprus was 3 Parachute Regiment together with support troops. 2 Para regiment, to which I was assigned, remained standing on the airstrip looking at the line of Valetta and Hastings aircraft which were on standby ready to fly us out if El Gamil airfield in Egypt was not taken in the first assault. It was a time of great anticipation and very little was said amongst the men as night moved towards dawn. By now we had been fully briefed and given photographs to study so we knew our landing prospects. We were at the peak of fitness after all the preparatory training and so it was just a matter of receiving the order to get into those planes with our canisters and gear ready for the off. We stood there in silent contemplation, lined up, waiting and waiting for several hours before the announcement came. The airport had been successfully taken and the second wave was stood down. It was a huge anti climax and the disappointment we felt is hard to explain. As our posting to Egypt no longer had any urgency the plan was to abandon the aircraft and take us over there by sea from Famagusta but our landing craft had engine trouble and we never set off which was of no consequence anyway as the others were swiftly returned. The invasion of Suez had been launched amidst considerable world criticism and immediately after the initial attack both the Americans and Soviets threatened reprisals against the British and the French unless they withdrew. Consequently the British Prime Minister, Anthony Eden, under great pressure, stopped the campaign only a day after it had begun. After the huge training effort in Cyprus, the call up of reservists, the positioning of the Royal Navy and the gathering together of the cream of the RAF whose Canberra's had paved the way prior to the invasion, it was all called off. What an absolute bundle up. Eden was heavily criticised and eventually resigned.

After this debacle we worked hard in Cyprus returning the build up of machinery and equipment back to the UK. EOKA activities also appeared to have subsided somewhat as we settled back into our old role. Things were pretty quiet and I was preparing for my demob in a couple of months when we got some really good news: the whole Parachute Brigade was to be sent home for Christmas! The mass exodus was handled by Coastal Command with whatever planes were available and a couple of us found some spare room in the forward gun turret of a Shackleton. Sitting in its perspex bubble my thoughts were with the gunners who had sat in the same position repeatedly during the last war. They must have been extremely brave guys as they worked in this terribly vulnerable and awesomely cold position. After a long and cold trip the Shackleton made its approach towards Britain. It was a bright and clear night as we saw the welcoming cliffs of Dover and a little later the friendly lights of London.

Once we had sorted ourselves out we were free to go so I contacted the folks and told them that I would be home next day. As I turned into Windsor Road there to greet me outside the house were some welcome home banners, the front door was open and I walked in. Mum was quietly going about her tasks in the kitchen and there were plates of buffet food everywhere for what appeared to be my welcome home party. Slowly and quietly I put my bag in the hall, leaned round the door and watched her for a moment or two until she turned and saw me. For a couple of seconds she froze until I walked over and held her when she finally let go and gently wept.

Two Year Holiday: Notes

(1) During the Second World War Malta had stood up to a terrible battering and in 1964 was awarded the George Cross in recognition. This was also the year that Malta gained its independence from Britain. Our other close relationship with the island involves the legendary footballer Stanley Matthews who went to live in Malta where he was very well respected and he set up a football school there. Previously, at the peak of his career whilst playing with Blackpool, he trained by running on the beach and using continuous deep breathing exercises: in for five, hold for five, out for five. Try it; you won't keep it up for long.

(2) We would meet up with the RAF police for our street patrols. They would be in their very smart Land Rover whilst we had an impressive Austin Champ. We would liaise near the entrance to the old town and decide on our route for that night. I suppose life is a lottery because one night EOKA planted a bomb near the archway entrance into the old town, which we had to pass through, and blew up an RAF vehicle which was on patrol that night. All of the crew were killed instantly. If it had been the night before when we were on duty we would have been right behind them or even leading the patrol and taking the hit as it was something of a lottery which of us set off first. Following the incident the regular meeting place was abandoned in favour of a random rendezvous.

(3) EOKA, like all terrorist groups, quietly killed a few soldiers each week adding a multiple killing occasionally. This may be the tactic that drives us out of Afghanistan combined with road bombs and suicide bombers; it is aimed at changing the opinion of public and politicians.

(4) The antique Sten guns were possibly one of the poorest weapons issued to the British Army; they had a poor safety catch and no stopping power. If dropped on the floor when loaded they would often go off like a rip rap and many soldiers died this way.

Up Up and Away -
Around the World in Eighteen Months

Do not squander time; for that's the stuff life is made of - Benjamin Franklin

After clearing the Army and spending just over a month at home I was about to leave once again. In some of my last letters from Army life I had put a proposition to the old man: would he agree if I did not return to the family business immediately as I wanted to take eighteen months out to try to hitch hike round the world before settling down? Dad was quietly encouraging and supportive, smoothing the way with Mum who was concerned about my going off again after a two year absence. Was I being selfish? Mum wanted to see me settled whilst Dad had been looking forward to my joining him again in the family firm but the arrangements were made and so, with their blessing, I set off once more. It was the 7th March 1957 when Dad drove me to Ringway Airport in Manchester for the 10.30 a.m. flight to Shannon Airport. From Shannon there was a flight with KLM Flying Dutchman which was headed for New York although my ultimate destination was Montreal. From Montreal, on the east coast of Canada, the plan was to hitch hike south into the USA, then west across the states and finally north back into Canada but this time to the Pacific coast from where I hoped to get work on a ship headed anywhere.

In 1957 Ringway airport was a very different place from the multi terminal international airport it is today. In fact the departure area consisted of just one hangar, none of the posh shops and restaurants you find now; there was only a single runway and the number of planes visible could be counted on the fingers of one hand. Before getting on the waiting plane I gave Dad a big hug and thanked him for his support. 'Do the best you can Will,' he said, 'keep in touch and don't worry about Mum, she will be OK.' Looking out of the porthole at Dad standing there, pockets bulging with his usual paraphernalia, I had an uneasy moment but put it down to the uncertainty of my trip.

The flight from Shannon was carrying about seventy eight passengers. It was half past midnight and we were New York bound. The cabin crew consisted of two stewards and two cracking Dutch air hostesses who served a meal to us before handing out pillows and blankets and as we settled down for the night one of the girls took the spare seat next to me. We chatted whilst her gorgeous scent enveloped me until I finally drifted off to sleep, her fragrant head resting on my shoulder – what a great start to my journey! Eventually, twenty six hours, four planes and a five hour time adjustment later, we banked over the St Lawrence River as we came into Montreal. The view from the porthole was of a world turned absolutely white with snow and a patchwork of black lines which were actually highways, intersections and train lines. It was like a painting. Travelling into the city and gazing around at this different world full of multi traffic lanes, motels, eateries, advertising boards, and cars in many different colours, was truly amazing. I felt as though I had been dropped onto a previously unknown, snow white planet.

Once in downtown Montreal I began to search out a YMCA in which to spend the night. There are many of these inexpensive hostels all over the world, and they are ideal for people in transit to use. Back home I had been a member of the YMCA since the age of fifteen when I was boxing under the guidance of Harry Lawton, a good friend and ex RAF Physical Training Instructor. Even now, some sixty odd years later, I am still a member and as well as doing circuit classes at the Manchester 'Y' each week I have also spent several years on the Board. I am deeply indebted to the YMCA for teaching me the discipline of training at an early age and so it was to that organisation that I looked for help. Of course I found one and once installed there my many plans were mulled over and my address book consulted. The book listed contacts in Canada as well as many other countries who would hopefully offer advice or hospitality if called upon. Sure enough I soon realised that I was only seven miles away from Barbara whose brother, John Laxton (1), had been a good friend of mine until he emigrated together with his wife Val and made it 'big' in Vancouver. A meeting with her was fixed and she helped me to get my bearings and suss the winter travel situation whilst we had a very British cup of tea and caught up on each others news.

The next day was Sunday and there were blizzards but still a trawl around the city and along the wharves by Victoria Bridge was in order. Montreal seemed like an island set within the St Lawrence Seaway, most of which was frozen. Barbara had told me that it was almost time for the ice breakers to arrive again in order to re open the shipping lanes and that this event was always celebrated with a huge ceremony in the city. This is a cold place, several degrees below freezing and a check on the weather for Monday told me that it would be cold again but bright and sunny. Sounds good, time to hit the road. Leaving the YMCA around 7 a.m. I position myself on the No 2 highway in the direction of Toronto which will put me nicely on the way to Hamilton where my address book tells me there is a good contact. Standing at the side of the road in Montreal waiting for a lift I must have looked a curious figure to the casual passer by. My rucksack had a Union Jack stitched on the top flap advertising my nationality and my feet were buried in the deep snow. Not only that, but there were no other hitch hikers desperate or daft enough to travel in that wintry weather. Eventually an American Indian guy pulled over and the first part of my journey in Canada began. I can't remember his name, if indeed I ever knew it, but I do recall that he talked in a series of grunts between smoking a huge cigar. Some sixty miles on he drops me at the Ottawa Toronto branch road to wait for my next lift. Quite soon a Buick with a New Hampshire plate pulls over. This is Floyd Smith, a salesman clearing the Ontario province and he is en route to Toronto which is right on course for me. We hit it off well from the start and that's good as this will be a long ride. His job is to sell newly hatched chicks to the feeding farms and he proceeded to tell me all about it. Hatched in incubators, within twelve hours the chicks are packed and dispatched with enough food to last twenty four hours by which time they will be at the feeding farm. They are then reared for ten weeks before entering the food chain and this is their total life span! Floyd was very friendly and chatty: 'John, we don't see a right lot of people doing what you are about at this time of year,' says Floyd. I explain it was a go or stay situation and whatever the weather I intended to travel. Floyd was very interesting to listen to as he related lots of detail about Canada and the USA. For example I was told that in Ontario all dogs had to be kept on a lead in public places and all traffic had to stop when the yellow school buses were collecting or depositing children; this is the minutiae of everyday life which often goes unnoticed by the tourist. What didn't go unnoticed though was the fact that after about fifty miles the cut out on the Buick burnt out: 'First trouble for two years,' moans Floyd who had only just been telling me how well the car ran. Car fixed we were on our way again, passing the massive DuPont complex which produced man made fabrics, and then on to the excavation project which aimed to join Toronto to the St Lawrence Seaway. Unlike the Panama Canal which was dug out by hand, this operation is covered in huge digging machines; Canada in 1957 was a very modern place. 'You are one of very few Brits who will see this work in progress,' Floyd chips in, clarifying the fact that not many British travellers got to Canada in those days; in fact I was a novelty. As soon as Floyd had spotted the regimental wings on my blazer pocket he seemed to view me as a fantastic sales aid. Consequently he introduced me to everyone we met and as I had recently been involved with the Suez debacle they were all exceptionally keen to talk to me and tell me their opinion. In Aurora, north of Toronto, we visit a customer who welcomed me very warmly and treated us to a conducted tour of his chicken plant. Once the chicks have been fed to the optimum they are hooked up on a conveyor belt, flapping and panicking, their feathers flying everywhere; then they enter a tunnel where they are stunned and killed. As the dead birds emerge at the other end they are stripped of their feathers before being moved on again by the conveyor until they almost immediately reappear again pre packed and ready to cook! That was 1957; god knows what is happening now but back then the speed of the operation was mind blowing. They were big on chickens in Canada and the US when I was there, Kentucky Fried chicken and fast food were already huge businesses whilst back in the UK we were lucky if we got chicken for an occasional weekend treat. Sadly for chickens they appear on all our menus now and the intensive industry surrounding the rearing and preparation of them must be even more advanced and speedier!

Leaving the chicken plant we motor on but around 7 p.m. ice forms on the road so we pull into a motel. We park the car right outside the chalet, just as you see in the movies, and the room is really well kitted out with a shower, TV, fridge, and coffee maker; these things are virtually unknown in the UK. Suitably impressed we tidy ourselves and freshen up then pop along to the eatery for a steak which arrives with a neat sign sticking out of it telling you just how it has been cooked. A jug of water is already on the table; this is standard everywhere in Canada and the USA, never do you have to ask for it. After a good night's rest Floyd and I set off again. As we travelled along the Queens Highway, passing through clover leaf interchanges, it seemed like a hitch hikers dream but eventually I was dropped off outside the YMCA in Hamilton. Floyd was sorry to leave me: 'Now John, you gotta long way to go, let me know how it goes,' he says as we shake hands, say goodbye and promise to keep in touch. In fact we did keep in touch until his death and I sent Floyd a thick ex army string vest for Christmas as he had been very impressed with mine; such an item was unbelievably not available in that land of plenty!

Hamilton is a town that has a considerable ex pat population as many British people emigrated there at the encouragement of the Canadian government support scheme after the war. One such family was that of Jackie Brierley and her family who originated from Oldham. Although sharing the same surname Jackie was no relation to the randy ladies man, Derek Brierley, who had served his apprenticeship with me back home. I had been invited to drop in if 'passing' so on my second night in Hamilton I joined Jackie's family for dinner and they related their adventures in this land of opportunity as we talked late into the night. Upon leaving the next morning they told me to be sure to 'take a look at Niagara Falls, it's only a bus ride away.' An amazing amount of water is teeming over the half moon panorama and wearing oil skins you can walk under the falls although visibility is difficult because of the masses of spray. Standing there I try to imagine some of the stunts people have staged as they go over the edge; strangely barrels were very popular as were tightrope walkers! I am always up for a stunt but no way would I mix it here; it's awesome stuff! Eventually I returned to the bus to make my way back to Hamilton but, as we went down the hill above the river, the driver stopped to call in at a shop for some fags. I was sat at the back of the bus so was possibly one of the last to realise that we were slowly moving forwards down the hill. Someone must make a move but no one does, so amidst a lot of commotion and screaming it seemed it was left to me to belt down the aisle and into the vacant drivers seat pressing all the pedals with my feet until eventually finding the handbrake and yanking it on. The bus juddered erratically before finally stopping its manic downwards journey. The passengers applauded and a rather large lady spontaneously hugged me then we all piled off the bus to meet the heavy driver as he puffed his way downhill towards us; he escaped being lynched but received a severe tongue lashing.

After many more, thankfully uneventful, miles I eventually found myself over the border in the USA. The lifts had been plentiful and one of the drivers, a guy called Ron Grant, had a job as a mover which involved visiting army camps to give estimates for relocating service families. This chap went out of his way to drop me at the border where I crossed the Blue Water Bridge and checked in as a visitor with the US customs. Next I hitched a lift with four girls from Emmett before boarding a lorry to Highway 13 and Saginaw where my address book told me that Eric Hibbertson and his family had settled after being sponsored for emigration to the USA after the war. A guy with a trailer dropped me almost directly at Eric's door and stood me a meal on the way. It couldn't get any better than that I thought but it did as I got a very good welcome from Eric and his family. It seemed amazing that these people had originated from Oldham as they seemed to be an altogether American family, complete with accent! Eric had been a joiner back at APAS in the early days of my apprenticeship and we had often worked together. He was a tough cookie, a true task master with a short fuse and most people stayed clear of him. On one occasion I was assisting him in the laying of a new upper floor when I fell between the joists resulting in my becoming stuck, legs dangling into the living room below, surrounded by showers of plaster and dust. Rather than help me out he tore downstairs where he proceeded to hit my legs with a plank until the lady of the house restrained him. Nevertheless I liked Eric and had learnt a great deal from him. Whilst there I found out that he had built his American home whilst running his own business in which he was very successful. I ended up staying for three days, sleeping on a camp bed, whilst Eric took great delight in showing me round the area which included amazing Shopping Malls with acres of parking space and self service stores, an idea that would greatly influence my own business in later years. We went to the local TV studio where I was pushed into a doing a brief interview as apparently I was an 'interesting' guy being British, 'a traveller an' all.' Eventually it was time to leave Saginaw and make my way to Michigan and as we said our goodbyes Eric presented me with a home made notice board. The message emblazoned on the board in painted letters was: 'Around the World'. This was my farewell gift and it immediately brought a response as a car passed me then reversed back at speed, the driver laughing at the board propped on top of my rucksack and saying: 'Are you serious? Get in man.'

By now I have been on my travels for ten days although it seems much longer. Lifts are no problem with the aid of the notice board and about two hundred miles from Michigan a guy with a trailer bearing two boats pulls over; he is bound for Minneapolis some five hundred miles further on which suits me fine. Later on he drops the trailer with a customer and says he will pick it up on his way back. Hugh Fraser is his name and he is an interesting guy. He was a salesman and although I cannot remember what he officially sold I do remember his many sidelines: the boats on the trailer, cameras, camping gear, and motorcycles. In fact he was a hot off the shelf universal salesman and it is absolutely entertaining as he recalls the detail of many of his past deals and the miles are quickly shed. We pass through Illinois and Dubuque then onwards to Iowa where we find a motel for the night. As well as being a sharp salesman Hugh is also a big snorer ensuring an early start on my part as I drag Hugh out of his noise zone and out for an all American breakfast of short stack which consists of layers of pancakes drenched in Maple syrup and pouring cream, absolutely gorgeous. All this food is washed down with loads of coffee (tea – what's that?) and by 8 a.m. we are on the road again. By midday we are in Minneapolis where Hugh is booked in on a study course so it is another YMCA for me. That evening we meet up again and set out to hunt for food and entertainment: 'John, there's a show in town I'm gonna take you to,' he tells me as he drives along and eventually we turn into a drive in cinema. We park up in front of a huge screen and are surrounded by about two hundred cars. Waiters are circulating amongst the vehicles taking orders for burgers, short stack, ice cream sodas, Knickerbocker glories; whatever you wanted. Nothing was unavailable it seemed. It was amazing and really cool. 'John, you might pick up some tips from this guy, watch along,' said Hugh as the film starts and we watch David Niven travel *Around the World in Eighty Days*. Hugh and I got on really well together and although we spent five hundred miles in good company, when we eventually parted and shook hands we both knew we would never meet again.

Another day, another highway but today it takes four hours to travel just one hundred miles as only short local lifts seem to be available. Then bingo! A brand new Buick pulls over. The driver is called Bill and he tells me he is heading west and invites me to hop in. Bill was well into World War Two, he had served as an engineer in the American Navy, often in critical areas of the various Pacific campaigns such as against the Japanese at Iwo Jima. He relates many of his war tales as we drive through the night and as he drops me off at dawn the next morning I realise the guy must be a robot as we have travelled hundreds of miles non stop through state after state. After a quick scrub up at an Eater I am back on the highway at 7 a.m. A series of short lifts gets me mid prairie near to a town called Chester in Montana but things grind to a halt here as there are no rides available at all. After standing at the roadside for a few hours a guy eventually pulls over to tell me: 'buddy you ain't gonna get a lift in these parts. Short time ago a hitcher worked a guy over, left him for dead on the road and took his motor.' Not news I really wanted to hear but he went on: 'the train comes thro' daily at 1.40 p.m. and there is only the one.' Chester is out in the sticks, a small township set in the mid prairies at the approach to the Rockies. It is surrounded by absolutely endless fields, a few houses, a bar and some large farms and as it is now clear that a lift is unlikely the train station becomes my target. Upon arrival I book a ticket for a train called *The Empire Builder* which will soon arrive having started its journey in Chicago. Whilst waiting the Station Master shows me around the place with its huge storage sheds, silos and elevators which load grain into the mighty rolling stock. There is no evidence of any other passenger except for me, not one, only commercial cargoes awaiting collection by the trains.

Bang on time the mighty engine approaches the station from across the prairie, clanging and hissing as it eventually halts at my feet. The dome observation carriages sparkle in the cold clear sunlight and it feels rather like a movie; it wouldn't be out of place for John Wayne and a posse of cowboys to come galloping round the corner towards us! The train is very long, maybe twenty coaches with two engines, one leading and one at the rear. As the carriage door opens out pops an immaculately attired black train attendant who proceeds to lower a small step ladder in order to assist with boarding as the ascent is about four feet! He wears a uniform which is very reminiscent of the ultra smart black and white attire worn by the staff on the GWR Cornish Riviera trains of my childhood. His shoes have a mirrored shine, his hands are encased in snowy white gloves and his neat bow tie and waistcoat finish off a perfect job. I hand up my travel stained rucksack before climbing aboard, not always a welcome piece of kit I often sense although it is certainly a point of interest. The guard is a really nice guy, right out of Alabama or New Orleans it would seem and, as he shows me to a well appointed compartment, he enlightens me about mealtimes and the various procedures that apply whilst on his train. The train departs and makes its way across miles of flat prairie until eventually we are climbing into and through the Rockies. There is a sea of freshly fallen snow and the trees are overloaded with the weight of it as we travel through seemingly endless frozen forests, the train often forced to slow down as the track becomes a series of slow twisting turns. I look backwards from the dome viewing carriage and see the long snake of the train behind me, gently climbing as we pass ravines, aqueducts, lakes, and massive expanses of bridges. There does not appear to be any human activity outside although there is the occasional isolated ranger post used by hunters and trackers; however there are many animal tracks in the snow and suddenly I see herds of Elk and Caribou. At times the train is only moving at about fifteen miles per hour due to the terrain but this allows a little more time to take in the breathtaking panorama; a wilderness of beauty and quietness that is only briefly interrupted by the passing visit of the train. As I sit and muse I notice that a lot of the passengers are wearing ten gallon hats and high heeled boots and sporting Bowie knives at their belts although nothing more serious than that. They are a quiet lot, unlike their fellow men who have happily and chattily driven me around from state to state. No, these guys are sizing me up but I ignore them. Following a much needed meal I am dog tired and lay out on the seat to sleep with my rucksack fastened to my leg for security! As I sleep the train travels through the nine mile long Cascade Tunnel which runs under the Cascade Mountains in Washington State until at around 5 a.m. the train attendant awakens me: 'Hey Mister, come on man we're at Everett and you need to change here to make a Vancouver connection.' Staggering off the train I find it is pitch black and I am no longer in the sticks, I am back into city life, and indeed, Canada.

My next target is Victoria BC which is a ferry ride from Vancouver where a Bank of Montreal cash transfer is waiting for me as funds are low; I must find some work soon. So I make my way to Vancouver from Everett and stay overnight in a pretty dodgy place called the Gresham Hotel as my preferred place of rest, the YMCA, is full. The poor standard of accommodation ensures an extremely early start the next morning, that and the fact that I have forgotten to adjust my watch having entered a different time zone! The city is very quiet and not yet wakened so I amble along until everywhere is finally open when I grab a hair cut to smarten myself up only to find it costs three times more than it would have in the UK! My next move is to get a bus to the pier head from where I will catch the Victoria Ferry but I leave the bus at the wrong stop and have to hire a cab to drive me manically to the ferry which I boarded with only two minutes to spare. Victoria was particularly on my list of places to visit as it was there that my grandmother's sister, Iphis Watts, also known as Fizz, lived with her husband on Yate Street in the Oak Bay district. There was also a chance that with their help and contacts I would be able to find a job on a ship when I was ready to leave the USA and Canada for other places. A short two mile bus ride dropped me off at the end of their road and although Mrs Watts was out, old Mr Watts got a brew going and welcomed me; I was indeed made embarrassingly welcome by all. Their daughter, Joan, was married to a teacher called Kyrle and they had three children: Diana, Gay and Philip. Kyrle took time out to show me around the place in what was to be a mad few days and one time we take a forty mile ride to Duncan where his eldest daughter Diana is head girl of her school. Needless to say it was a little embarrassing being a twenty three year old guy visiting a school full of adolescent girls! Another trip took us to the Canadian Parliament where they were discussing whether or not sport should be played on Sunday. We went to Beacon and Thunderbird Parks, had a trip around the buildings in Victoria to admire the architecture which was so much ahead of Britain's, and visited a few museums. One evening we attended a lecture at the school where Kyrle was a teacher. The lecture was about the Forbidden Plateau, an expanse of land at the north end of Vancouver Island. The professor giving the talk explained how it got its name from an old Indian legend; he was an experienced climber and also related many of his climbing adventures which were fascinating.

Sightseeing completed, Kyrle introduced me to a contact for assistance in getting a job, a chap called Maddock who was the manager of a shipyard. As he showed us round we saw the first destroyer to be built wholly in Victoria and only the second to be built in Canada itself. Named *Fraser*, she looked very sleek and smooth and we were informed that she could fight blind using just her radar, wireless and whatever other electronics were installed. Her decks were very smooth and we were told that this was in order to shed atomic fall out. I enquired about the possibility of getting a job on board a ship but was told that it may not be too easy. To work on board an ocean going ship was my first choice of work but plan B was to get a job for a short time with a ferry company for which a union ticket is needed. There followed an interview at the immigration office with a stern and uncompromising officer. An argument ensued with this 'poker face' about the necessity of buying a Union ticket at a cost of $80 but I finally stump up the money, get my ticket and find myself allocated a job working on the ferries on the Alaskan deep sea run. Work starts the following Monday so my whirlwind of visits is hastily completed in the few days remaining. Returning to the Watts' one evening after another hectic day of sightseeing there is a phone message from a bloke that Maddock had introduced me to. Mr Ridout worked for King Brothers Shipping Agency and, wondering what he wanted I returned his call although it was about 6.30 p.m. 'John, did you listen to the local news this morning? Three members of one of our ships crews got into a brawl and there was a stabbing. It may be possible to sign on that ship if you get down there quick as they are now short of a man but they are due to sail at 10 p.m.' We had heard the news that a man was in hospital after suffering multiple stab wounds. He was reported to be in a critical condition after undergoing a six hour operation whilst several others were also wounded or imprisoned. At the time I had thought no more about the incident believing it to be nothing to do with me but now here was Mr Ridout offering me the job vacated by the guy on the operating table. My first instinct was to say no as the ferry job was all lined up and my very expensive ticket purchased but then again this was a real chance for me; the ship was bound for South Africa via Panama and Trinidad, oceans and worlds away. So, after asking Kyle to make my apologies to the ferry company, I grabbed a lift to the quay and there she was, the *MV Baron Inchcape* with her full cargo of timber. Her Skipper, Stanley Williams, was a slight chap, and only about 5 foot tall. He gave me papers to sign and within minutes I had joined the crew as second cook with a salary of £27 per month. There followed a hurried trip back to the Watts' to get my belongings and explain to them what was happening. They were, of course, very surprised by the turn of events and seemed genuinely sorry to see me leave; in fact as I thanked them for their hospitality and said my goodbyes old Mrs Watts was quite cut up. But the decision had been made and there was no stopping me now so I rushed to the quayside and boarded the *Baron Inchcape* with seemingly only fifteen minutes to spare before she was due to sail. Fifteen minutes to spare, surely that was cutting it very fine to catch a ship that was to take me a third of the way round the world. But there it is again – the edge of time.

1. Departure … Ringway Airport 1957. Last view of a healthy and well Dad.

2 KLM Super Constellation arriving in New York

3. Floyd the chicken man – note the background sign in a nation of coffee drinkers

4. My hand made sign demonstrated not by me

5. Niagara – the Canadian side

6. Scene from The Empire Builder as she approaches the Rockies

7. Beacon Hill Park, Victoria, British Columbia – the tallest Totem Pole in the world

8. MV Baron Inchcape mixed cargo – built 1956. Tonnage 5490 grt/2849 nrt/ 9460 dwt; Length: 461 feet; Breadth: 58 feet; Draught: 25 feet

9. Hairdressing on board – always a queue – notice his tackle balancing on the ship's rail

Up Up and Away – Around the World in Eighteen Months: Notes

(1) John Noel Laxton – from nothing to something – his brief:
John left the U.K. with an Honours degree in Law and an undistinguished National Service: 'never rising above the bottom rank, my only honour being a member of the British Army on the Rhine boxing team where I won a medal as the "Best Loser".' He was newly married after a very short courtship to Val whose parents: 'didn't want her to see me so we got married instead.' They were a gutsy, determined couple, always ahead of the pack, a good act together. Val quit first year Honours French at Durham University so that she could join John in a move to Canada. On the 1st June 1957 they boarded one of the Cunard Line ships, *The Saxonia*, bound for Montreal where they arrived on June 6th 1957. Whilst on board the couple had managed to amass a kitty of £100 by winning games of brag which: 'we played every day on board.' John had developed his card skills by: 'playing every Sunday night after Church with school buddies.' Once established in Montreal John became a door to door salesman in the French quarter, selling Electrolux Vacuum Cleaners where he: 'did quite well financially, it was the best training for trial lawyers.' After six months the couple had saved enough to buy a 1950 Ford Station Wagon and heeding the call of 'go west young man' off they went travelling across Canada. 'It took a month … but eventually we arrived in Calgary which was advertised as being at the foot of the Rockies but we couldn't see the bloody Rockies so we drove on to Vancouver.'

John and Val arrived in Vancouver on October 1st 1957 and: 'instantly fell in love with the most beautiful city in the world and the Canadian lifestyle of no class barriers and unlimited entrepreneurial opportunities.' John couldn't find any regular work so went back to selling vacuum cleaners door to door for another eighteen months eventually deciding: 'I had no option but to become a lawyer, reluctantly.' There followed one year at UBC Law School then articles for a further year.

> Val found work with BA Oil, as a computer expert (she bluffed her way in);
> taught French for four years and helped put me through UBC for one year.
> Amazingly I totally fell in love with the law and litigation in particular;
> enjoyed sufficient success that I was made a partner after three years, and,
> after six years, I started my own firm. I've never looked back since.
> My legal career allowed me to invest in real estate and also become a developer.

John and Val also built a stunning house overlooking Vancouver Bay which had a lift down to a private beach and they raised three daughters, Chandra, Glenda and Jenna, all of whom attended university.

'After forty odd years Val and I divorced but we are good friends and we still meet regularly at family gatherings'. Prior to that John and Val were featured in a BBC programme called 'Across the Great Divide' presented by Cliff Michelmore who interviewed and filmed Brits who had become successful across the pond. It was shown to about twenty million viewers in the UK. 'It showed Val and I helicopter skiing at Whistler and left the impression we owned the mountain.'

Some guys don't like to quit and after a transition from selling vacuum cleaners to law, from law to estate, John Noel (so called because he had the misfortune to be born on Christmas Day) does not slacken off. Together with a mutual friend, Peter Sellers, I think it's time we went out there to see what the b****r is up to these days. Meanwhile Val spends six months of the year in Vancouver and the other six months in Valbonne, France where the rest of the family are based.

MV Baron Inchcape - Pacific, Panama, Atlantic

Opportunity is missed by most people because it is dressed in overalls and looks like work – Thomas Edison

The *Baron Inchcape* was one of the Baron line of ships owned and operated by H. Hogarth and Co. of Glasgow and when I enlisted she was only one year old. Modern and well fitted out, she had a capacity of around 5500 tons and as a Tramp Steamer she could pick up cargo from anywhere in the world. When I joined the ship she had holds full of grain from Vancouver and an additional deck cargo of timber which she had collected here in Victoria. Although I had made it with only a few minutes to spare before she was due to sail, I could not detect any signs of imminent departure, only an air of uncertainty as a mixture of crew, customs and immigration men congregated on deck around a large white canvas sheet. On closer inspection I realised that deposited on the sheet were a vast array of knives, knuckle dusters, chains, and all other kinds of light weaponry. Customs men were watching over the hoard and I was told that the ship had been searched as a result of the stabbing which had landed me the job as second cook. I stood and surveyed the scene realising that there was little chance of us going anywhere at that moment so I prepared for a long wait. The assembled crew consisted of about thirty five to forty men who were mostly Scousers and Glaswegians and, as I looked once more at the confiscated tools they had possessed, I began to wonder just exactly what kind of guys I was getting mixed up with! After what seemed hours, so impatient was I to get going, the immigration men called us all to order as they wanted to check our papers. As I stood there I recognised the poker faced guy who had interviewed me for the ferry job a couple of days ago when I got my ticket so I shuffled to the most subdued spot in the line where I kept my head down until he had passed. I had his work permit in my pocket but fortunately he didn't recognise me. In due course all the artillery was packed up and removed from the ship, the Customs and Immigration Officers left and preparations were made to get under way. Bill Legg, the cook, seeks me out and takes me to the cabin recently vacated by the injured crew member I am to replace. Apparently the poor lad had sustained four stab wounds to his chest and was in a critical condition, as was his cabin which was in an unbelievable mess although I was assured that there was a bed in there somewhere! 'See you at 0530 hours in the galley,' said Bill as he left me to sort out the upheaval which took well over an hour. The clearing up was actually worth it though, as I had the cabin all to myself and the accommodation surpassed my best expectations. The ship had been due to sail at 10 p.m. but with the customs and immigration inspections and delays it must have been nearer to midnight when we eventually left the docks.

Although my job title was 'Second Cook' any initial thoughts of actually being allowed to do any cooking needed to be crossed off right away. If you have ever been a professional dish washer and vegetable preparation skivvy, then second cook on board the *Baron Inchcape* was the job for you. However I saw it as an enjoyable challenge and after three days I was in a good routine. With breakfast out of the way by nine O'clock the spud and veg bashing would commence after carting the rations out of a huge walk in fridge. There is food everywhere and certainly no shortages; everyone eats really well on this ship which put into dispute the fact that the crew refer to the *Baron's* owners as 'Hungry Hogarth's'. This nick name had been given to the shipping line as their ships are out so long at sea before returning home that the food runs out, or, the food that is available is rotten or in very short supply. That was certainly not my experience as in fact there was tons of stuff to eat and I quickly added six pounds to my figure with the lame excuse that I didn't know exactly where my next meal would be coming from! The statistics of my daily potato peeling are quite interesting if analysed: a good half a sack per day over a month is fifteen sacks and I mean 'big' sacks! Veg follow and anything else that needs peeling is also my department. After each meal I do a mammoth washing up session then mop out the galley before cleaning the huge cookers. I have a break each afternoon about 3 p.m. then it is back to work at 5.45 p.m. for the final stint which is finished by about 9 p.m.; it's a long day. I get along fine with Bill, the quiet cook. He is married with a child of ten but he is in the middle of a divorce, hardly surprising as in those days guys could be out at sea for nearly twelve months which does not fit in well with home life. It is not easy being a seaman; the isolation out at sea, camaraderie with their mates, parties in port, and their own space for much of the time means life back at home on shore is a definite challenge. There they face the real world of mortgages, bills, schooling, in laws, and an unsettled partner. Regardless of their general moans about life on ship some of these guys can't get back to sea quick enough! The life of a sailor is definitely not the job for a family oriented man.

After a couple of days we had already sailed six hundred and twenty four miles as we were travelling on average three hundred miles a day at twelve knots. We sailed on southwards into warmer weather passing along the coast of California: San Francisco, Los Angeles, and San Diego are all put behind us as we head towards Mexico. We have not seen any ships for a few days although we have dolphins swimming alongside and many birds who continue to fly around us probably in anticipation of my peelings as nearly all waste from the kitchens goes over the side. At one point we are followed by two Albatross' who drift in the thermals above, barely moving; later still turtles appear and one of them has a bird feeding off his shell as he swims along. Being new to all this wildlife I was also innocent of what could happen if you left your porthole wide open at night. One warm evening I was rudely awakened by a slap on the face. I leapt from my bunk, fists ready to defend myself from some crazed crew member only to find a flying fish lying among my sheets! Attracted to the ships lights it had jumped through my open porthole. In fact as I looked around I realised that my cabin was actually full of the things; some were already dead whilst others were flapping about on the floor and the next day I found that there were many more on deck. My porthole remained ajar rather than wide open after that. During the darkness of night as the ship gently sailed along the phosphorescence from her bows cut through the water and it was a beautiful sight. The further south we travelled the more brilliant became the sunsets and I had to pinch myself to believe that this was happening to me; a great trip across America from the east to the west coast; the making of many new friends and meeting up with old ones; and now a free trip to South Africa! All this together with the beauty of the ocean! My job was a cinch and it was really great to be alive.

I was not the only new crew member as it happened, a guy called Glen was working as a stoker in the engine room and on land he was a light heavyweight boxer. A black lad with Caribbean ancestry, he had been fighting in America and Canada and said he had a good record at world class levels. We got on well together and frequently trained on deck when not working but unsurprisingly there was no rush from any of the crew, or from me, to spar with Glen! Friday night on board sees the traditional rum issue. The event gets crew and officers together for an hour as we sup one glass which is the allowance but we are also usually allowed a top up. The stuff they distribute is white in colour and to me it's like fire water but I go with the flow. After the second shot I feel like diving overboard for a swim, I am so hot, but there is good banter, and the event is a nice touch. On Sunday mornings the skipper and the first mate carry out an inspection of the ship and crews quarters. However, compared to the Army inspection at the RMP depot in Woking, where folds were measured and dust particles analysed, this inspection was a light hearted picnic! All in all the crew are OK with me; I help to feed them so I am needed, but onshore I feel it could be somewhat different for they are a pretty motley lot and when booze takes over it's anyone's call!

We sail on and the weather really warms up. Out there somewhere we are passing Guatemala, Salvador, and Costa Rica; our schedule is something on the lines of: fourteen days sailing to Panama, five days to Trinidad where we will bunker (fuel and provisions), then nineteen days to Cape Town; some thirty eight days in all. Eventually we arrive in Panama and after days without seeing any other ships we start to see lots of activity as we enter the Gulf of Panama where there are many other merchant ships anchored and awaiting their slot to go through the canal. This short cut, between the Atlantic and Pacific oceans, actually saves three to five thousand miles on a journey by avoiding Cape Horn; likewise we aim to do the same and so we set anchor eight miles away from the first lock at Miraflores to await our turn. As we enter the lock it is mid morning and I am sunning myself on deck in the midst of my daily peeling routine wearing a tight right hand glove. The glove has become a necessity as I have worn the skin off most of my fingers with the continual peeling! When the slop bucket is full I confidently tip the contents over the side of the ship as I have done every day so far. I continue with my work when suddenly I am aroused from my calming routine by the sounds of whistle blowing and as I glance up I meet with the sight of two policemen on the side of the lock waving and shouting at me. They are really mad but I am having difficulty understanding why. Fortunately the first mate arrives to sort out the fuss which appears to be due to my peelings having gone overboard. Apparently there is one simple rule in these locks and there are signs everywhere stating that nothing, absolutely nothing, is to be discharged into the water or indeed into the entire stretch of the canal. As a rookie I was totally unaware of this but come on, its common sense you dope! The levying of a fine was being discussed as I drifted away amidst the commotion; I never did find out exactly how much my daft action cost the ship. Nevertheless we continued through the Miraflores locks; it was a great experience to be lifted through the lock system and set into the artificial lake which lies at an altitude of eighty five feet above sea level. As you pass through the locks another merchantman will be a few yards alongside as it transits the canal in the opposite direction and the whole episode is quite fascinating. After another lock at Pedro Miguel we eventually arrive at Lake Gatun where we pause before making our descent through the last set of locks. At last we glide out into the large natural harbour of Limon Bay which is busy with hove to ships waiting to pass through the canal in the opposite direction. Each lock is about three hundred metres long and the whole journey through the canal is a distance of forty seven point nine miles, or seventy seven kilometres, and it should take about a day to complete unless hold ups occur. The Panama Canal is said to be the eighth wonder of the world, and considering that it was dug out entirely by hand and cost the lives of thousands of men, it surely merits that award. I cast my mind back to the St Lawrence Seaway project that I passed whilst travelling with Floyd Smith en route to Hamilton in Canada. Thankfully in this day and age such an endeavour would not have to be dug by hand and would hopefully not be the cause of any fatalities among the workers!

Leaving the Canal behind the ship gets back into her rhythm as we sail into the Caribbean heading for Trinidad where we will refuel and take on supplies. We have been doing some stocktaking and have a large shopping list for the next leg of around nineteen days. Now the weather gets really hot; it is truly energising and we all lap it up. Eventually we dock in Port of Spain,

Trinidad, and we are the only ship alongside at the time. Consequently we are the only target for the local kids who are waiting for us, ready to demonstrate their skills to a stranger. 'Ten cents Johnny, I catch you shark,' they shout, and as I glance over the edge of the quay one of them is clutching a baby shark. I am intrigued so I 'pays my money' and into the sea he dives. After a minute or so up he pops but he is empty handed; down he goes again and bingo, this time the head of his catch emerges before the boy does, he is gripping it around its middle as he places it on the pontoon. The young shark he has caught for me is about three foot long and I study it admiringly before it is thrown back into the sea. These 'fishermen' were great little guys, so quick and skilled, often staying below the surface for a couple of minutes in search of their prey. However as soon as it is apparent that they have extracted what money they can from us they eventually melt away; their swimming and diving skills make for a steady earner in these fishy waters!

As we were to be berthed in Trinidad for around six hours this left an opportunity for a few of us to hire a taxi for a quick tour of the area. The single road we travelled along was surrounded by thick forest and some very basic shacks, a few of them lifted off the ground on stilts. The taxi driver tells us that the people are poor and you can easily see that although some of the kids that we see are finely turned out in school uniform. Poor or not, everyone seems to be happy and they are all laughing and waving at us. Further on a lonely washing line announces there must be a home tucked away somewhere in the prolific vegetation, and the odd wrecked car lies around, none of them in much worse condition than the taxi we are travelling in! The beer and local mango mixture lunch lightened the day and we were encouraged to try the local rum and, as we were paying, Charlie the taxi driver joined us even though he was driving! Actually he seemed to drive better after consuming half a bottle of rum. The roads were terrible but the alcohol softened our return journey and by early evening we were back on the *Baron Inchcape* who was now fuelled up and ready to leave. The provisions we ordered had been taken aboard by the two young pantry boys under the supervision of the second steward and everything was stored away so there was nothing for me to do except carry on as before: meals, prep, peel, wash up, etc., etc. As I said previously there is no shortage of good food on board although, by today's standards, Bill Legg, the cook, would not be a candidate for anything attempting a Michelin star whilst being quite adequate for this role and these guys.

A couple of days out from Trinidad the turquoise crystal clear waters of the Caribbean start to change colour and the further south we travel the ocean turns green and then brown. Suddenly debris and trees start appearing in the previously immaculate water together with plant life and birds although there is no land in sight. I ask what is happening: 'simple,' is the answer; 'we are passing the Amazon basin outflow.' The Amazon flows for four thousand miles from the Andes to the Atlantic Ocean and the sheer volume of this outfall of fresh water and silt colours the sea and dilutes its saltiness up to around one hundred miles from shore. What a mighty river system; seven miles wide in parts with thousands of tributaries pouring into it. It is actually the largest river system in the world but it not the longest; that honour belongs to the Nile in Egypt although the lengths of both rivers are constantly being recalculated as it is such a close thing.

Eventually we find clear blue waters again and it gets hotter still as we sail through the South Atlantic. The only signs of land we see are the lights of Ascension Island and St Helena; it is very remote down here but we catch sight of two ships which are possibly heading towards Dakar en route to Europe. After another couple of days with no ships in sight one suddenly crosses our bow some two hundred yards abeam. Around midday we pick up an SOS from the same ship, a cargo boat that has had an explosion in her engine room leaving four of her men seriously injured. Although we are quite near to her another ship, *The City of New York,* is even closer and they immediately mark her position to put a doctor on board. It was a close call; we would have been her rescuer otherwise.

The days passed and we followed the same routine only varying the menu slightly during the Easter period when we made Hot Cross Buns. My peeling duties continue and the sacks of spuds diminish. As we approach the equator it gets even hotter and one evening, having finished my chores of washing up and scrubbing down, I am relaxing in my cabin when there is an awful din outside. Peter, one of the officer apprentices, bursts in with a gang of men, all of them togged up in very strange attire. Peter himself appears to be dressed as King Neptune and his servants are in the guises of various sea objects; one of them is dressed as a merman, whilst they are all equipped with forks, staffs, cans, and odd musical objects. Amongst the noise I hear them demand my 'honourable presence' and I am seized, stripped down to my briefs, blindfolded and led forth onto the deck where, judging by the racket, the rest of the crew seems to be waiting. Now what? I am invited to share 'Neptune's brew' as I am lifted into a foul, slimy mess. Of course I struggle but I am ineffective against four burly arms which are screwing me down into the horrible substance. A couple of buckets of smelly stuff are also chucked on me whilst another guy is busy with the hair clippers. It would be bad even if I could see but I couldn't and I feel as if I am drowning in the morass. Finally they extract me and I once again enter the world of light as my blindfold is removed. The skipper and officers are looking on, Neptune is sat on his throne which appears to be a large arm chair and everyone is cheering enthusiastically. I look down to find that I have been scrubbed all over with a horrible swill consisting of fish heads, bones, curry, and any other leftovers from the kitchen, the smellier the better! They point the hose at me and someone throws a couple of towels over but as I dry myself I realise that great chunks of my hair have gone. My ordeal may have ended but now it is Glen's turn which will be very interesting I reckon as he is the boxing champ: let's see if he can box his way out of this! Initially he stands in the vile mess but however hard they try his legs will not bend so he cannot be immersed in it. He still gets plastered with the brew but makes sure that the two guys he has in a head lock, one under each arm, also get covered. When his blindfold was eventually removed it seemed for a moment he would chuck someone overboard and it was a while before he calmed down enough for the Skipper to hand over our documents. At last we began to understand what was going on as he quoted an old fashioned rite:

> To have the customary rights of his Oceanic Majesty King Neptune which he saw fit to establish, that all vilifying and humbling potions mixed and brewed to the entire satisfaction of His Majesty and Retinue, though it was thought that Mr Shark bitterly complained about not being able to stomach the aroma arising from this ancient menu. However the initiation of most respecting subject J.P. was well received by all.

Signed and dated by His Majesty and his official witnesses, Glen and I receive our 'Equatorial Certificates' timed and dated, 5 p.m., 23rd April 1957. Apparently it is a long standing tradition for anyone daft enough to admit he has never crossed the equator to be initiated by the more experienced crew members. But, to make amends, out comes the rum and there are handshakes all round; Glen is calmer and more settled and he also enters into the party spirit. You live and learn but I wouldn't have missed it or would I? Time to shave the rest of my hair off.

For every working Sunday at sea we get an extra day's shore leave; there are also some overtime hours and basic pay has, for some reason, escalated from £27 per month to £29 and 10 shillings. All this and I am enjoying myself as well! As we sail across time zones we add twenty minutes to the clock each night and for a couple of days now we have been accompanied by a large shark, a phenomenon which I am told is unusual. We believe its presence must be connected with the rubbish we are putting overboard so we monitor him and sure enough when we tip the rubbish into the sea he hangs back to sift through it all before catching up with us again, waiting for our next dump. As we sail into the mid Atlantic we come across loads of trash, forever circling where the sea currents cross. Worst of it all are the large deposits of thick, unrefined oil flattening the sea, a sign that the oil tankers have flushed their empty tanks whilst returning from a trip. It is well to reflect at this point on the work of Jacques-Yves Cousteau, the environmentalist and pioneer of sub aqua diving. In October 1960 he organised a campaign against the French Government who wanted to discharge radioactive waste into the Mediterranean. Subsequently Jacques and his wife, Simone, carried out research into oceanic problems on their boat *Calypso* which was actually part laboratory and their findings resulted in a warning to the world of many problems to come in the future due to our mismanagement of the seas. In the 1950's and 60's ships were discharging all kinds of rubbish, as was the *Baron Inchcape*, and we are still paying the price today although thanks to Jacques Cousteau we are more enlightened and the bulk of the rubbish dumping is being addressed. I have no doubt whatever that without him we would not be where we are today with pollution awareness and remedies; the world is now beginning to realise there is a hell of a lot of catching up to do.

Eventually, around nineteen days out from Trinidad, we are approaching Cape Town in South Africa where our cargo of grain will be unloaded before we sail on to Durban with the deck cargo of timber. I have been thinking about things and decide it is time to talk to Stan, the skipper, although I will have to be canny about this. The thing is I do not want to be stuck in South Africa indefinitely which I would be if I left the ship, but I would like to see some of the country. I have heard a rumour that the *Baron* will be taking a cargo from Durban to Mozambique before returning to Cape Town so I could have an opportunity for some extensive shore leave if I can swing things my way. The skipper is a good guy so I really hope that he won't hold me to the articles of signing on and after some small talk I go for it: 'could I take time on shore at Durban?' I ask. To my surprise he readily agrees and tells me I will have about a week before they return from Mozambique; furthermore, he tells me, once in Durban he will lose his ship's carpenter or 'Chippy' and asks me if I would like the job: 'you have that trade John, the job is yours if you want it.' I couldn't believe my luck; it just gets better and better! God only knew what a Chippy's duties were but I knew it would involve an increase in pay, the Bosun's super twin cabin aft, and, as this was a definite promotion, a more respected role. And then, the final surprise; the ship will be taking a cargo out of Cape Town to the east side of the states and will then set sail for Japan. Wow! Never could I have imagined such luck but, being an opportunist, I push my luck even further and test the water regarding possible discharge from the ship once in Japan in order to resume my travels from that far off place. The skipper said we would cross that bridge when we came to it which sounded very hopeful to me! My only other alternative would be to jump ship once in Japan but I didn't really want to do that as I very much appreciated his confidence in me and would do my best to fulfil his expectations.

I was thrilled as I resumed my duties and my happiness only increased when the fragrances of a foreign place wafted over the ship; the lads had told me that before you even see land you can smell it and it is true. After almost three weeks at sea there is a great buzz of activity as the crew get the scent and prepare for landfall, there are clouds on the far horizon and as we get nearer to land, we see the spectacular sight of Table Mountain breaking just above them – wow! Left and right of Table Mountain are the tops of Devils Peak and Lion Head and the whole thing provides a mighty backdrop to the foreground of Table Bay. As we ease into the bay we pass the infamous Robben Island which lies about seven kilometres out. This was the island where Nelson Mandela would later be imprisoned and which is now a World Heritage Site and museum. We are shepherded into the Victoria and Albert waterfront in Cape Town by a small tug boat which takes us to our dock in one of the busy quays. It was 10 a.m. on the 7th May and we were on schedule. As we waited to unload I gazed at the large ocean traders surrounding us, they were so huge they made our ship look very small indeed! The skipper was unsettled as there was some disagreement and the unloading is slow; as we are only spending four days here there is also great impatience from the men who are dying to get on shore. Eventually we are set free into Cape Town which, in 1957, is a modern city with blocks of flats twelve stories high curving round the sea front; a sharp contrast to the harsh lesson I would later receive when I encountered the environment inhabited by the black communities. I had not really given much thought to apartheid before arriving in South Africa but I was soon to see the true hardship the indigenous people had to endure under the enforced discipline and suppression. I had a lot to learn. Eagerly I join some of the other lads on a sightseeing tour and at one point we call into the Parliament Building where they are discussing the native employment problem. On one side of the House are the ruling National Party made up of Afrikaans of Dutch origin whilst the opposition is a mixed bag of the English element. The Dutch are pressing for a colour bar in church which just about sums up the entire apartheid situation in this country. We visit the Cathedral which is not an elaborate copy of British cathedrals but a modest and simple building and then, sightseeing over, we swim in the warm ocean in good surf conditions and later lie on a beautiful sandy beach. Twice we try to take the cable up Table Mountain but on both occasions due to wind and weather it is not possible. In the evening, after a few drinks, we have a flutter in a first class Italian Restaurant and it's good to do it properly on shore even though the ships food is good. All these experiences are enabled by the fact that we have taken a sub on our pay before we left the ship but it was well worth it!

Whilst we were ashore having fun some of the crew had to stay on board and Skipper Stan was one of them. However it was a known fact that a Japanese lady regularly visited him so he didn't miss out! (Sorry Stan). Eventually our fun is over and it is time to weigh anchor and at 9 p.m. on Friday 10th May we leave Cape Town and head for the port of Durban. The ship is lighter now without its grain cargo and we are soon round the Cape of Good Hope where the crossing of oceans and currents cause us to roll about in the swell; consequently it was very difficult to sleep that first night. As we follow part of South Africa's extensive coastline we can see sand dunes in the distance; we sail by East London and thankfully, in more settled seas, we eventually arrive at Durban where we move straight into our berth. It is 3 p.m. on Monday 13th May. Durban harbour is a fantastic size with its three huge basins and at a rough guess there must have been fifty or so ocean giants loading and unloading around us whilst there were tugs everywhere orchestrating a multitude of roles. We are here for a couple of days and I will stay with the ship until she leaves Durban for Mozambique when my impromptu shore leave will begin.

South Africa

Four hundred and seventy fighting Voortrekkers took on between ten and fifteen thousand Zulu warriors of which over three thousand were killed compared to three wounded Voortrekkers. Thereafter the River Ncome became known as Blood River
- Facts from the Battle of Blood River

Although I enjoyed life on the *Baron Inchcape* I was itching to begin my extended shore leave. At sea you are among a working, routine community where options don't exist but once in port there are many choices to be made. Life on board was in some ways cramping my style as I was only a casual seaman working a passage to get me around the world, the primary purpose of my trip being to roam around foreign places. However being on the ship was a means to an end and here I was in South Africa. As we approached Durban out came my extremely useful address book and sure enough I find a contact in that city; Keith Morris, an accountant, and his wife Joyce who was the daughter of our local doctor back home and sister to Heather, who we allowed to join our VJ day bonfire many years ago. By 8 p.m. I had completed all my duties and was cleaned up and ready to go ashore to seek them out. The *Baron Inchcape* was berthed at the end of a mass of warehouse sheds some half mile from the dock entrance and it was pitch black as I left the ship to make my unannounced call. Heading down the network of silent alleys in the dockyard I try to step on it as it is getting late and the lads have told me that the dockyard is not a place to hang around. I hurry on but begin to get a strong feeling that I have company as there seems to be a faint swishing sound coming from the direction of the sheds. I stop and turn around but there is nothing to be seen and the swishing noise stops only to be replaced by a grunting sound. As I round the next shed and see the illuminated dock entrance in the distance some quarter of a mile away, I step on it even more. By now though, whatever is behind me is closing fast, and this time the gentle jingle of some kind of bell can be heard. I stop and it stops; I stop again and once more whatever is following me also stops. As it gets a bit lighter nearer the dock entrance I look back once more and this time I can see the outline of two gigantic dark figures with flashes of white on them. Alarmed, I sprint for the dock yard gate hotly pursued by my shadows and as I reach the relative safety of the entrance they finally catch up with me. They are two huge Zulu's in full war dress carrying spears and huge shields; they are also sporting tall headdresses which make their total height about nine foot. Instead of attacking they smile broadly as they tower above me; they are truly intimidating but I soon relax and we share some banter as I realise they are enjoying this, being fully aware of their effect on me. Obviously this stunt has been pulled before! As I look at them my mind flashes to images of the Anglo Zulu War when thousands of these very serious warriors swept down onto the British Army and I could now imagine how their very appearance must have stricken the fear of God into their opponents. But they are not warriors thank goodness – they are off duty workers on their way to a Zulu dance. Relaxed once more I leave the dock yard only to find myself surrounded by even more of these giant men and women who were also on their way to the dance. I was startled to see that one of the female Zulu's was an albino, completely white and exceptionally tall at around six and a half feet.

Leaving the Zulus behind I make my way into the city. Even at night, Durban in 1957 was very impressive; there was a rich waterfront of hotels, restaurants and buildings with lovely architecture, all facing onto a beautiful golden beach. Of course the city had escaped the damage inflicted by a World War which had only recently ended in other parts of the world, which may partly have explained the grandeur, but as I was to find out, living conditions for the black people in South Africa were very different from this scene which housed whites only. I made my way to Keith and Joyce Morris' address and although it was turned 9 O'clock by this time and I was totally unexpected I was still very well received. They had heard I was hitchhiking in the States but they had no idea of my arrival in their part of the world. We chatted for a while and arranged to meet for dinner the following evening.

Back on board Skipper Stan asks to see me and he confirms that the *Baron Inchcape* is to depart for Mozambique to pick up some copper ore and that on the way back they will be docking at Cape Town. He gives me the necessary permission and documentation to absent myself from this trip and to stay on shore and travel around South Africa although he impresses upon me that I must be in Cape Town without fail when they dock. The next bit of good news was that this will be in three weeks time rather than one as I had previously been told. Three weeks to travel around South Africa – excellent!!! Stan also confirms that the ship will definitely be going to Japan after delivering her next cargo to the USA and although this suits me down to the ground it will not please a lot of the crew as it means the ship could be away for almost a full year. Japan will probably not be a popular run except with me!

The following day is Friday and I watch the *Baron Inchcape* depart from the shore before hurrying off to do some quick sightseeing and book in somewhere for a couple of nights. Later that evening I join the Morris' for dinner in their impressive sea view flat. They have a nine month old baby girl and Joyce's mother, Kath, is staying with them on a visit from the UK. From what I could see Joyce would get plenty of help around the home even without her mother; a house girl serves the food to us in a very pretty way and on the table is a hand bell which can be used to summon her presence when required. I believe there was also a cook. Europeans in South Africa in the fifties employed plenty of staff from the black population but the pay was poor and colonialism was still very much in evidence. However the Morris' were a happy family lucky enough to live on the right side of the tracks in a vibrant country which had plenty of opportunity and good weather to boot! As we chatted over dinner they mentioned some recent news they had heard from home: 'do you know David Lamb?' I was asked. 'Sure do,' I replied, 'we did a walking and climbing trip in Norway about three years ago and had a fantastic time.' (1) They then told me the dreadful news about David's fatal accident whilst riding on his scooter with his beautiful fiancée, Shirley. David had been a good friend and I was totally blown over at what had happened. The next day I am kept busy, being hosted here and there by Keith, and I find that Durban is another impressive city like Cape Town. However it becomes abundantly clear that South Africa is a white mans place; apartheid keeps the black people down as I can see in every encounter we have with these suppressed folk.

Before moving on to the interior of this beautiful country I make sure to enjoy the sea and surf and after bathing hire a rickshaw for a ride through the city. The rickshaw is pulled by a huge guy dressed as a Zulu warrior who turns out to be great fun. His party trick is to run headlong at full speed with me bouncing around behind him before he leaps up into the air at a thirty degree angle. Whilst suspended in the air his legs are still going like the clappers, just like the action you see in a cartoon. His accompanying war cry finishes me off and laughingly we haggle and negotiate the price of the fare as is the tradition in this country. Another day I take a trip to a regular tourist trap, the Valley of a Thousand Hills. There is a recreated Zulu reserve for the tourists so that we can witness how life used to be for the natives. Wise and adaptable, the old warriors in the reserve have their daughters dancing for us; one of them calls his daughter Jane Russell which really cracks me up and the girls gyrate, heavily topless, in a special dance. I'm not sure if M & S cup sizes would have coped with those lasses! Later the Zulu chief tells us the history and manners of his people whilst the girls do a spot of impromptu cooking. A man's wealth, he assures us, is gauged by the number of wives he has which in turn have cost a great number of cattle; therefore cattle or wives reflect wealth and there is hardly any difference between them it seems although I notice it was a wife he offered in return for dollars or currency and not a cow! I thank him for the offer and decline but think about the vacancy for second cook on the *Baron Inchcape*, a position which one of these wives would fill very nicely! Further trips took me to view a Hindu temple and a Roman Catholic Mission but to my great regret I did not get to visit Soweto. Originally a suppressed black township, Soweto was later one of the main settings in the struggle against apartheid. The township is also famous for having the only street in the world where two Nobel Prize winners have lived: Nelson Mandela and Archbishop Desmond Tutu. In stark contrast to Soweto Keith and I finish up one evening in a very surprising place - Claridge's! Yes, really. Whilst there enjoying the British influenced elegance of our surroundings and our cocktails, Keith introduced me to an auditing friend of his who tells me that he is going to Johannesburg on Sunday and would I like a lift? What a great offer, Jo'burg was the next place I wanted to visit and this lift will save me hitch hiking; wonderful things just keep happening – it's just too good to be true.

Sunday morning arrives, my day of departure, and as I say cheerio to Keith and Joyce Morris, who have been so friendly and hospitable since I

1.

2.

4.

3.

1. Approaching Cape Town and Table
Mountain
2. Some of my ship mates – mostly
Scousers and Glaswegians, although one
of them now lives locally in Dukinfield.
Small world!
3. Ken with a flying fish
4. Bill Legg the cook and I – we got
along well together
5. Spud bashing on deck – not a care in
the world

5.

6.

7.

8.

9.

10.

6. The leaping Rickshaw Boy in Durban
7. He really wanted to sell me one of his daughters!
8. With Reg at the Gold Mine
9. and 10. The Zulu's dance in the arena at the mine, zombified on liquor

wandered in late one evening, I think about how settled and happy they seem to be here. My promised lift arrives in the form of a Wolseley 4-40 which is already crowded with three other passengers and their associated luggage. Even so there somehow seems to be room for me and my embarrassingly large rucksack. We drive throughout the day and into the night until we eventually arrive in Johannesburg at about 3 a.m. Although I was very grateful for the lift I was glad to get out of the cramped accommodation and stretch my legs at last as I booked into a cheap commercial hotel. The next morning was spent taking a good walk round the city and getting my stiff legs back in working order. In my trusty notebook I find there are contacts on my father's side living in Johannesburg; Kathy, referred to as Aunt Kate, lived with her daughter Florence, son in law Reg, and their two children, Rosemary aged fourteen and Evelyn aged eight. Their home was in a district of Johannesburg called Florida and by mid afternoon I was on their doorstep, yet another unannounced arrival which receives a warm welcome. Reg is a top man in the St John's Ambulance Brigade and he is tied up until the weekend so I entertain myself until then by exploring the city and delving into its history. Johannesburg, whilst being very large, is not the capital of South Africa; in fact there are three capitals: Cape Town is the legislative capital, Pretoria the administrative capital and Bloemfontein the judicial capital amongst the nine provinces. The republic of South Africa is not a small place, it is actually equal in size to the land mass of Germany, France and Italy put together and that is a lot of space even with a population of around forty four million. Around seventy seven per cent of this population are black people whilst only ten per cent are white; the remainder is made up of mixed race, Indians and Asians.

One day I travel thirty miles to Pretoria in order to see the huge monument to the Voortrekkers. In 1652 a mass of Dutch settlers arrived in the Cape and by 1800 there were about forty thousand of them, known as Boers. Due to several complicated reasons a large group of these people left the Cape for the interior and this sub group became known as the Voortrekkers. As they were encroaching on native Zulu land many disputes with the indigenous people naturally followed and on the 16th December 1838, around four hundred and seventy four Voortrekkers fought against approximately fifteen thousand Zulus. Surprisingly the Zulus were defeated after having lost around three thousand warriors whilst the Boers suffered no losses and had only three injuries, or so it is claimed. This was probably due to the fact that the Boers had fire power on their side whilst the defeated Zulu's were armed with only short spears and stretched leather shields. However it was won, this decisive battle became known as the Battle of Blood River and it heralded the beginning of the end for the mighty Zulu kingdom. The city of Pretoria is named after the Boer commander Andries Pretorius who became a national hero and to commemorate the brave Voortrekkers the monument I had travelled to Pretoria to see was erected in the late 1940's. Although enormous, I was disappointed and found it to be rather unattractive. The edifice is supported by the statues of four of the Voortrekker leaders, one being set at each corner, and the dedication refers to the struggles of the pioneers, a bizarre but god fearing band of settlers and fine fighting men.

Eventually weekend arrives, Reg is free from work and he takes me to a gold mine on the Sunday to view some tribal dancing. The Zulu's perform in full warrior dress with spears and shields and one group at a time they enter the camp's large arena and begin to stamp their feet in time with the beating drum. Ear piercing war cries accompany their movements as the dust rises around them and as they dance they begin to look as though they are in some form of trance. Eventually at some invisible signal they stop and the next group comes along. Their dance movements appear to be choreographed by the sound of a whistle and, depending on how it is blown, the entire group of thirty to forty dancers immediately respond by turning one way or another, faster than the tick of a clock. It is a vision of a fantastic, uniform undulating energy, similar to a Mexican wave but these people are using their entire bodies. The dancing is accompanied by the drinking of some kind of hooch which makes the participants appear drunk and zombified. Reg tells me that they will dance all day long, into the evening and the darkness of night until they drop to the floor with exhaustion; and all this on their day off from grafting in the mine! The Zulu's came down from their tribal territories in the hills to live and work at the gold mine in the hope of a better, or richer, life but their allocated accommodation is very basic; they have no running water, just a stand pipe on a concreted area. For lunch we sample the workers food which consists of mealy rice and beans and I get the feeling of a POW situation; there are two thousand native workers at this mine and I will not bother to say how much they earn, it is such a tiny amount. In this particular mine most of the processing of the gold is done on the surface but later we visit a privately owned gold mine where we pull into the surface office and manage to talk our way into being taken underground to the workings. Suitably kitted up we descend six hundred feet to the face of the gold seam and it was a great experience as they explained and demonstrated the processes of extracting gold in the stifling underground heat. Today twenty per cent of the world's gold still comes from South Africa with gold remaining a good investment.

Leaving the mines and the Zulu dancers behind, Reg and I return to Johannesburg and drive around the suburbs looking at the various buildings and studying the architecture which surprisingly turns out to be very much on the lines of what I have seen in the USA. It was in great contrast to the miner's accommodation which we had seen that morning at the mine; the indigenous blacks were truly second or even third class citizens under the ruling white Afrikaners. Apartheid was so embedded in South African culture that to my surprise even Reg looked down on the black people and in 1957 this was a totally accepted attitude although as an outsider I felt the uncertainty and exploitation of their lot and a great degree of concern.

I was very glad to have met our distant relatives in South Africa but all too soon it was time for me to take my leave again. I say farewell and thanks to Aunt Kate, Florence and Reg for their generous hospitality and set off to continue my journey. The next port of call is Kruger National Park, as part of a here and must see trip organised by a company called 'Trans African Safaris'. The tour bus picks me up and I join an already established and very odd bunch of passengers in a nine seater coach. The driver is a guy who weighs about twenty stone and my other companions for the trip consist of an old American lady; a grumpy German; Tony aged nineteen and his father who live in Cape Town; two middle aged English spinsters; and a silent, middle aged, English male. With this gang my trip does not seem likely, at least initially, to be a barrel of laughs. Eventually we arrive at our first camp where we are to stay in traditional native Rondavel huts. After a comfortable night I am up and ready very early and whilst I am waiting for the others I take a drink of tea to the elderly American lady who promptly yells at me: 'go to hell!' I am rather surprised at her response of course but also very amused. It turns out that she has some kind of medical problem, anaemia I think, and has to inject regularly. That morning she had not had her 'fix' when I approached her. Bad health or not, at the age of seventy one she is travelling round the world for the second time; she was a real trooper and a great contrast to the two English women in the party who worried their way all through the trip.

The safari gets going and we do all the usual things such as attending the water holes at first light, searching for the various animals and photographing both them and the lovely landscape. When I think back now I realise how much a digital camera would have been of use on my trip as in those days camera film had a very limited exposure; extremely frustrating when there was so much to capture! The coach in which we were driven around had a very temperamental carburettor and Fatty, the driver, was unable to fit himself under the vehicle to carry out any repairs so I volunteered and solved the problems by stuffing soap in the base of the leaking carburettor thus managing a temporary fix, or at least saving Fatty from becoming fast under the chassis! The evenings out there in the bush are sublime; the house lads, who do everything, prepare food on a barbeque and then we sit there in the warm evening air, strange sounds around us, eating and drinking and looking at the lovely scenery; we don't have to lift a finger. The Kruger National Park covers almost nineteen thousand square kilometres and stretches from Crocodile River in the south to the Limpopo River in the north. Travel whilst on safari is from sunrise to sunset as after dark one has to stay in the fenced rest camps for safety reasons. Witnessing sunset and dawn within the park is a truly beautiful experience and my only disappointment was the scarcity of the animals, the presence of which can never be guaranteed. However a crocodile search lifted the beat for us a little and taking everything into account I would still award the tour seven out of ten.

We were due back in Johannesburg on the evening of 31st May and as I couldn't risk being late a flight was booked for me from there to Cape Town so that I could meet up with the *Baron Inchcape* again. On our last night in the bush we were camped in the Drakensberg Mountain area and Tony and his father offered me a free lift back to Cape Town if I would share the driving. Another bit of luck, I couldn't believe it. Back in Johannesburg I cancel my flight and join them in their huge automatic Chevrolet which I am asked if I am OK to drive. My immediate response is: 'no problem,' although automatic cars had hardly been discovered in the UK and I had never driven one. Tony and his father take it in turns to drive until about 9 p.m. when we stop to have a snack and then it is my turn and everything goes well but just fancy – a car where you do not change gear! Fortunately the route from Jo'burg to Cape Town was fairly straightforward as I gingerly felt my way around the mechanics. I actually found the Chevrolet to be a real pleasure to drive and it was incredibly comfortable gliding along at a good pace without having to change gears. By 10 p.m. my hosts are fast asleep in the back of the car and we have nearly a thousand miles to go to Cape Town. As I drive through the night it starts to rain, and rain, and rain. The wind blows the stuff at the car and the wipers struggle to move the torrent of water; and someone said that winter in South Africa was the dry season! Then we hit an electric storm with terrific flashes of lightning and as I drive through it the lads in the back of the car do not even stir. I couldn't believe it as the conditions were so noisy and terrible. After almost twelve hours, just before 9 a.m., they eventually wake up; I am whacked and have been fighting sleep, determined not to stop the car. As I tried to explain what we had driven through the reality of it did not seem to register with them and something was said on the lines of: 'you should have woken us.' Nevertheless I really appreciated the lift and driving the large Yankee automatic car was a pleasant challenge.

Once back in Cape Town I had a little time to kill before the arrival of the *Baron Inchcape* but fortunately, with the help of my trusty notebook, the digs kept coming along and I tracked down Aunt Kate's other daughter, Jean, who lived alone in a very select area of Cape Town called Sea Point. Her immaculate house was beautifully situated on a rocky bay overlooking the shore where the last of the Atlantic rollers were breaking; the surroundings were beautiful and the air was crisp and pure. Jean was already aware that I may wander in as she had been told of my travels by her sister so she had been partly expecting me. However what I had not anticipated was that she had also been notified of my proposed flight and had been to the airport to meet me – oh dear! Once again I have to pinch myself to believe what is happening; here I am in a beautiful house standing in a gorgeously appointed room which is not, however, enhanced by my travel stained rucksack dumped by the window. Standing and looking out at the stupendous ocean view I thank my lucky stars once again but I am really tired after the mammoth drive from the Drakensberg hills and I am glad to turn in. However the next day finds me walking out of the lovely white house and right into the surf of the Atlantic – it does not come much better than that. Jean was out at work all day so I was left to my own devices but that night we had dinner together and I found out a great deal more about life in South Africa which is a very complex country. Although imperialism and colonialism can be quite correctly criticised, it is a fact that less people were starving under that regime than they are presently Jean tells me. She also explains the system of government which was split between the Boer majority and the English minority and about apartheid, the system inflicted on the black people by the Afrikaans (Boers) in order to keep them subjugated and the effects of which I have witnessed during my stay here. For three great days I stay in the beautiful house resting and swimming either in the sea or the super outdoor pool on the front. Very nice indeed.

All in all, during my three weeks shore leave it would have been difficult to see any more than I did as every hour was taken up. Living with local people is definitely the way to learn a lot about a foreign place in a short time and wherever I travelled I was made to feel welcome. Jean, like everyone else, was great, giving me all her trust and the run of her home; we actually got on very well together and she would have liked me to stay longer. I would have liked that too but I had a ship to catch.

South Africa: Notes

(1) Just a couple of years previously David Lamb and I took a trip to Norway for some trekking and climbing. We travelled to Bergen and from there to Voss and onwards to the Hardangervidda mountain plateau where we travelled using the Norwegian system of DNT huts (Den Norske Turistforening). A red letter 'T' painted onto rocks and cairns clearly indicates the route through the mountains and there are 20,000 kilometres of marked tracks. Eventually we left the Hardanger Mountains passing through mighty glaciers before bussing out to the Jotunheimen National Park where there is the largest concentration of mountains above 2000 metres. After three weeks of fantastic mountainous scenery, very fresh air, exercise, good food and companionship we sailed for home; broke, tired but very impressed and invigorated. Once home we settled back down into our respective lives. David planned to take his articles in Architecture and I was due to finish my apprenticeship and join the Army for my National Service. David was engaged to an absolutely beautiful girl called Shirley who was tall and blonde; they were very seriously in love and planned to get married the following year. However just a few short years later a really sickening disaster struck. David had a Lambretta scooter and as he was taking Shirley home on it one night, for a reason no one can understand, an accident occurred and they were both killed. Everyone was shocked at this terrible accident, God, not so long ago David, at only twenty one, was literally on top of the world on a mountain in Norway. I think back to how we both stood on those mountains, full of life and vigour with our futures to look forward to. Where is the justice?

Cape Town for Japan - Or Not

If you do not know true disappointment, you do not know true happiness

Out of Cape Town – into storms and sorrow.

I thought that I might beat the *Baron Inchcape* to the docks in Cape Town but it was not so for as I approached the quay she was already there, set comfortably and fully loaded up to her plimsoll line. It was good to see everyone again and as they regaled me with tales of the voyage to Mozambique I was welcomed with a nod or a mighty slap on the back and a ribbing about laying claim to the Bosun's quarters. Later on Skipper Stan sends for me; he was not the kind of man who wasted words but even so he managed to make me feel welcome as he passed me over to the First Mate to whom I would report and who was to talk me through my new job. As the management of the ballast tanks will be foremost amongst my new responsibilities we descend into the bowels of the ship where there are six seawater tanks and two which contain drinking water. My job is to balance the tanks regularly by moving water from one to another in accordance with the current sea conditions, weight of cargo etc. The tanks are fitted with dials and valves from which readings have to be taken first thing in the morning and again in the evening thus indicating if any adjustments are necessary to maintain the ships trim. In addition to this important task I have to ensure that any deck cargo is monitored and stowed according to the prevailing sea conditions as well as carrying out all general repairs around the ship which is where my trade as Joiner will come in. Briefly then, these are the tasks of a ships carpenter and as the *Baron* had a fine workshop containing absolutely everything I may need I was all set to go.

Instruction over I am finally installed in my new cabin which has its own eating facilities as well as a bathroom with shower. It is absolutely amazing how everything has fallen into place for me and I count my blessings putting it all down to fate or extremely good luck. Later on I call in the kitchens to see Bill, the cook, who welcomes me back and we share a good crack together. A new guy has replaced me as second chef, and I wish him luck with all the peeling!

As the ship leaves Cape Town behind I work late into the first night, familiarising myself with my new routine and the checks I have to make whilst the First Mate goes through the paperwork showing me the records which have to be entered up daily. I am more than happy with my lot but that contentment wasn't to last long for as we head full into the Atlantic Ocean against prevailing tides the gales set in and the *Baron* has to fight her way through a bow on sea. The deck cargo is carefully checked as the ship is wildly rolling and pitching and whilst I am checking through my itinerary the gales turn into a near full on storm. It is truly the worst weather I have encountered so far and it ain't letting up. Bill is having a rough time in the galley, his menu's are adjusted to the conditions and are still good although the rough seas mean that appetites are soon satisfied for most of the men. The next morning sees me up and about early after a very rocky night and making my way down into the bowels of the ship to take the soundings. Down gangways of metal steps and through the engine room and I am in the bottom of the ship with its overwhelming smell of oil, almost unbearable heat and tremendous noise. I trim a couple of the tanks to maintain the stability of the ship and enter the figures in the 'bible'. Emerging back on deck the early morning reveals leaden, grey skies with really terrible sea conditions; I begin to feel very groggy and put it down to suddenly emerging into the fresh air from the heavy atmosphere in the bowels of the boat. I try to ignore it and pass on breakfast in order to get on with the job in hand but by midday I am vomiting even though I try very hard not to. Suddenly I seem to be having bloody bad luck just when I have to give it my best shot. Heavy seas for two days saw me feeling wretched although I still managed to make my two vital daily visits to the water tanks. The experience seemed to cure me however because ever since that trip I have sailed as part of a crew and solo in really bad weather but have never again suffered from sea sickness. Eventually the sailing conditions improve and I perk up. The job is working out well, there is plenty to do round the ship and I get lots of tips and help from the First Mate. We are now closing back over the equator as we head for Philadelphia on the east coast of America and the routine of rum ration, good grub, music, films, company, interesting work, fine quarters, and brilliant weather continues. I am truly enjoying *le bonne vie,* with not a worry in the world.

A couple of weeks out of Cape Town we are passing the Ascension Islands on our starboard side as one of the lads seeks me out. 'John, the skipper wants to see you,' he says. We don't normally see much of Stan on a voyage other than the Friday night rum allocation or the Sunday inspection so I begin to think that maybe I have screwed up in some way. Entering his cabin he gets straight to the point: 'John, we have had a ship to shore communication from your mother to say that your father is ill and you have to get back home as soon as possible. I intend to divert the ship and put you ashore in Trinidad where all the arrangements have been made for an immediate flight home.' For a moment I am speechless; what could possibly have happened for my Mother to be calling me home from the other side of the world; could it all be a mistake? The Skipper has been given no details of Dad's illness; he had been well when I left him at Ringway airport some months ago but then I recall the uneasiness I felt as I waved goodbye to him from the aeroplane and I begin to feel very anxious. The Skipper adds: 'John, you have done well on this ship, we shall be very sorry to see you leave us.' I thank him for everything he has done and tell him how much I have appreciated his guidance before making my way from his cabin in a daze.

The message was truly a bolt out of the blue and just proves that often in life, especially when you seem to be home and dry, things can change in an instant; life and luck can be very fragile. I went over and over the situation in my mind; what had happened? Would I be home in time? Accident; illness; Mum would not have taken this step unless something was very seriously wrong. By diverting to Trinidad then getting back on course an extra two days and six hundred miles would be added to the ships schedule; however at sea any SOS or a similar situation is responded to immediately and time and money does not come into it. Many years later whilst cruising on the QE2 we were en route from Gibraltar to Southampton when one of the ship's officers had a heart attack. The ship changed course and headed towards Portugal, getting closer to land to enable a helicopter pick up. The deck was prepared for the helicopter to land, the patient was collected, and then the ship returned to its course. Because of the delay we were behind schedule and the whole ships complement would have to spend an extra night on board which would incur extra food costs as well as all the expense involved in having to operate the ship for an extra day. It must have cost hundreds of thousands but there was no alternative or choice to be made and the *Baron Inchcape* was in a similar situation as she altered her course just for me.

So far on my journey I had had more than my fair share of good luck and I wonder if sometimes this makes one feel immune to any setbacks. It was certainly an awful shock to have my positive and progressive existence shattered in this way, there must be real trouble at home. I returned to my cabin to re- check recent mail; there had been two references made about Dad having trouble with his voice but the Doctor had checked him and tests were negative. He was advised to take a holiday so he teamed up with two other members of the Sunbeam Owners Club and the three of them were planning to take their cars on a trip to Norway. By now they should have had their holiday and returned home, what could have happened? What could justify asking for my immediate return? I began to realise the enormity of my recall, they would not bring me back home from my trip unless it was absolutely essential; car accident, heart attack; would Dad still be alive when I got home? All these unanswered questions were going round inside my head and I felt as though the stuffing had really been knocked out of me. I remember shaking with the uncertainty of it all and the waiting was unbearable. After only a couple of weeks in my new role as Chippy I felt I had got the measure of things and was determined to carry on doing my job until we arrived in Trinidad which was about twenty four hours away. Apart from anything else carrying out my tasks would hopefully take my mind off things so off I went into the basement to balance the tanks although I was certainly feeling less than my best. I opened the valve to one of the freshwater tanks in order to spread some of the water into the other one and in doing so somehow managed to allow sea water in. It was the stokers who were the first to spot a degree of salt in the drinking water, Christ, were we in trouble. These lads working in the engine room had enormous thirsts as it was so hot down there and due to my error they would have to ration the small amount of bottled water we had on board; I had let them down. Bill Legg, the cook, boiled up some containers from the least contaminated tank for drinking but what an unforgivable mistake I had made. The situation with the water right on top of the news from home really got me down but I was determined to get a grip of things and leave my duties in good order for a hand over. By the time the ship docked in Trinidad I had everything sorted and before disembarking made sure to empty the contaminated tanks and refill them.

Sadly I signed off the *Baron Inchcape* and went to meet the ships agent who took me to the Seaman's Mission where I would stay the night before catching my flight home. 'There's a dance tonight, might take your mind off things,' he said as he dropped me off: 'you'll be picked up at 6.30 a.m. tomorrow and taken to the airstrip.' The Mission turned out to be a friendly chummy place although I was not in the mood to make the best of it. These hostelries are situated in most ports where they are used by visiting crews, men waiting to join a ship, those in transit, any sailor who is ill, for companionship; in fact, anything at all associated with the lives of seamen. I pondered on my situation and decided that for one night at least, I was in a 'missionary' position. Well I had to try and brighten myself up somehow but that night in the Seaman's Mission I definitely wasn't feeling up to any of that kind of thing nor was I up to the dancing. There was a Hattie Jacques kind of lady organising the evening's entertainment who was bossily trying to rustle up some enthusiasm amongst the few males that were about as four very well dressed white ladies arrived. Even with the musicians there were scarcely more than a dozen of us but nothing daunted, 'Hattie Jacques' mustered us together and the dancing commenced. We were in a huge room where a couple of full ship's complements may have made an impact but in which our small number made very little impression. There were so few of us that the other side of the dance floor looked like a runway, it was so big and empty. Under Hattie's direction I do my best with my limited steps and my injured mind and find out that the girls are all married and live on the island in the best way they can as they have husbands who apparently don't dance. These seemingly poor neglected wives watch out daily for visiting ships so that they can cheer up the sailors as well as themselves. The husbands are quite happy that their wives should attend the Mission they tell me, and obviously they hope to find a good dancer amongst the sailors but if they are desperate they will dance with each other. Meanwhile the guy with the music is hammering it out, he is a bit over enthusiastic with his microphone and, as I recollect the situation now I realise what a great skit Alan Bennett could make of it! Part way through the evening 'Hattie Jacques' organises a spot waltz and some balloons are released and I troll on as long as I can, defending politeness. Naturally my mind is not on the job and around 10.30 p.m. I excuse myself. It was a hard night. All I can say is that any sailor calling at this particular Seaman's Mission won't be left sitting in his room. In fact it did not escape me that on a good night the phrase I had amused myself with earlier may have been apt for some of these lads and lassies as I felt sure that some of Hattie's friends came for more than just a dance partner!

Alone in my room, tossing and turning, sleep does not come easily and I am up and about well ahead of pick up time. Phoning home from Trinidad in those days would have been very difficult; phone calls had to be booked in advance and anyway I preferred not to know any more whilst away from home and so I was taken to the airport still mystified as to what could possibly be happening to Dad. After a couple of interconnecting flights I eventually arrive in New York where there is a direct flight to Manchester. The whole journey had been well planned and no time was wasted thanks to Hogarth's, the owners of the Baron line; it was truly excellent how they organised my repatriation. Arriving at Ringway, a very minor airport in those days, I was soon cleared through customs and Mum was there to meet me. Seeing her in the distance all I can think about is the news she is about to tell me. It should have been a further year or so before I came home but now, after just a few months, here I was. Mum looked tired and sad but relieved to see me, we did not speak as my rucksack slid off my shoulder and I put my arms out to hold her for a while until the tears passed. 'Dad didn't want to send for you, I'm sorry,' she said. 'Don't worry about that Mum, I'm here now, come on let's go home.' Over the past two years whilst I had been doing my National Service my parents had rarely seen me and then after just a month at home I had gone away again; and now this. I felt guilty at having left them; they only had me after all. It is at difficult family times like this that I always feel it would be good to have a brother or sister as the onus on a single child can be heavy indeed and the responsibility of looking after your parents is better shared. However family always comes first and there was no hesitation or regret as I accompanied my mother out of the airport and into whatever trouble was waiting for me at home.

Homecoming

Courage is being scared to death – but saddling up anyway -
John Wayne

'John, your Dad had a voice problem some time ago. We didn't take it too seriously at first although it didn't improve then the Doctor said we should take a break so we went to Norway in the car with two other couples from the Sunbeam Club. Poor soul got tired and his voice got weaker and weaker; he was not himself at all. Then he started to get back pains so it was back to the hospital for more tests and eventually the surgeon looking after him said the news wasn't good. I'm sorry John but he has been diagnosed with lung cancer and secondary cancers which are affecting his neck and back.' This was the bad, bad news my Mother had to tell me as we met at Manchester airport on my impromptu return from travelling. I had braced myself for something terrible, it had to be serious for my mother to track me down, as she had in mid ocean but I still believed that where there's life there's hope and Dad was still alive. As I have mentioned my father had always been a heavy smoker, Churchman's Number 1 packets everywhere – dimp burning his lip before he removed it – and his lung cancer had spread with great speed. 'How long have we got Mum?' I asked. 'The Doctors say about six weeks if they cannot operate to remove the cancer; he's gone from twelve stone to about seven or eight and he's looking poorly John.' How could this happen in such a short time? What is this disease? Surely something could be done. My mind was racing with unanswered questions and the Christie Hospital flashed into my mind, they were cancer specialists. 'Let's have some magic God,' I prayed, 'he's only fifty two.' It seemed so unfair, my father had always worked hard, often late into the night, he was truly one of a kind, a great guy – damn those Churchman cigarettes.

As we left the airport it was mid morning so we had time to return home for me to freshen up before going to Ancoats Hospital where visiting was at 2 p.m. We got into the car which was being driven by Ernest, the ex yard foreman who had taken on the role of family retainer since Dad's illness. I greet him and put my arm on his shoulder; he looks really down as he whispers: 'sorry John.' Once at home it seemed an eternity since last being there; things had changed so much, this was not the order of play when I had left on that cold morning earlier in the year and somehow I felt uncertain and confused. Later, as we got near to the hospital, Mum let me go on ahead as Dad was often waiting outside when she arrived. 'He doesn't look one hundred per cent,' she reminded me as I set off feeling unsettled and rather frightened; everything seemed to be happening so quickly and it was unreal. As I walk down the road I see a person that I do not recognise leaning on a stick as he perches on a shallow wall. As I get nearer this stranger sees me and rises slowly. The gap between us closes and a thousand thoughts rush through my mind as I recognise my Dad and I am so glad to be with him at last. I put my arms around him with a reassuring hug, he drops his stick and we say nothing at all for a few moments. Eventually he breaks the silence: 'Good to see you Will,' he whispers, but then there is a pause; he was not a kissing or emotional type of person; 'I told Mum not to call you back home, you were getting on so well,' he finally murmured. By this time Mum had joined us and we linked him on either side as we walked through the archway into the Hospital. As we drank our tea Mum's eyes were full of tears which she did not want Dad to see so we discussed my trip instead of talking about the illness; we were doing our best to be upbeat but the only good thing was the fact that we were all three together again. It became obvious to me that my father was terminally ill although Mum had not told me this directly; she had been positive, supportive and strong and these qualities would be much in evidence in the weeks to come. Several days later Mum and I met with the surgeon, a tall red headed fellow who looked like he might have played in the second row of the Saracens rugby squad. He was the type of bloke who called a spade a spade and he told us that an exploratory operation had revealed that the cancer was deep rooted and no further surgery was possible. Mum asked for the worst case scenario and we were again told that we had no longer than six weeks. The doctor then went on to suggest how best to spend this short time and before we left he made a point of asking me not to smoke, a promise that I have upheld all my life.

We brought Dad home and the next few weeks are only recollected as a blur. If I did have time to think it was to wonder how things could have changed so much in such a short time. Only a few days ago I had been in a cracking position, everything going well for me, climate and company as good as you could wish for and now this. My previous life had become a mirage as we concentrated on the reality of this seemingly irreversible situation. Today there are many advances in the treatment of cancer; chemotherapy may have helped although I have my doubts as the cancer was in too many places; those cigarettes had truly taken their lethal toll. Our local GP Sammy Adler was kind and helpful, administering the necessary pain killers and drugs as we watched helplessly whilst even more weight dropped off Dad's frail body. Going back through his life as I desperately looked for reasons why, I once again recalled the bad motoring accident he had in the Jowett Jupiter. That incident had really shaken him, had it sparked off his illness? It didn't matter how much I searched for the answer, nothing could be done now. We moved him into one of the bedrooms with twin beds so that he would not be left alone at any time, day or night; one of us would always be there to calm and comfort him as the need arose. His face grew even thinner and his eyes seemed so far away but the flash of mischief was still there sometimes. We had shared real fun together as my Dad was a true kid at heart, a prolific practical joker and I travelled back in time to those better days when…

Frank Thompson was a wealthy wholesale green grocer who lived two doors away from us on Windsor Road. He was the proud owner of one of the poshest American cars in Oldham, a huge Chrysler and, come the firework season, it was Dad's tradition to treat Frank to a big cannon firework down his exhaust pipe. As a child I was employed to give a timely knock on Frank's front door before disappearing to join Dad in his hiding place and from there we would watch as Frank emerged from his house only to be met with a huge vibrating explosion and smoke gushing out from under his car. Of course there was no one to be seen but even so he would call out: 'Lewis Pellowe I know you are out there,' and he would rant and curse for some time before slamming the door shut… On other occasions we would fasten cotton to the front door knockers of a few houses on opposite sides of the street. We would then hide from sight and pull the cotton in unison ensuring that all our neighbours would answer their doors simultaneously. It was great fun to see them peering at each other suspiciously across the road as they realised there was nobody on the doorstep. We had this manoeuvre off to a fine art. My father loved climbing chimneys, clambering over roofs, playing table tennis late into the night (fag in mouth), being a night owl. He was a great dancer; he loved competing in motor sports and driving his car down to Falmouth; he was a maverick who disappeared from home when things got a bit 'hot' and stayed at the Edinburgh Hotel at the top of Park Road for a couple of nights until it felt safe to return. He was a kind, generous and popular chap who liked his own space very much whilst also being happy in company…

Back to reality. At the untimely age of fifty two my father was condemned to a slow death. Mum was an absolute brick throughout those terrible weeks with her constant gentle nursing and her words of encouragement as she tried to keep hope alive. Eventually even Dad realised that he was fighting a losing battle but we never talked about it. Prayers were said all the time and maybe we believed in miracles for a short while but from what I can remember my father was not a religious person although he was a true Christian in spirit. He was always there for people and very understanding of their problems. His work force adored him.

Towards the end of those interminable weeks the pain became unbearable so Dr Adler administered whatever he possibly could to alleviate things and called at the house daily. Poor Dad; we constantly bathed his parched lips as his mouth was so dry. Slowly everything that propelled life was shutting down and now all hope had gone. We were still praying although now our prayers asked for a peaceful end to this terrible disease and on the 7th September 1957 as Mum sat with him Dad's suffering finally came to an end. She awoke me to say it was all over and whatever our thoughts when the end comes and a life shuts down I remember finding it very hard to understand as I asked the question 'why?' I cannot remember going into the bedroom but I do remember the undertaker, Mr Barlow, one of our neighbours, coming soon afterwards. He was friendly and very helpful to Mum as she organised all the arrangements.

In due course the funeral service took place at Oldham Crematorium and as we drove in through the gates there were cars and people milling about everywhere; in fact there were so many mourners that many had to stand outside the chapel and the crowd was about four or five people deep. The entire building fraternity of Oldham was there, all the Pellowe workforce, the complete membership of the Liberal Club, the players from the Table Tennis league, the local ex home guard who Dad had served with during the war, and many other friends and acquaintances. The doors of the chapel were left open in the hope that the people who were standing outside would be able to hear the service and I was told afterwards that none of them moved or murmured during its duration. Such was the popularity and respect my dad had engendered throughout his life. He was a super guy.

Just a few short months before this terrible period I had been enjoying absolute freedom but now I had lost my father and had new responsibilities; I really had to get a grip of the situation particularly as things soon became unsettled within the family business. It was time to buckle down and do as well as possible at whatever it was I chose to do. Life had been rather a playground for me, thanks to the love and generosity of my parents, but I knew that was over; it was my turn to deliver, take on responsibility and ensure that my mother was as happy and secure as possible whilst Dad's work would be carried on in whatever way it turned out. From this time it was apparent that life was to change.

One of Life's Crossroads

Those who have succeeded at anything and don't mention luck
are kidding themselves - Larry L King

Following the death of my father I set to and got on with my work in the family business whilst simultaneously picking up a social life again. The sequence of events, of comings and goings, from Dellow days to disappearing into the Army, a trip round the world to a sudden recall home, all this meant that I was well behind my counterparts who were busy courting, getting engaged, and married. Regular weekend slots at Froggats Dance Hall, after imbibing alcohol in the 'Hole in the Wall' for pre dance nerves, had not featured heavily in my events calendar. Margaret, the trainee physiotherapist, was courting someone else by now, things move on and at heart I was a free spirit and much preferred it that way, particularly after all the freedom I had enjoyed in the past three years. Also, the loss of my greatest pal, my Dad, meant that I was now facing the serious side of life as I settled into the family business where I had previously served my time as an apprentice joiner.

Sad and uncertain about the future, Mother and I were still living at Windsor Road; and so it was that a time of great assessment began. There would be no returning to motor sports, that was gone and yesterday, however I did get back into playing some rugby at weekends and still managed some climbing on Saddleworth's beautiful crags. It was now late summer, 1957, and on my return to work I found myself out of touch with the day to day running of APAS. Dad's absence really affected the staff and whilst Dad's brother, Arthur, handled the office side of things, he had always had a very different approach to my father who had managed the building sites, the surveying, estimating, and all the industrial, mill and cinema work. Site visits were not Arthur's thing at all and I don't recall ever seeing him on a building location although he was heavily involved with the joinery shop, office and administration, and one of his hobbies was wood carving. No, I'm afraid that Dad and Arthur, although brothers, had very different views on life and work and may not always have seen eye to eye. Whilst I had been away in the Army, Arthur had brought his youngest son, Peter, to work in the family firm. Peter had already completed his National Service and so was now a permanent member of the team. His brother, Guy, a giant of a fellow at six foot four inches, had also arrived in my absence and he too worked at APAS although at this stage I wasn't sure exactly where he fitted in. Arthur was sympathetic and helpful as we tried to rearrange all Dads' responsibilities following his death; they say no one is indispensable but we would see. After many chats to try to decide what was to be my role it was eventually agreed that I would get involved with the outside foreman, carry out some estimating work, work on the industrial jobs and allocate the morning job worksheets. I was a qualified joiner with a National Certificate from Oldham Technical College and a first year surveying course qualification so I was comfortable taking on these responsibilities. Arthur, meanwhile, was to deal with outside contracts, the building sites and the whole joinery programme. The day to day business of the office and company accounts was very competently looked after by Harry Howard, a most conscientious company secretary who provided invaluable support. At this time the fireplace trade was considerable and we were busy competing with Duncan's, our friendly rivals; there was also a steady stream of plumbing work and business seemed good in general. Arthur and my dad, Lewis, had recruited a great team, many of whom had been working with us all through their apprenticeships, breaking off for war service then returning to APAS as tradesmen and I'm sure these lads must have many stories to tell; some of them were certainly very interesting chaps.

Even though there was change all round it was still a sad time for me. I did my best to handle my new role and responsibilities but I felt in a minority situation working with Arthur and his two sons whom I had never spent any time with and barely knew. I began to get restless. Peter, Arthur's youngest son, was the complete opposite of me and we didn't get on. We were poles apart in our definition of work and I would never have run a business with him out of choice whilst Arthur's other son, Guy, seemed to come and go and didn't really appear to have any concrete role. When he was around he usually based himself at a small office and yard that the company owned in Hollinwood which was called Housing Units, a small builder's merchants used as a buying lever for the vast amounts of materials APAS used on the house building front. Merchants get extra over rider settlement discounts varying from 2.5% to 7.5% and this applies to cement, plasterboard plumbing, bricks, drainage, doors etc and so it was a good move to establish this merchant's yard. All the discounted material added up to great savings when you were purchasing for a building site of between thirty and sixty new builds. However as Guy didn't have any building experience that I knew of he couldn't have been in his comfort zone at Housing Units; likewise Peter who must also have felt a bit out of place at APAS.

A couple of years passed by with me getting involved in my job and starting to make some plans but gradually it began to dawn on me that I seemed to be working twice the hours that the other, strictly 9 – 5, family players did and I began to feel increasingly uncomfortable about the situation. One day my interest was aroused by a waggon load of prepared joinery which was waiting to depart from our yard. I asked where the window and door frames, all primed and ready for installation, were going and was told it was a regular load which was sent to Cornwall. I knew that Arthur was dabbling in some building work down there but for how long and to what extent it had been going on I had no idea. Later that evening, when everyone had gone, I checked the company accounts and work sheets but could find nothing for the consignment sent out on the waggon that day. Now things began to make sense; Guy, always missing, must be running a building operation down south but where were the bloody accounts? I confronted Arthur and asked to see the paperwork which of course he could not produce. Previously Mum had also been upset by Arthur when she found out that he had not paid Dad's National Insurance stamp when he was ill which caused her pension to be less than it should have been. Although I didn't take it very seriously at the time my mother was very annoyed and now when I think back to how much money she lost in pensions, as she lived to be ninety nine, I can see why she was so bothered. Considering how it would be for me if Arthur retired or died and I was left working with his two sons I decided it was time for a head to head, laying all cards on the table.

Prior to entering into discussions regarding the future of APAS I had quietly, and perhaps rather selfishly, been pursuing an interest that began to get me thinking; something so completely different that it would involve starting a completely new life if I decided to take it on as a career. The world was already aware of Jacques Yves Cousteau, the campaigner against oceanic pollution, and he was now famous again for having co-developed the Aqua Lung underwater breathing set and I was intrigued. The apparatus he had developed to follow his studies allowed a diver to breathe in air from a compressed air bottle which was fed through a reducer valve thus allowing one to dive to considerable depths. At the same time I also heard about the BUC, British Underwater Centre, operated by Captain Trevor Hampton (1) in Warfleet Creek, Dartmouth, and I couldn't wait to join one of their diving courses. The Hampton's were offering a three day aqua lung course at a cost of five guineas and other courses would follow such as oxygen re-breather diving and the standard diving dress course, best understood by the large suit, helmet and weighted boots! I had problems at work and no steady girlfriend, although again it has to be said that I truly didn't want to get involved with anyone, so I felt relatively free and able to commit myself to whatever I chose to do. Consequently I enrolled on a weekend course at BUC but as I was working this meant a very early start in order to get to Dartmouth by 8.30 a.m. on a Friday morning ready for a first diving briefing. I left home at 3.30 a.m. and really flogged my car to make it in time; fortunately I had good wheels in the shape of a TR2. The weekend course consisted of four hours of practical work regarding diving procedures and equipment, and three dive sessions all of which had to be completed by Sunday tea time.

After only the first dive I was really hooked even though visibility had been affected by inclement weather, but - oh boy, how wonderful it was! The diving school operated from the three levels of Boat House Cottage which had been built on the tidal Warfleet Creek in Dartmouth by the Hampton's. There was also a workshop and storage area from which stone steps led down to the flat bottomed diving boat moored in the creek which had a swivel ladder at the bow to allow easy entry into the water. There is an easy way to tell if a diver is using CA (Compressed Air Aqualung Diver) or oxygen because CA will leave a tell tale trail of bubbles on the surface of the water whereas oxygen doesn't. Also oxygen equipment restricts the diver to a depth of approximately thirty foot whereas you can go deeper with CA. Captain Hampton taught divers both methods and he was chosen by the BBC to train their naturalists and feature film makers, amongst them Tony Soper and Johnny Morris, who both subsequently qualified as British Master Divers. In fact in 1960 Johnny Morris made a film about the training entitled *Master Diver* and very soon professionals were coming from all over the world to this small creek in Devon for the very best, professional, one to one training. Sir John Wedgwood, of pottery fame, qualified CA/O (oxygen); David Dimbleby came to make a film; and ex Royal Navy divers, now in Civvy Street, were asked if they were BUDS (British Underwater Diving Centre) as this qualification was often recognised in preference to the training provided by the Royal Navy. The school's record was exceptional and no diver had ever got the bends (compressed air illness) whilst under the instruction of Trevor Hampton.

When I was down in Dartmouth, which was as often as I could possibly manage it, I often met up with, and accompanied, a Siamese diver, Prince Benyasakt Kritakara, who was over here in the UK studying to become a doctor. We usually stayed in the Victoria Hotel and we had some great times partying there; hangovers didn't seem a great problem in those days. One weekend I had gone to Dartmouth for some free diving whilst the skipper trained two or three new clients when I suddenly found myself in company with David Attenborough and Tony Soper. The skipper suggested we had a competition whereby we were to collect as many spider crabs as we could in one diving trip, the winner being the one who could bring the most up in one dive. Spider crabs have a very small body but enormously long legs with a span somewhere between eighteen and thirty inches and they live at a depth somewhere between thirty and fifty feet. Down we went and collected several, fighting our way back to the surface as we tried to keep our catch intact by holding them against our chests using only our flippers to propel ourselves upwards. The contest was not easy at all and gave some measure of the type of guy Trevor Hampton was! I only managed to bring four or five crabs up but this was well short of David Attenborough's clutch of eight which were clinging and struggling against him as he emerged from the sea. He really was in his natural element dealing with creatures as the world would find out; a great man. Competition over we returned to the steps at the centre, splashed our way up to stow the gear away in the storage area then looked for Gwen Hampton who would dispense some much needed hot coffee. Then it was down to the Victoria Hotel where we met up with the Prince and party time began. Nothing could beat it.

Having discovered Dartmouth and diving I was tackling the Master Diving qualification in stages as I could not get the necessary two weeks off work; simultaneously I was also pondering an alternative career in diving.

1.

 2.

3.

4.

1. Dartmouth Fronts, the Royal British Naval College
2. Trevor Hampton supervising Aqualung diving off one of his swinging ladder dive boats
3. Boat Cottage previously the home of BUC. Great memories
4. Two ferries still ply the river as building of a bridge is banned

Things were really coming to a head at APAS by now and I felt that we had arrived at a make or break situation so I decided to speak to Mum and explain my plans. I told her how I was hoping to qualify as a Master Diver and then live and work down in Dartmouth, anticipating an opportunity. I thought she would go through the roof but no, she heard me out and agreed to my offer of taking her down to see the place, meet the Hampton's and see what happened from there. We booked in at the Gunfield Hotel which was across the creek from the school but the weather was horrible and the hotel was a very odd place. If you think of Fawlty Towers you've got it only this place was far worse! Run by rather eccentric twin brothers called Llewellyn, we checked in and were served some form of dinner. Following a very cold night we went down for breakfast at the normal time next morning but looked in vain for someone to serve us. There was no one around. We hunted high and low and eventually made our own breakfast in the hotel kitchen and still no one showed up. This has to have been the most casual hotel I have ever visited in my life! However, amusing though it sounds now, all this bother did not help to get Mum in good spirits and when we called to visit the Hampton's later that day she was hesitant in relating to my enthusiasm. I admired her for hearing me out and making the trip but in the final analysis it came down to priorities. Mum would be more settled staying in Oldham and in any case earning a living as a diver could have proved to be very hard; the North Sea Gas fields were well in the future so the opportunities for diving jobs in those days were very limited. Pulling myself together and realising that back in the real world there was a challenge and a job to address at home, my dreams of living and working in Dartmouth were left behind (2). I never did fully complete the Master Diving qualification much to my enduring regret.

As previously mentioned APAS had purchased a yard at Hollinwood where Guy would hang out when not in Cornwall. Originally the site had been the Hollinwood Smithy which was a very old brick building with a small loft. Also on site there was a partially covered barn and a shed in which was installed a circular saw and a cross cut saw; three bays had been built for holding loose sand, ballast and granite and although the supplies in the yard were for APAS' use, the yard itself not being required to trade or grow, some of the local builders also used it for convenience. The staff at Hollinwood consisted of only two people and a part time cleaner but even so a neat double storey office showroom had been built with a fifty to sixty foot frontage on the main Oldham to Manchester Road. In this building there was an extremely fine staircase installed by Frank Lees who was an excellent tradesman, and it was a real jewel in the crown. Frank would never know the huge number of people destined to use his stairs when the place eventually became Housing Units under my ownership. To the right of the showroom was a tarmac forecourt area and to the left were five small stone cottages which the company owned but rented out to tenants, the middle one actually being a shop which sold Hegginbottom's tripe! From one end to the other the whole thing presented a good frontage on a busy road. Mum, realising I was unsettled working with Arthur and his sons, would support me whatever happened; so, even though it seemed there may be a difficult road ahead, we forced a meeting to thrash things out. I suppose I was still pretty naïve at the time as the odds were definitely stacked in Arthur's corner but we talked quite sensibly and Mum was a real brick, giving as good as she got.

During our talks the possibility of my taking over Housing Units was discussed and, as part of the proposed deal, a financial package for Mum was suggested, to be paid over six years (selling Dad's shares for cash over that period). However to this day who exactly made the suggestion about separating APAS and Housing Units remains unclear in my mind. We did some maths over Dad's half share in the firm and eventually agreed a settlement after the completion of valuations and various other legal formalities. Suddenly I had a business of my own to run and grow (3), Mother had an income and Arthur and his sons remained at APAS with all the assets loaded in their favour. Even so I had some real doubts about the ability of APAS to continue without Lewis Pellowe, and was concerned for the future of the workforce; later on these concerns would become a reality (4).

For me and Mum it was a clean break from the past and certainly an opportunity I was personally ready for. Back at the Grammar School my performance had been dismal; then I had bummed around for several years but losing Dad as we did changed me overnight. Now was the moment of truth and with a certain sadness I realised that my 'hands on' career had completely changed direction. I was now destined to become a merchant and retailer but in actual fact the way things proceeded at Housing Units meant that my building background would prove to be extremely valuable. It is a fact that the business would not have developed as it did without those skills; dead true, and so it is to the building trade that I owe any success.

One of Life's Crossroads: Notes

(1.) Trevor Hampton was an extremely interesting man and certainly influenced me during the time that I knew him. We already shared some traits before meeting – we both owned a Bond Minicar and later ditto with an Austin Countryman. I suppose I could say that his was the kind of life that that appeals to me most and that is why I find him so fascinating. Jill, his daughter, wrote a biography of her Dad *Wheels, Wings and Water*, it's a great read but as it has been published privately the only way you will get to peruse it is to go to Dartmouth Library where there is a copy available. In it his life reads like a *Boy's Own* adventure; born at the right time, a time of opportunity with a world war thrown in, he earned his title 'Captain' both for flying and small boat sailing. Straight from school he was apprenticed to the Austin car factory in the midlands which gave him the mechanical know how of all things that moved. Racing motorcycles under the name *New Imperial* he competed at Donnington, the Ulster Grand Prix and the amateur Manx Grand Prix where he had a class win. During WW2 he would captain Wellington Bombers in the mission *M for Mother;* unable to make one of the sorties due to an ear problem his loyal crew put aside their concern but fatefully did not return from that trip. Later Hampton would flight test Lancaster Bombers and he was awarded the Air Force Cross for his services to aviation. After a spell as a test pilot flying Spitfire's the next adventure in his life was to be on the water where he experienced a series of small yacht sailing. It was during this time that he met his second wife, Gwyneth Harding, rather coincidentally related to the big boss in Cyprus during National Service, Sir John Harding. Trevor and Gwyneth went on to share a challenging life together and, as she had been brought up around boats, Gwyneth was quite happy to live on a thirty foot yacht even having a young daughter, the aforementioned Jill, there. Eventually the family upped sticks and moved to a thirty five foot motor cruiser before buying a shack at Warfleet Creek, Dartmouth which they eventually rebuilt as Boat Cottage which is where I found them. Having given his first diving lesson in 1953, Hampton continued until 1976 when, at the age of 63, he sold the business. Trevor Hampton's life contained all the ingredients of adventure that boys read about and long for; a mixture of air and sea adventures with a good helping of danger and uncertainty. I can definitely identify with that, the adrenalin, excitement and hardship instead of a life behind an office desk! Hampton died in February 2002 aged eighty nine. Gwyneth, now in her later years, still bathes at high water from the steps at the bottom of Boat Cottage in that once busy creek. She maintains that the salt water is good for her skin which I also believe to be true.

(2.) Many years later we bought a flat in Dartmouth to use for holidays. It was a super place and as we now had a permanent home by the sea my dreams of diving and owning my own boat seemed to be coming to fruition. Firstly Tim and I bought a small Dory dinghy from the Liverpool area which had a 25hp outboard motor on the back. As we couldn't wait to test it out in Dartmouth we enthusiastically rushed up to the Lakes, got it in the water and shot off; I don't think we even bothered to read the instructions. We had been a bit too keen though and something went wrong or jammed; the engine was revving flat out as the boat shot out of the water and up onto the beach until we eventually stopped it amidst a lot of shouting. We managed to get it back on the trailer and returned it to the supplier for some adjustments. Once it was fixed and we had read the instructions we got the lot down to Devon and began charging around in the harbour. The Dory dinghies and the flat are long gone but are very fondly remembered. We swapped the flat for a house and the dinghies were replaced by a small seventeen foot leisure yacht which I bought from a boat yard in Chesterfield of all places; later I progressed to a twenty four and a half foot British Hunter cruiser. Both these yachts were named *One Day* – why? Because one day we will live permanently in Dartmouth – we'd better hurry up!

(3.) The legal agreement which separated APAS from Housing Units was dated 24th August 1960. Interestingly my agreement to hand over Housing Units to a new owner (over a four year period) was dated 24th August 1999 – only thirty nine years on. There are lots of parallels when you look for them.

(4.) Following Dad's death the demise of APAS was ongoing as it was reduced and eventually closed down. Lewis Pellowe would not have let that happen. At its lowest ebb and with a much reduced workforce, I pondered whether to make an offer to buy the business with Dad in mind. If I had done that, however, it could have diluted the intake into Housing Units which was growing rapidly. Sorry Dad.

1.

2.

4.

3.

6.

5.

1. First version of *One Day* the 17' leisure yacht
2. Current 24'5" Hunter ready to go back in the water after her spring overhaul. Spurred on by Dennis and Eleanor.
3. Viv – courting times in *Reggie*
4. Family all abourd *One Day* during Regatta week
5. Louanne, Claire, Viv and terrier, Meg, in our first Dory, *Nervous Wreck*
6. Viv prefers the peace of the harbour

I'll Marry You One Day

I was the last knight in dull armour after other shining knights had moved on –
John Pellowe

Around the same time as I became the owner of a small business I suddenly found myself facing yet another life changing event as literally just around the corner there was a surprise waiting for me. Amongst my friends was a girl called Pam Hoyland. I had known her since childhood when her family and mine used to holiday together each summer in Anglesey or on the Norfolk Broads. By now, of course, she was all grown up and married to a doctor called Ken Ansell. They lived in Germany as Ken was doing his National Service in the Army Medical Corps but Pam was over here visiting her parents, as she did frequently, when I bumped into her one day in the late 1950's. Now Pam could turn heads with her beauty and she was often recognised by people as she had appeared on TV as the hostess in a programme called 'Spot the Tune' presented by Ken Platt. She knew she was in safe hands with me when we arranged to visit the Galleon Open Air Swimming Pool in Didsbury one summer evening and when she suggested that she brought a friend along the next time that was fine by me. Apparently this friend of hers had recently visited Pam and her husband in Germany and had never been without an escort, having had the odd officer thrown in on her visit. An attractive girl then, I thought, but I wasn't particularly interested even though I had the distinct feeling that I was being set up. Many of my pals and the girls I had known from earlier days were engaged or even married by now so the playing field was thinning out but I had no concern about it, I was a confirmed member of the singles club and definitely had no plans to have it any otherwise, for now at least. I already knew the girl, Pam told me, but again I didn't pay much attention.

And so it was that the following Friday evening I finished up with two for one in my pink TR2, Pam and 'our' friend: enter Vivienne Critchley of course......and indeed it was good to see her. One time pal and former classmate at Werneth School, you may remember that at the age of five she had said to me as she sat on the toilet: 'You're my sweetheart and one day I'll marry you.' Now that is tough stuff from someone so young but as the years passed we had drifted apart although it had not escaped my notice that she never seemed short of suitors, albeit of a 'mixed' nature.

Having discharged her matchmaking responsibilities Pam returned to her husband in BOAR Germany, whilst Viv and I continued to go out together as a couple. On Friday evenings we would visit the pool then go on for a swank night out at the Shambles (1) in Manchester where we would always sit in the corner of the back tap room opposite the gent's toilet. We would settle down for Viv's preferred alcoholic beverage, Tetley's Bitter, and one of the rather good pork pies which was about all you could get in the way of bar food in those days. Sitting on the solid wooden seats under the low ceiling which was amber stained from years and years of cigarette smoke, Viv would add to the colour by smoking a cigarette or two of her own as the room filled up with regulars. As the night progressed the atmosphere gradually thickened with the aromas of beer, cigarette smoke and the smell which wafted from the gent's toilets each time the door opened and closed! Truly romantic, but the lack of grandeur did not seem to worry Viv and we were quite content there. At closing time as the bell was sounding for last orders the older regulars would nod and wave knowingly as we left and moved outside into the night air with our clothes smelling of smoke.

On Saturday evenings we would often also meet up after my rugby game, assuming the team coach was not seriously delayed by various necessary stops on the way back from a match. Rugby was a Saturday ritual and should I be delayed I didn't worry too much. One Saturday the coach was late back into Oldham and even though I wasn't seeing Viv that evening I hurriedly got into my TR2 to make a mad dash down to the Avenue Cinema in Blackley so that I wouldn't miss the beginning of the Jack Hawkins film, *The Cruel Sea*. The stretch of road down Hollinwood Avenue is long and wide and in my haste I did not realise I actually overtook the police in their Riley Pathfinder. Just as I was paying for a 2/9d ticket at the cinema kiosk I felt a hand on my shoulder and, as I turned around, I came face to face with two large coppers, one of whom calmly said: 'you passed us at 96 miles per hour and disappeared into the distance,' as he handed me a ticket. I felt a bit shame faced but they were actually quite humorous about the whole thing as they cracked their Stirling Moss jokes although their banter ensured that I missed the opening credits of the film! A few weeks later I had to attend court about the incident and I was accompanied by John Lord, a Barrister. I knew it would be tricky but John made a great effort and produced a handful of blown up photographs which had been taken with the camera placed flat on the surface of the centre of the road on Hollinwood Avenue – honestly it looked like Silverstone – and he pleaded the case for a reclassified speed restriction. Despite his efforts I lost my licence for six months and as we came out of court John asked me if I wanted a lift but I replied that I was OK as my car was there. 'You can't drive', he said, 'you have just lost your licence.' The consequences of my punishment had not immediately occurred to me and I found it very hard to restrain myself from using my car. I managed a couple of weeks but once the dust had settled I risked driving now and again and it was on one of these illegal trips, with Viv that I had another brush with the law.

We were parked up in a quiet spot in Bardsley when a police car suddenly appeared from nowhere. As our windows were a little steamed up shall we say, the policeman tapped on the roof to get our attention and after checking us out he got back into his car and left. Just to be on the safe side as we left our courting ground Viv took the wheel of my car although she had never driven it before and, as a banned driver I was not a suitable instructor. The usual excuse, we were young etc, and as we emerged onto Ashton Road to our horror the police car was lying in wait for us damn it! Quick as a flash I said to Viv: 'tell them you have been driving all night,' but unfortunately, for good measure, Viv also told the policeman that her name was Pam Ansell as she knew that Pam had a driving licence whereas her own was only a provisional one. Sorry Pam! A chit was issued demanding that documents be produced but fortunately one of the coppers turned out to be a rugby colleague called Roy Hamer (2), a good traditional copper. Obviously Roy knew us and had realised what was going on so over he came and tried to help: 'John, you have to come clean on this, I know this isn't Pam Ansell,' he said, and so, with his help, we changed the official documentation to Viv's name although this meant that she was later charged for driving without a qualified driver. Had Roy not been on the scene things could have got very serious and, showing true love, Viv took it all in her stride (3). This whole evening's episode could literally be referred to as 'getting your knickers in a twist'! Shortly afterwards when I met Roy at a match he told me to take care as the local police were aware I may be driving whilst banned. Other people had also cautioned me and so I refrained as I only had two more months of the ban to go.

Viv had proved to be a reliable friend and as she radiated fun we continued to go out together and, whilst it was never the love affair of the century, meeting as we did rather later on should we say, we grew very fond of each other. I was surprised she had not settled down before as there seemed to have been many opportunities but there we are. On her way to the tennis club Viv would have to walk past 307 Windsor Road where my mother would often be stood in the window as she talked to Willie, her large red and grey African parrot. As Willie was a good talker he and mother always had a good prattle together but she would break off from chatting to him and say to me: 'there's a nice girl,' as Viv walked by. This happened so often that even the bloody parrot started to say 'there's a nice girl;' it was time to get worried! I'm sure the old girl was thinking it was time to off load me, was there a conspiracy one wonders? Vivienne did seem to play a lot of tennis! Whatever, our courting continued and things were going well until one night Viv got tickets to see *South Pacific* at the Odeon in Manchester. The evening was a disaster; I had work problems on my mind and I was about to take a diving holiday in Spain with Ian Platt (4) and Ian Hilton whereas I think Viv had been hoping that I would ask her to go; and probably I should have. I think the song from *South Pacific* entitled, *I'm Gonna Wash that Man Right Outta my Hair*, really came into play and before the night was over our relationship was off. Viv, no doubt obeying the words of her mother: 'God helps those who help themselves', threw herself into another affair; she never has been one to let the grass grow under her feet! As for me, whilst en route across France towards Spain my co driver drove my Morris Traveller off the road after hitting a stone sign because a bloody wasp had flown into the car! Punishment? We managed to find a French farmer with his own forge and with his help we rebuilt the wheel arch and suspension and, after many hard hours of work, we celebrated the resurrection of the car by drinking the farmers wine and eating his food. From there we limped onwards to Spain and the rest of the holiday but before we knew it we were back home and although I have never been able to explain why, somehow Viv and I were back together again. Truly I had missed her whilst she put the whole thing down to a wake up call for me! Looking back I should have spent less time with my 'toys', got off my backside and been a bit more active in certain departments of life. I have real regrets that I did not begin a relationship with Viv earlier, rather than emerging a long way down the queue; we may then have enjoyed that elusive, real, love affair. Yes I truly feel that.

In the summer of 1959 I introduced Vivienne to Dartmouth where we stayed at a bed and breakfast in Victoria Road but spent all our time in the posher Victoria Hotel where we would have our drinks and meals. Whilst in Dartmouth we hired *Reggie*, a clinker, or rowing boat, which was varnished to a shiny brown. We would load up with Tetley's bitter and pork pies, (this being well before we became more aware and opted for a healthy diet of salads and Dubonnet), and we would row around the coves and backwaters of the area. Perhaps we were finally in love; certainly I had abandoned my diving gear on this trip so I was surely on a slippery road!

Whilst Viv and I were getting on with our courting her mum and dad, Tom and Edith Critchley, were quietly tucked away in their home in the Enfield Avenue cul-de-sac (5). One time owners of the grocer's shop I had frequented as a child they were now leading a quieter life with Tom working as a machine engineer at Sampson's on Gainsborough Avenue. The work was only moderately paid but Tom was very content, an attitude that is sadly lacking today. He was a quiet, relaxed, conscientious, unfussy kind of guy, a true product of pre war families. In his spare time he was a serious grower of chrysanthemums and was president of the Oldham Chrysanthemum Society so, in order to give myself some 'street cred' with Tom I helped him to rebuild his aging greenhouse which was the nerve centre of his hobby. As well as owning Vivienne the Critchley's also had a solidly built Corgi dog called Justin, a good dog although a little daft. Getting a dog had been Vivienne's idea although of course she was never around to look after him and it was all left to her parents – you know how it is. The first time I picked Viv up from her home I was introduced to Justin who I thought looked quite amusing with his large head and neck. Later, as I started the car to commence our date something made me turn round to survey the back seat and there was the bloody dog, waiting expectantly to go somewhere. Justin specialised in taking long trips to sniff out any bitches he thought may need his attention and he also enjoyed getting lost so I was frequently drawn into search parties when he went missing on his amorous adventures.

Meanwhile I was having my own amorous adventures with Viv. Our relationship deepened and we spent more time together doing all the various activities we enjoyed which included dancing. Viv was a particularly good dancer and whilst I was not in her league we were always up and cracking when *Rock Around the Clock* or Buddy Holly let loose. We had also been hiking together on our great Saddleworth gritstone moors and as this had not presented any problems for Viv we decided to visit Pont-pen-y-Benglog in Snowdonia one Easter. Just before we made the trip I decided to speak to Viv's father, and, as I had rejuvenated his glasshouse by the laying of a concrete floor and the building of base walls, I felt I had cleared my way to ask permission to marry his daughter. One evening Viv and her Mum faded away upstairs on some pretext whilst I asked Tom for his

Vivienne and her dad delivering his prize blooms to the Annual Show.
He was a keen and good competitor.

permission and of course there were no objections just utter relief in Tom's features as I heard him humming *As Time Goes By*. The deed being completed in a couple of minutes we didn't have a celebratory drink, as Tom never had alcohol in the house, but we spent a good half hour discussing the merits of Oldham Rugby League who were a great team at that time. Just a matter of priorities you see! So, permission granted, Viv and I made our way to Wales where we stayed in a barn which was handy for the pub that we patronised before literally hitting the hay. The following morning we washed in a nearby stream then went off to climb a couple of high peaks, one of them being Glyder Fawr which is a tricky edge leading to Tryfan. It was here that I gave Viv an engagement ring and finally asked her to marry me as, out of the corner of my eye, I saw the Aston Martin and associated lifestyle I had envisaged falling off the cliff.

Viv and I were married on New Years Eve 1960 and Tom had vibes from his greenhouse that the weather would be good that day which it was. The service was held at St Thomas's in Werneth and our good friend Stuart Driver, a popular guy whom we had known for years, was to be the minister. Following the ceremony our reception would be held at the Midland Hotel, real top drawer stuff (6), and Viv and her Mum had it all worked out whilst my mother nosed in as much as she dared. I always chuckle about weddings; all the adrenaline, nervous tension, fuss and worry that precede these events seem pointless as they inevitably go off really well, and our wedding was no exception being executed with near military precision. Of course there had been the usual panic moments such as the attempted decimation of the bride's wedding outfit. Viv had ordered a lovely white velvet dress which was trimmed round the neckline with a single mink pelt but unfortunately, a couple of days before the wedding, Justin, the amorous Corgi, located the mink which was carefully wrapped up in crepe paper and not realising its significance decided to chew it up. Now I was not in the Critchley household when the girls found him but this time he had really put his foot, or should I say his teeth, in it and this really must have been Justin's finest hour although Viv may have thought it should have been his final hour! There followed a frantic time of careful remedial work to patch and reposition the trim and Viv appeared on the day looking one hundred per cent believe me. Bob Lees, my cousin, did a good job as Best Man despite him being quite young and although that was the role my old pal Ian Platt had hoped to fill he was happy enough with being one of the other officials together with Jimmy Gerraghty, Philip Jackson, Peter Wild and Kelvin Hall. I rather think most chaps getting married become mesmerised during the whole affair and can hardly believe they are doing it; all these people and well wishers slapping you on the back whilst the marriage is pictured in your mind as a cloud with two huge gates sporting 'freedom' signs slowly closing in the mist. On the other side of the gates stands your coveted Lamborghini which gradually disappears from view; at least that is how I saw it and indeed those dreams certainly became extremely distant as the following year we were to see a lot of changes.

After our marriage we were going to live in the house at Windsor Road, as my mother had moved to a bungalow on Northgate in Garden Suburb, Oldham and I stayed there with her the night before the do. On the morning of the wedding I remember walking down to the chemist's shop to purchase some 'gentlemen's requirements' for the honeymoon which we were to spend on a skiing holiday in Fulpmes, Austria, a place that had been recommended to us by Peter Whitworth (7) an old friend. Skiing in 1960 was not quite what it is today and from Innsbruck you had to clatter your way up to Fulpmes on a single line funicular railway very reminiscent of something made from an old fashioned Meccano set. Along the way there were several stops at tiny snow covered villages where we collected the odd traveller or two but eventually we arrived at our destination, still clad in city overcoats and black leather shoes. As we slid our way through the snow laden, silent, Hansel and Gretel village in search of our hotel I remember knocking on the door of a chalet style house at about 10.30 p.m., looking totally out of place and asking in apologetic English where the Hotel Lutz could be! Eventually we found it and settled in before making our way to the ski slopes the next morning where we reported for our first lesson. We were issued with pairs of skis much taller than we were and in our huge uncoordinated boots we ventured forth. The bloody instructor, basic in his deliverance, never considered the skis and boots to be other than the best as he bellowed to us: 'Benz your ness Englishmen,' and we couldn't wait for lunch time which was between 12 and 1 p.m. Drifting back quite late from our respite, about two-ish, the instructor shouted: 'Where's you been Englishmen's,' to which I politely replied: 'held up on honeymoon Fritz!' After two or three days of this suffering we exchanged our huge skis for a toboggan and thereafter enjoyed a more leisurely honeymoon and lunch breaks! Whilst staying in Fulpmes we palled up with the son of the hotel's owners and Heidi, a waitress who would join us after her evening shift. We had all developed a taste for cherry brandy which had the effect of making us feel better and better by the glass and one drunken night the four of us were joined by another guest, a German Sales Representative. As the others gradually departed, Viv going off to be sick at one point but returning very briefly and showing true grit in my opinion, the German and I continued drinking right through until dawn. He didn't speak any English and I didn't speak a word of German but we managed to converse all night long and I recall interpreting his actions to mean that he was very apologetic about Hitler whilst I ran round the room pretending to be a Spitfire; a unique exercise in rebuilding relationships which even Tony Blair could not match! Eventually the German finished his umpteenth cherry brandy, had his breakfast and set off on his rounds whilst I went to bed.

Honeymoon over we returned home and poor Viv started to be sick; we had not planned such a quick start family so I spent some time considering the shelf life of the products I had purchased for use on our honeymoon from the friendly chemist's shop in Garden Suburb. All too soon Tim was born and unfortunately he was a troublesome baby. You couldn't put him down after his feed and winding him was a feat in itself. His birth coincided with my new responsibilities at Housing Units and I would often be out all day from 7 a.m. until around 10 p.m. and even though both Viv's mum and mine were always fluttering about trying to help Viv was exhausted. When I arrived home late at night chubby cheeked Tim would still be full of wind with no intention of settling; he really wore us down and we became desperate. Fortunately one night a friend of ours, Raymond, who worked at the Christie Hospital, called in. He picked up our squawking son, held him upside down by his feet, gently shook him and to our sheer amazement the wind came out! However just as we got on top of that problem the little fella began to curl up with severe bouts of pain and this time it was really frightening. Definitely not wind we thought although our GP didn't appear to agree with us so we asked for a second opinion and that evening a young, turbaned and bearded Indian doctor called to the house. He also felt there was something serious going on, possibly an intersection of the bowel but he couldn't be sure. Nevertheless he immediately admitted Tim to hospital where he was operated on and sure enough the Indian doctor was correct; our baby's condition had been very serious and would have led to a gangrenous bowel had it been left. He saved your life Tim! Following that episode Tim became much more settled and nothing much seems to have slowed him down since! Later, when Louanne eventually showed up, she was a lot easier to look after initially but soon enough she too started to have trouble. After her feeds she would have the most fearful projectile vomiting and the milk came out with such force it was frightening. Eventually and thankfully she was hospitalised and was slowly cured.

As I have mentioned previously, around the time Viv and I married and had Tim I had left the family business, APAS, and moved to the yard in Hollinwood. APAS had been an established and prestigious organisation but my legacy, Housing Units, was still finding its feet and only had a very basic turnover. Although I felt very confident we could succeed, having a new wife and a baby suddenly in the equation really put the pressure on and it seemed only time would tell what would become of my project.

I'll Marry You One Day: Notes

(1) Many years later, after the IRA bomb attack on Manchester, our pub, The Shambles (Old Wellington Inn), together with the neighbouring Sinclair's Oyster Bar were picked up in their medieval entirety and moved a short distance away to make room for Selfridges, Marks and Spencer and a whole bank of designer shops. It's still the same inside just in a different location! Time Viv and I popped in after fifty years plus!

(2) Roy played at Keb Lane in the second row whilst I was hooker and we would sometimes turn out for the same team. He was a typical 1950's well respected bobby. He lived in a police house on Hollins Road and his beat included the large Limeside estate, now known as Limehurst, where he was not without trouble it has to be said. He was rather like the policeman in *Dixon of Dock Green*, a popular 1950's TV series with Jack Warner; that was Roy. If the kids went out of line a thick ear would be in the offing or he would take the child home and talk to the parents. Roy's presence, words and action commanded a respect which is not seen today. He was a great policeman of that time and a help in times of need – thanks Roy.

(3) That wasn't the only time Viv had a brush with the law whilst in my car. Many years later we were driving back from a long trip to France intending to stop over at our house in Dartmouth before making our way back 'up north'. I must have been tired or something after leaving the ferry because just ten miles away from our Devon home I foolishly moved across the road obviously thinking for a moment that I was still travelling on the continent. Driving down the wrong side of the road we hit an Audi which was coming uphill and round a blind bend. There was a head on crash and both cars were burnt out but fortunately the farmer and his wife in the Audi were not seriously injured and neither were we. I was of course full of remorse and to this day Viv cannot relax when I am driving her anywhere.

(4) One weekend Viv and I drove down to Worcestershire to stay with my pal, Ian Platt, who was working for Metal Box in that area at the time. He lived in a lovely rented cottage complete with beams and its own orchard. We had a fine time and Ian, being a social creature, was well suited to his role as head of PR where it seemed to me that he spent all his time golfing and meeting clients. Always very well turned out (remember he was the MP on the motorbike who looked the job, always out to impress the ladies), he

had enjoyed a bucketful of girlfriends and his latest conquest was a Scottish girl called Beryl who had just qualified as an air hostess with American Airlines and was away on her first trip with them.

On the Saturday evening Viv and I were pubbing it with Ian and his friends and he told us how keen he was on Beryl. He said he had led a very colourful life but felt it was now time to settle down and get married, much to my surprise! He must be really smitten we thought. As we arrived back at his cottage later that night there was a message from Beryl asking Ian to phone her the following morning. It seemed that there must be something important to discuss as she was in the USA on duty for the airline so we sat and talked it over into the early hours, considering what the nature of the call may be whilst passing round a drop of one thing or another. Obviously you didn't have to be Einstein to arrive at the most likely conclusion and eventually we all ambled to bed to pass the time until our suspicions could be confirmed. The next morning, via a very poor line, Beryl confirmed what we had suspected and without any hesitation Ian said they would get married and he would make plans to get her back home quickly. Unfortunately she would have to leave her much wanted job after just starting it but that's life and as we talked it all over Ian asked me if I would be his Best Man at the wedding which would take place in Scotland.

Beryl and Ian eventually married, had their baby who they named Karen, and, in the course of time, Ian left his job at Metal Box, moved to Scotland and started his own business specialising in selected foods produced in the area. We had talked the business idea through together, both feeling that the timing was right and it was a good plan but realising that much capital and machinery would be required as well as locating suitable premises. Nothing daunted, Ian and Beryl made a steady start distributing tinned, bottled and packed products, later planning to do mail order. It was all looking very encouraging then, as so often happens in life, wham! Playing golf one day Ian felt a pain in his ankle which persisted and later moved to his back. It was a real mystery, very hard to diagnose initially and many tests were made until eventually a cancer was located. He was in Scotland in 1978 and there mustn't have been any facilities up there because he was referred to Christies in Manchester for treatment which he had to undergo every three months. He would drive down and stay with us whilst having his treatment, driving back to Scotland afterwards until the next session. Ian and I would spend a lot of time talking when he visited but as time passed I saw that he was growing weaker and weaker. It was very, very sad. One evening we were sat in front of the fire with Whiskers the Second, another black and white cat, curled up beside me on the rug. Viv had gone to bed and Ian was looking particularly jiggered as he announced: 'This will be my last trip John, the treatment hasn't worked so tomorrow it will be goodbye.' Those are tough words for a guy of about forty five to have to utter and I am not sure now how I replied. The next morning we shook hands and hugged each other and he was gone. On January 25th 1979, my forty fourth birthday, I helped carry Ian's coffin at his funeral. A colourful pal who I had known since childhood had played his last round.

(5) Whilst Tom enjoyed a steady life and his Chrysanthemums, he was also a good artist and had a great love of music, often attending the Halle Orchestra concerts in Manchester to which he would also take Vivienne. On one of their visits Tom came across Sir Malcolm Sergeant during the interval and passed a comment to him about the performance. Apparently the great man misunderstood and saying: 'follow me,' led a very confused Tom into the Gents toilets! Vivienne's mother, Edith, did not have good health having been badly affected by the birth of a still born baby boy many years earlier. Consequently she didn't go out to work after selling the shop but she excelled at being prudent with money and probably had the spending down to the last bob or two as she was always very much in control. Mr and Mrs Critchley didn't go out often although they did sometimes visit The Liberal Club or the Roxy Cinema whilst Tom would go to The Druid's pub for his Friday night pint. However they never failed to attend the flower show which was held every autumn in the conservatory at Werneth Park. It was here that Tom's horticultural skills would shine as, with great dedication, he would display his chrysanthemum blooms which were timed to perfection for the great day. As the couple didn't have a car and would never have considered taking a taxi, a long walk was required to the venue and on the day of the show, around 1968, Edith, unwell with bouts of indigestion, still insisted on walking home. During the course of the walk she had a heart attack which was swiftly followed by a second, fatal one. She was a really good person who did her best for her daughter and whose whole purpose in life seemed to be to steer Viv towards being 'married well', just like Mrs Bennett in *Pride and Prejudice*! If she could see us now I am sure she wouldn't be disappointed. Tom and Edith had married in 1928 and upon his wife's death Tom's life was greatly changed. Exploring the space that is created when you lose your life partner, he eventually settled for becoming a member of the bowling club at Werneth.

(6) At our wedding reception at the Midland Hotel we had Baked Alaska (baked ice cream!) a real first. Robin Eglin, a friend, was working in the kitchen at the hotel. Nice job Robin!

(7) Peter's family business, some may remember, was the well established 'Whitworth's' in Oldham Market Hall which sold ironmongery and household requisites. Peter eventually retired and the tradition of the family business came to an end as shopping styles changed.

You Make Your Bed - You Lie In It

Permanently is a huge milestone to carry

Running the small operation at Housing Units in Hollinwood of which I was now the apprehensive owner, was Derek Delhide. He had originally joined APAS straight from school but as he worked in the office I didn't know him too well as all my time was spent in the joinery workshop, out on sites and with the other apprentices. Derek was in his late twenties and so was of a similar age to me. He was very loyal and reliable and had been sent to the Hollinwood site to take over from Harold Berry who had initially opened it. Following the split of APAS Derek was to stay in Hollinwood and work with me together with a couple of other guys and, as I had no clear idea of exactly what had been going on down there, this was a good thing.

Upon my arrival little time was wasted in getting things sorted out; I asked many questions and took stock of what was what. The name of the business 'Housing Units' had been given to the site by its parent company APAS, and I'm not really sure why they called it that but we never considered changing it. In the showroom at the front of the yard there were a few miscellaneous products such as ironmongery, fire parts, some paint, a few tools, buckets, shovels, and several 'All Night' Firemaster Insert Grates. These things were a revolution in heating; they were fitted with a draught control and did exactly what they said – maintained warmth in the house throughout the night. The yard products consisted of: timber, sand, boards, ballast, cement, plaster, a few doors, plasterboard, and, in the barn, a glass cutting shop complete with sheets of glass held in racks. Regarding customers, we had convenient business with the local tradesmen for the yard sales but the showroom seemed to need some promotion. Traditionally the locals in Failsworth would come to us one day in every month to pay their gas bills and we would set up a table and chair in the showroom where the gas man from Oldham would sit and collect his money. I was told this was done to encourage people to call in and whilst it was a good idea it was not enough. So basically the business consisted of a nucleus of stock for the local jobbing builder, together with a small turn over from the showroom and a very useful timber cutting service.

After this initial assessment of my fledgling business I felt it was really unclear where the main emphasis of sales was in the showroom whilst the yard products were more defined and slowly turning over. My reflections about those early days are somewhat unclear now it has to be said, as everything happened so quickly, but I recall feeling that despite some minor problems there was some real potential here. The existing small showroom with its first floor space and its fine staircase, together with the cottages and forecourt on either side, had good frontal prospects and I was itching to get going and make this work. However before doing anything I took the time to evaluate how the place had been run by APAS, respecting Derek who had been virtually in sole charge. As I was very familiar with the building and timber sales side of things that is where I initially positioned myself whilst Derek saw to the book keeping and office work. Hours worked were 8.0 a.m. until 5.30 p.m. Monday to Saturday with a half day closing on Tuesday. Working alongside Derek was Ron Jackson, a good bench joiner who was in charge of the outside sales and the few deliveries we made; there was also a young lad called Frank Richardson who was his assistant and completing the team was the morning cleaner, the very jolly and very round Mrs Ball (I know!). There was one more inherited asset – a three ton Bedford Tipper waggon and as Saturday mornings were our busiest time we hired a part time waggon driver called Joe Brennan who worked for APAS during week days. Joe would make our local deliveries which were mainly in the Failsworth area and included Lord Lane where several large housing estates were springing up; in fact these burgeoning estates were to give Housing Units terrific business in the future. By now it was about 1959/60 and I would not be far out if I said the turnover was around £100 - £150 a week.

I began to slowly formulate my strategy for growth and after everyone had left for the evening I would get to work drawing up plans and carefully listing the ranges of merchandise I felt we should introduce to the business.

The one thing running constantly through my mind was developing a system of self service similar to that I had seen briefly whilst on my travels in the States. I believed that this was indeed the way forward and hoped that HU would be able to lead the way in DIY self selection. In fact I had noticed that some customers were already heading in that direction, for as they browsed or waited for their orders in the timber shop, they would eagerly rummage amongst the various off cuts of Formica that were lying around already chalk marked with a price. The conclusion was that my customers were already unwittingly serving themselves and, as I wanted to cash in on this trait, I removed the counter where they normally waited to be served and let them select their own merchandise. I worked all hours building new shelves to display our extra products; ideas could not be put into action quickly enough and, from being a convenience depot for local builders, the birth of self service was about to happen. Derek was very supportive and we got on well together; in fact later on he would say to me: 'it was the best thing that happened to me when you came here.' Derek was a bachelor; a Liberal councillor for Saddleworth he eventually became Chairman of the Council and a magistrate. He was ever so popular in the Saddleworth area, undoubtedly a people's man who always remained a loyal rock to me even though at times I must have been quite overwhelming as my enthusiasm was so great; however he took it all on the chin – mostly anyway!

I believed that the formula for success followed a clear route; we would:

- turn our selling area into self service
- introduce merchandise that was needed in the local area
- shop fit the showroom; build sheds, ramps and racks outside and enhance the whole premises.
- buy in bulk, increase our margins, then sell competitively and offer a prompt, responsive, service.
- eventually open six days a week, defying the council who said we had to close for half a day on Tuesdays. Thursday would be our late night and we would open all day on Saturday.
- not borrow cash but reinvest by increased trading.

If we stuck to this plan I felt sure we would not fail but good luck was on our side as well as we were fortunate to be there at the right time. Fate is a strange thing, never underestimate it – I didn't!

Whilst out and about in the truck during the week delivering our limited range of building materials, I noticed all the new drives outside the houses on the estates and the lack of garden walls. This was obviously another opportunity for us to expand as there was a huge market for flags for the drives and bricks for the walls. A company from Sale called Bettercrete were frequently delivering building supplies in the area and we had an account with them so I wasn't impressed that they were trading on our pitch. So we changed our supplier and opened an account with Marshall's of Halifax. Back at the yard we erected a ramp at waggon level to make loading flags easier as we could 'walk' them on and off the waggon. Next to the ramp we built a cement storage shed so we could buy in ten ton loads at a discount, however all loose material had to be loaded onto our waggon by hand and it was back breaking work. There were approximately six or seven shovelfuls of sand to the hundredweight so an order for two tons meant an awful lot of shovelling! Fortunately it wasn't too long before we spotted a Chaseside Tractor, complete with front bucket, for sale at a farm in Denshaw. We hurriedly bought it and drove it down to Hollinwood the same night with no number plates and it was put into action the very next morning. This piece of equipment provided a revolution for whoever had to do the loading.

Our account with Marshall's grew rapidly as we also took on Tudor stone and walling stone and from one waggon load of goods a week we were soon receiving three or four. Every time we spotted a new housing estate nearing completion we would do a leaflet drop advertising ourselves and thus increasing business. Initially I had sketched our products for the leaflets myself but I came across a really good fellow called Norman Bocking who was a draughtsman and artist so this task was transferred to him. In fact we now needed to produce brochures rather than leaflets, due to our ever increasing stock, and Norman's artwork truly helped pioneer our business as not many firms had sales literature at this time. He literally earned tons for me with his artwork; initially we ran off about five hundred copies but that soon grew to be about three thousand. We extended the timber range, stocked decorative board, and hardboard on pallets was delivered to us straight from the docks. Interwoven and Waney edged fencing panels filled the yard as did huge loads of rustic poles from Cumbria and we had a carrier with a bulk truck who would collect stone direct from the quarry. Inside the showroom was a shelf system of spur

6.

8.

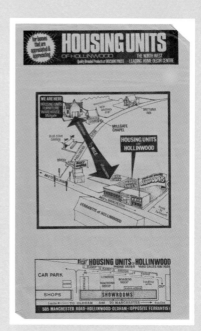

7.

9.

1. Brochure 1960 – hand written by myself
2. 1965 – enter Norman Bocking. Images 2-9 all his artwork.
3. Second effort
4. Simple Fireplace handout – handed out thousands and earned thousands
5. Blitz full page typed copy advert in the Oldham Chronicle and the Manchester Evening News – we changed the selection of goods on it continually
6. Some you win others you lose – the postage strike didn't help with this one
7. The converted Sunday School was rather tucked away so we put these fliers in the shopping bags and handed out thousands. Norman Bocking's artwork
8. We used these long ads on the right hand side of the outside edge of the newspapers – it worked again – Norman again
9. An identifiable image is important and here's how ours changed over the years – starting with 'Fred' right through to using a colour of green similar to that used by Harrods

uprights and brackets which allowed flexibility of levels and width; we stocked a full range of Leyland paints together with brushes etc; we had a wall full of shelves displaying tools and pre packed fittings which had just been launched; Hoover products were sold and we introduced a whole range of electrical appliances and LEC fridges. Every week we introduced new lines and the Wholesalers were flocking in as our buying was now getting serious. Ron, who had been running the yard, moved to Blackpool so I asked David Johnson (1), an ex joiner colleague from APAS, to join us. We chatted and when I had talked him into it he saw his new job in sales as a challenge although he would have to leave the 'tools'. In fact David provided the kick start we needed and indeed it was with his help that Housing Units grew and progressed.

The area sales manager for Hoover was Joe Gerraghty, the father of Jimmy (2) who was a good pal from the old days on 'the block' and one of my groomsmen when I got married. Joe was urging us to stock the full range of Hoover products rather than just a few spares and in fact the Hoover brand was very good and very popular; do you recall when they brought out the twin tub washer? It washed in one side and spun in the other. That model was followed by the Keymatic single tub washer which further revolutionised washing day. Previous to both these Hoover models Hotpoint had produced a washer with a rotating centre paddle and an electric mangle; I remember that my own Mother bought one and it was a far cry from the boiler, posser, tub and huge antiquated mangle of my childhood. Things had certainly moved on and we did extremely well with the revolutionary washing products by Hoover and there was also a good market for reconditioned models. It was around this time that a guy called Flatley invented a drying cabinet, a thing so incredibly simple you may have thought it was a joke. It consisted of a square metal box which stood about thirty three inches high. In the base of the box there was an electric heating element and when you lifted the metal wrapped top lid there were five or six rails on which to hang your wet washing. These driers may have been a little expensive at £5 19/6d but after they were advertised on TV they sold very well indeed and the public flocked in for them. Prior to this invention if it wasn't fit to dry damp clothes outside they had to be hung on a clothes maiden or on the ever so popular rack which was fastened to the kitchen ceiling and lowered using a rope and pulley system (we sold those too!). Houses were not usually centrally heated in those days and so it

1.

2.

3.

1. Young and entuhusiastic March 1964. Left to right: Me, David Johnson, Derek Delhide. All of us under the age of 30 when nothing was impossible – well we thought so

2. The saddest news – summer 2006 – David and his wife Sheila were killed in a road accident. David's input into Housing Units was critical in the 1960s and 70s when he left to start his own building and joinery business.

3. The Bridge at Mumps, Oldham had a permanent Housing Units advert displayed on it for many years courtesy of artist Bill Porter before it was demolished in 2011. It was a landmark

was a real chore to get the washing dry. It is no wonder that Flatley created an immediate market with his wonderful box drier and his invention certainly helped my turnover!

Sales were growing and we were doing well. One minute we would be outside serving sand and cement, timber or fencing, and then we would dash back inside to sell paint, washing machines, a Flatley or some hardware. We were seriously multi tasking so we looked at getting more help. Joe, our Saturday driver, left APAS to come and work full time for us as our deliveries were growing and growing with all the new estates springing up. He was tall and thin, strong as an ox and lugging flags around seemed to present no problem for him even though each 3'x2' flags weighed one and a half hundredweight! I am still much beholden to Joe who, at the critical growth time of the company, was an absolute key player. When he was on holiday I would take over the deliveries and if 'Mr Smith' wanted thirty flags at the rear of his house then each flag would have to be 'walked' around the building if we couldn't get the truck round the back. If we delivered walling stones they had to be handballed and stocked at each house. Boy was I glad when Joe returned! Order a ton of sand nowadays and it will arrive in a wonderful white canvas bag which is lifted off the waggon by mechanical means but you can't have your goods delivered to the rear of the property if there is no vehicular access. At the end of his busy day Joe would always finish up at the Woodman Inn across the road from the shop where he would enjoy two or three pints although by that time in the evening he could be rather 'high' having perspired throughout the day with his backbreaking work!

The whole business was thriving and each week the turnover increased, as did the product range. Initially Derek and I worked in a tiny office measuring approximately nine foot by five; there was no room to sit down so we had a stand up bench and it was like working in a box. We knew it was going to be hard going for the first few years as it is in any business so we pegged our wages equally, initially at around £20 per week. Vivienne's wage as a teacher really helped until she had to give up work when Tim was born. Each week thereafter I gave Viv £8 which she allocated with care between the necessities: £2 greengrocery, £3 groceries, £1 cleaning, £1 fuel etc. She has always been good with money and has always paid the household bills; she really takes after her mother in this respect. At Christmas

Derek and I would try to salvage an extra pay packet for ourselves and the staff and we always bought Capons for the workforce and had a night out.

By now we had many trade accounts which meant we were giving extended credit but to ensure that accounts were paid promptly we offered a 5% discount if they were paid within seven days of issue. Even so getting money in was not easy. Fortunately we had the retail trade to fall back on as this was cash over the counter. Cash flow was critical as we were pressing our suppliers to give us a similar seven day settlement discount, something I have always been keen on but obviously it meant we had to have the ready cash to pay. Exasperated I would take my trade customer's outstanding invoices home before posting them out and I would place them on the floor of the lounge in piles headed 'one month overdue', 'two months overdue' etc. I would then write on each statement out of frustration: 'a fat lot of good that did!' Things ticked along but eventually one wise guy got us. He had conducted his account reasonably well so far although he was still a relatively new customer. One day he asked if we could supply asbestos roofing sheets for an engineering works on Lees Road. I gave him a good quote at a cost of approximately £1500 and the delivery was arranged to go to site direct from the factory. The roof went on but we didn't get paid. Experience had taught me that pleading for payment was a waste of time so I would camp outside debtor's houses blocking their driveways and when they realised I wasn't going away they would usually give in and pay. However this technique did not always work such as the time when a builder, who sidelined as a bookie in Hollinwood, opened an account with us. He was something of a maverick character having served some time 'away from home' shall we say. His business activities were very questionable and he was a poor payer. He partnered up with a friend of mine for one of his projects, a pub conversion in the Greenfield area, and, whilst I was very disappointed about my pal getting involved with this guy, I agreed to supply the necessary materials. Needless to say I didn't get paid. After working about fifteen hours at the shop you do not want to be charging round at night for your money but I tried and he continually brushed me off: 'tomorrow I will give you a cheque, OK?' But tomorrow never came. Amongst this character's many other 'interests' he owned a night club in Manchester and as a last stand I went there late one evening and made a fuss even though a couple of heavies were lurking around. I didn't care, I was really worked up. Eventually I found the debtor inside, surrounded by flashing lights, a smart bar and several lovely babes but my act was not convincing enough, he ignored me and I finally realised there is a time to quit. As I left the club I saw his huge American limousine parked outside, a top of the range Buick or similar, and, as the opportunity was too good to miss, I let the tyres down. I never did get my money.

By August 1965 we had around two hundred outstanding accounts which added up to a total value of £4464 2s 6d. There was about £2297 one month overdue whilst £1485 was well over a month late. It seemed to me that we were opening too many small accounts and I had a cash flow problem. It has always been my practice not to borrow money and therefore as time passed with no payment there was only one solution. Despite having wiped off more than we could afford we decided to wind up the trade accounts keeping only the regular payers. We had good cash flow on the retail side and that was where our future lay; no more parking in drives or pleading for our dues.

With all our developments there came the time when Derek and I had too much to do; we couldn't be everywhere at once, office work was increasing as more and more accounts were opened with suppliers and we looked for a book keeper. Enter Mr Alf Prebble who we were very glad to have join us. The site was filling up quickly, we needed more room and yet more staff. Next to our main building were the five cottages that we let out on small weekly rents of 12s 6d. Gradually they started to become vacant and when the cottage right next to the shop became empty we quickly banged an opening through, cleaned it up, gave it a lick of paint and moved stock in. It was around this time that Joan Pearton, a good friend of ours, came to work part time on the admin side and she would often bring her baby daughter to work with her. Zoë would spend her morning in a lovely large wheeled Silver Cross pram which one day happened to be parked in the area that had formerly been the front room of the cottage. Our cleaner, Mrs Ball, the very nice rounded lady, was busy cleaning in the room above when she somehow fell through the floor, scattering the really old lime washed ceiling of the downstairs room all over Zoë's pram! Attracted by the noise several of us arrived on the scene simultaneously to be confronted by Mrs Ball's short legs, contained in very large bloomers, wedged between the floor joists of the room above and dangling right over the pram. Unbelievably baby Zoë, covered in years of debris and dust, slept through the whole incident! The very last cottage to become vacant was the one in the middle, the tripe shop belonging to the Heginbottom family. Now I had never been able to eat tripe and we could often smell it when the fine art of triping was afoot but folks in Hollinwood seemed to like it. The smell would remind me of when I was young and my mother used to cook tripe and onions; I would never eat it even when it was served up to me again for my next meal. Dad loved to eat it raw with lashings of vinegar, salt and pepper which obviously disguised the awful taste! Mrs Heginbottom decided to transfer her shop to a stall in Oldham Market where she remained for many years and incidentally we later bought the tripe works on Wickentree Lane but that's another story.

Now that all the cottages were empty we obtained the necessary planning permission and demolished them. In their place we erected a high wood sectioned building measuring 80' x 35' and quoted by H. Peel Ltd., Sowerby Bridge at a cost of £2668 and 3 shillings! The date was 24th October 1964. When the new store was finally fitted out with all the necessary shop fittings the total cost was £7500 which was an awful lot of money but we managed it. Everything was worked out carefully; what we would sell, where it would go, and as soon as the paint was dry we worked late, long and weekends to get all the stuff in there. Whatever we were to do in the future this first 'grand design' more than gave us a huge push forward in our history. We were now in a situation to really set out our stall. The whole back wall of the showroom had a range of adjustable shelves under an illuminated canopy; island modules held different ranges of merchandise and there were no counters, just tills and wrapping points. In the entrance we laid a wonderful floor in Amtico which was the best flooring available and great attention was given to the lighting throughout the store. By now we were approaching 1965 and no one had done anything like this at the time. It wasn't just the shop that was expanding either; in the yard our builders merchandise range had really extended as had the outbuildings to contain it. Again we ensured that the stock was laid out in such a way as to encourage customers to explore, whilst outside our premises there was a splendid forecourt where we would display merchandise, really going to town with it on Saturday's. I would arrive around 6 a.m. to start putting things outside and it would be almost 8 a.m. when I had finished but boy what a frontage we had. It was such a good position, right on the main road into Manchester, and everyone that went past on a bus or in a car couldn't miss us. I was reminded recently of a Saturday boy who used to help with the sweeping and setting out of the frontage. His name was John Twigg and there was a piece in the local paper all about him. John is now the Group Planning Director at Manchester Airport and he is married to Margaret who he met whilst working with me; she worked in the dress shop next door to HU. Hollinwood never struck me as the most romantic place on the planet but there you go – they have been married thirty five years!

During the early 60's a guy called Barry Bucknell was hosting one of the first ever DIY programmes on TV, the public enthused and were up for all sorts of DIY projects they would never have tackled before. Barry did a show one night where he knocked a serving hatch into the wall between the dining room and kitchen of a house. The following weekend we had a high demand for lintels, sand, cement, bricks and plaster; whatever he did we watched and would be ready at weekend for the rush to copy his designs and projects. The UK had really taken to DIY and we had everything that was needed; the time was just right for us. The one activity that we did not carry on with was the glass shop; David Johnson and I ran weekly checks and found out we were smashing more glass than we were selling. Each of us would have a go but none of us emerged as a real glass cutter so we 'cut' our losses. I am proud to say this was the only line we ever rejected.

One of my initial aims remained unresolved and was niggling away at me. This was the fact that we were supposed to shut the retail shop for half a day on Tuesday's although we were still allowed to deal with trade supplies. Deciding to ignore the rules imposed by the council we opened the shop, but an assortment of council clerks were despatched from the town hall to tell us we must shut, and impressive legal notices were issued although we just binned them. We were polite but did not weaken. In fact I believe we actually got a summons but we bombarded the Oldham Chronicle and the council with letters indicating their short sightedness, lack of income for the town etc. I was a little concerned for Derek's position in all this, he was a local councillor after all, so I made this battle with the council my own personal one. Eventually I won my case about Tuesday opening and that bylaw was soon relaxed allowing other traders to follow our lead. Later on we would introduce our late night opening until 8 p.m. on Thursday's a practice which continues to this day and was also adopted by other traders.

Sunday trading is a different matter however. Personally I disagree with opening businesses on Sunday's and I believe twenty four hour trading is absolutely wrong. It seems to be hugely wasteful in view of the energy problems this planet faces and it is also economically questionable. Trading seven days a week, non stop, requires transport and infrastructure to back it all up; it's not just a matter of opening the door and switching the lights on. Twenty four hour trading creates seven days and nights of non stop energy and activity that involves extra staff, increased waste and cost. I have no objection to late night trading, that is good, but come on; if you cannot shop between 8 a.m. and 10 p.m. which is around eighty hours a week, there is something wrong. The French seem to have it right; on Sunday's the whole family eat together round the table which is a really important philosophy and habit in my opinion, one that is now sadly relinquished by most people as they have their meal on their knee whilst watching TV. Nevertheless in the late 1990's I had to bow down to consumer demand and start to open for business on Sunday's but I made sure to support my staff by making a point of being there with them although it was against my better judgement.

You Make Your Bed – You Lie In It: Notes

(1) David Johnson and I spent several years throughout the sixties working together at Housing Units but eventually he decided it was time to open his own business, a fine joiners shop. He was in partnership with his brother, Michael who had also worked at Housing Units and working alongside them was Sheila, David's wife, and Wendy their cheerful daughter. The company undertook refits for the National Westminster Bank and were also main contractors for Warburton's Bread factories. Work on several National Heritage schemes was also undertaken. David's was a successful, tough, professional and very well run operation with a quality client portfolio. Maybe he should have gone it alone earlier than he did but meanwhile I hope he learnt something whilst working with me that helped him on his way as he helped me. David eventually sold his business and the newly retired couple commenced on a full time life together. Nevertheless, as often seems to happen when things are going well, disaster struck.

In 2006, inspired by John McCombs painting classes, I arranged to go on a painting trip on my yacht with Dave Edwards, an artist friend I have exhibited with twice. As usual we were painting from dawn to dusk and on this particular trip we were moored high up the Carrick Roads in Cornwall, when I got a call from Vivienne who had bad news. I will always remember how the evening was settling, the colours and the atmosphere were idyllic as the sun lowered reflecting it's light in the waters of the creek we were moored in …when …………'wham'. Viv told me that David and Sheila Johnson had both been killed in a motoring accident. David was a good and experienced driver but as he and Sheila set off for their caravan which was kept just outside York, they were involved in a head on collision and David was killed instantly. I understand that Sheila died a short time afterwards whilst still on the roadside. Teachers and children from one of our local schools, SS Aidan and Oswald, were passing by as the accident happened and they said how the scene was: 'absolutely horrendous and nothing could prepare you for such a thing.' I was stunned as I asked Viv: 'when is the funeral, I must get back?' Viv tried to reassure me: 'I will be there with Tim and Louanne, there is nothing you can do John.' I talked it over with Dave Edwards and we considered leaving the boat in Falmouth under his care whilst I made the trip back north. However, following further conversations with Viv over the next twenty four hours I decided to stay on board. Of course Viv reported straight back to me when she returned from the funeral. Apparently the service was very brief as everyone was still absolutely stunned; there had been no reference to David and Sheila's wonderful life together although it would have been hard to find a more devoted couple. Viv said the whole thing was over in under half an hour which really shocked me; I had spent thousands of hours in David Johnson's company over the years and it was all over in half an hour. Memories came flooding back. In the 1980's I had organised a reunion of our era of APAS employees and David's speech full of memories, together with his wit and endless jokes was the highlight of the evening. David and Sheila had always played a straight, fair and kind hand so why should their lives end like that? I found it very hard to accept and the sadness I felt for his children, Wendy and Tony, cannot be explained in words. Driving round a bend in the road the respective lives of this outgoing couple were snuffed out.

As David Edwards and I returned from Carrick Roads we moored the yacht in Falmouth and I called into the church at the bottom of The Moor next to Jacob's Ladder which is an endless climb of stone steps to the top of the hill. In the church entrance there was a solo art exhibition consisting of pictures in abundance; definitely quantity rather than quality. Sitting there quietly in the Chapel I again reflected on the times David Johnson and I had spent together and his invaluable contribution in helping us get Housing Units going during those hard ground breaking years. Even further back were the fun times we had working together as apprentices fitting roofs. One of our stunts, whilst working on the Merton Avenue site in Hollins, was to sprint off a plank at roof wall plate level attempting to reach the sand pit. If you failed to get enough speed you would not make it and on one occasion David didn't and badly damaged his ankle. When Joe Hales the site foreman got stuck into us it was me who was held responsible and when my old man heard about it he was not at all pleased. My thoughts then turned to Sheila, David's wife, who had beaten breast cancer. They had loved each other dearly and had a marriage without flaws. David was so jolly; whenever I met him there would be ten minutes of jokes before we got down to discussing anything. When you hear of something tragic happening as suddenly as this, particularly after all the hard work the pair of them had put into things, it truly makes the other issues we moan and go on about so bloody unimportant.

(2) Jimmy was one of my groomsmen when I got married. He ran a decorating business with Trevor Styles – wheels mad the pair of them – they each owned a Morgan three wheeler which was propelled by a twin 'V' cylinder Japanese engine exposed on the front of the bonnet (that is how Morgan cars started). Very tragically he had a fatal accident in his works van whilst still very young. It was very sad. He was always buzzing with life and energy. He left a wife, Jean, and a son, John.

There's A Real Market Out There

If at first you don't succeed, try, try again. Then quit. No use being a damn fool
about it
W. C. Fields

In the 1970's there was a programme on TV hosted by a lovely chap called Arthur Negus and it was drawing a lot of attention. The programme was *The Antiques Road Show* and the public eagerly tuned into the programme each week with the result that old furniture and hidden treasures were much sought after. Unfortunately there was little chance the ordinary man in the street could afford to enter into this market but to assist with the stumbling block some firms were producing copies of old fashioned styles in mahogany and oak; it was reproduction furniture at a fraction of the price of the antique originals and we could see huge potential here. We put together a collection of wheel back chairs, dressers, tables and the really popular Marina cottage suite of which we were to sell hundreds. We had cracked the DIY self service and now it was time to pull this off. There was no doubt in my mind that reproduction furniture was one of the most important cards in our hand; the public had not seen it put over like this before and suddenly they could take everything away at a reasonable price and have their own 'Antique Roadshow'.

Whilst our furniture was going well, other things were also happening. The door market had been extremely dull, offering very basic designs, but now ambitious buyers were travelling to the Far East to search for products. Solid wood doors began to arrive from the Philippines and they were given attractive names such as: 'Kentucky', 'Madrid', 'Seville', and 'Elizabethan'. These lovely hardwood doors with carved or routed features were made even more attractive when we adorned them with brass or black, antique door furniture; perspex bull's-eye bullion window panes, and Georgian panel conversions; all for sale at our store naturally. At about the same time a craze for louvre doors took off and we stocked those as well. We were seriously going into top gear with a continual stream of new and innovative products, making sure we had plenty of stock and getting things delivered on time. It was all hands to the pump and most of the staff could turn their hands to anything although there was one occasion when it may have been better if they hadn't. There was a young lad called David Harlow who usually worked in the machine department but could always be called on to serve customers if we were stretched. One Saturday he was called to help in the shop but unfortunately as he was not over familiar with one of our cranky tills, he was having great trouble closing the drawer. Finally he gave it a very hard push which resulted in the heavy till sliding off the counter, smashing straight through a large plate glass window and landing on the pavement outside! David was definitely one of our most enthusiastic members of staff I think it is safe to say.

Meanwhile we had noticed a firm in Manchester who were doing well with natural stone fireplace kits so we decided to follow. We already had a growing account with Marshall's of Halifax who were able to supply a reconstructed, man made product called Tudor Stone. These blocks were ideal for building fireplaces; they came in four sizes and four subtle colours: natural, buff, grey and pink; we even arranged for Marshall's to make some 'pitch faced' stone as an alternative to the usual flat surface thus giving a dimensional feel. Easy to use and a third of the price of natural stone, Tudor blocks were the perfect solution. To complement the stone fireplaces we were able to provide slate for the hearth courtesy of a local lad called Eric who regularly visited the slate mines at Ffestiniog in Wales. He would fill up his small truck with the stuff, put it into bags containing enough slate to cover one square yard and then sell it to us for our customers. The remaining piece of the fireplace jigsaw was the mantle shelf but we soon managed to arrange for supplies of kiln dried teak and mahogany from a local timber importer. Having resourced all the necessary materials we drew up some designs and produced leaflets showing how to build a fireplace; we then erected a few demonstration models in the shop and waited for the customers to buy. As luck would have it Barry Bucknell once again inadvertently helped us by building a natural stone fireplace on

TV and our 'kits' literally flew out of the store. Once again we were there and ready at just the right time and it was fantastic.

Another craze in home décor was soon to follow. People were just starting to eat out, often in mock Tudor beamed pubs complete with roaring log fires and surrounded by brass and copper ware including chimney canopies; they loved it. So much so that we introduced a range of seven copper canopies and copper sheet hearths to our stock but the real problem to crack was the demand for Tudor styled beams. If a serious DIYer wanted to put beams into his home he faced great difficulty as firstly he would have to find them in a demolition yard and secondly they would inevitably be the wrong size and so he would have to bash his walls about to accommodate them. Even for a professional builder this would be very hard and heavy work, so I pondered the problem of how to provide what our customers wanted in an easy to use way. Luckily, whilst on my travels, I heard of Oakleaf Productions over towards Bradford. This outfit was run by Mr Bannister, an industrial chemist, who had found a way of making an injected urethane product which was identical in looks to wood. This was the breakthrough we needed. The imitation wood was not cheap but had the advantages of being easy to handle as it was very lightweight, and it could be cut to suit any size of room. At my meeting with Mr Bannister I mentioned that we hoped to sell his products, reproduction beams and planks in particular, to the public and that we would provide a simple instruction sheet for DIY installation purposes. Now he was a very astute, rather serious man who normally dealt with architects, authorities, and trade customers and I recall that he thought I was a little 'cuckoo' with my strange ideas. Never mind. Back in the showroom in Hollinwood we built a fireplace set complete with log alcove and seat. A copper canopy and a varnished slate hearth gave a lovely finish whilst above and around it we put Oakleaf beams, planking and a plate rack. To complete the installation we hung Edgar wooden light fittings from the ceiling and walls, set a gas fire in the fireplace opening and placed a burgundy rug on the floor in front of the hearth with a dummy cat curled up on it. Mr Bannister could not believe what we had achieved with his product and to be quite honest neither could we. The customers loved the display and were eager to copy it so we subsequently sold loads of Oakleaf beams.

The Ideal Home Show was held annually at Earls Court, London but it wasn't long before Manchester also had its own version, first at Belle Vue, then the City Hall on Deansgate and later at Platt Fields. Presenting innovative DIY ideas the 'Tudor Look' Housing Units stand was adorned with reproduction fittings and furniture and every year it proved to be the biggest puller in the place. Opening the shows over the years we had Princess Alexandra, Chay Blythe and Elsie Tanner and they were all genuinely impressed with our display and spent much time with us. Although it was really hard graft getting everything there and setting it all up in great detail at least with the new Manchester locale we didn't have to travel far but it was awkward sometimes as we rushed to get everything ready for the opening day only to be hampered by various tradesmen on site. Trade unions were strong and dominant at that time and we had to be very careful not to encroach on the territory of the professionals working at the venue by doing things ourselves. The electricians in particular were a real touchy lot of b*****s; if we dared to even lay a finger on a light bulb they would down tools and leave the stand! Even so we really benefited from the Manchester exhibitions which were well attended and we handed out lots of promotional material showing the products we had for sale, together with the prices. The result of this was that we attracted many new customers who eagerly made their way to Hollinwood, a place which was not the most well known venue on the planet!

So the pressure was on and obviously a lot of time had to be spent on buying stock to meet our customer's expectations. Derek and I worked well together and whilst he spent more time on the books I did more on the buying side of the business; however we would both attend the Furniture Exhibitions at Earls Court, Olympia and the many London West End hotels which held private viewings. These buying trips were demanding and we would often start the day at Earls Court at 9 a.m., move on to Olympia and finally on to the West End venues. We would eat on the hoof and it was often midnight by the time we finished and returned to our digs only to repeat the whole thing again the next day. Occasionally if I felt drowsy in the mid afternoon I would look for somewhere to have a cat nap for ten or fifteen minutes. In many of the West End hotels they had voluminous drapes hung at the windows which provided the perfect place – I would duck behind them and wedged upright against the window frame I would nod off. Derek never understood how I could do it but in fifteen minutes I would be back and ready for action, fully charged up.

Initially on our trips to London we watched the cash and stayed in basic accommodation but as times improved we found an excellent place to stay in the form of Dolphin Square in the Pimlico area. Built between 1935 and 1936 and claiming to be the largest self contained block of flats in Europe there was a good choice of accommodation on offer; anything from a single serviced flat to a multi bedroom suite; for just a few days, a year, or as a permanent home. Impeccably and attractively built near the river looking across to Battersea, the place was, and is, one of London's gems for it is still in use today and houses a swimming pool, a Squash and Fitness Club, an on site Bar and Restaurant, and several shops all surrounded by private gardens. If we were back at Dolphin Square early enough Derek and I would visit the local Pimlico restaurants and one of our favourites was the Italian where the actor Wilfred Bramble of *Steptoe and Son* fame sat in a corner on his own most nights. Best of all, however, was 'Grumbles'. We became what you would call regular customers there, so much so that I still receive a birthday card from them every year. The restaurant is still there so if you are ever in London pop in to 'Grumbles' with its scrub top tables and candles; dress casually or in city togs and you never know who you may be sitting next to. One night we were next to the American ambassador and we saw many well known faces such as Ayrton Senna during our times there.

Wherever we had spent our evening we would be back on our scouting mission by 9 a.m. the next morning, travelling to Earls Court or wherever the furniture event was being held that day. My tactics never altered over forty years of attending exhibitions. Be it a three or four day stint I would walk around for the first couple of days, carefully noting any likely purchases, and I would always try to stay behind after closing time so that I could view quietly, uninterrupted by agents and reps. I found this to be very valuable for covering real ground and whilst skulking around I would often bump into Richard Barker of Barker and Stonehouse, classic furnishers with stores in the North East of England. The night before the last day of the show I would make a final selection of the products I intended to purchase, list them, make out my travel plan and, if I was still happy with my selections on the second viewing, I would place the order there and then. As Derek and I made our way around the various venues we got to know many people and there were certainly some memorable ones. One of these 'characters' was the amusing Manny Cousins. As well as owning

Waring and Gillow Manny was also chairman of Leeds Football Club in the years when Don Revie managed a great team which included Jack Charlton. The 'Manny Cousins Circus', as he and his retinue were known, caused all the exhibiting companies to go on red alert when they visited, so great was their buying power. Sheltered by Ben Pomerance and another sidekick, Manny, who was a slightly built man, would come striding down the aisles quickly followed by other guys high up in his pecking order of associates. Trailing behind, as befitted their more lowly status, were the store managers, maybe twelve to fifteen of them. The massed group would completely block up the walkway and all the agents and owners of the furniture stands would eagerly await their interest. On one occasion I turned to Derek and said: 'just watch this, here comes the Pied Piper of furniture,' for Manny seemed to be exactly that, so great was his following. As they swooped through the show, the entourage would walk straight past most of the stands whilst the store managers following behind would try to view what they could without breaking rank. Suddenly Manny stops. His two henchmen know the form and are well to either side of him so they are OK but all those behind the advance party bumble into each other as they also hurriedly stop in their tracks. Then they all do an about turn as the 'boss' wants to inspect something he has just passed; the mild chaos he creates is great fun to watch, so much so that I sometimes think he did it on purpose.

Those were great days and a good pal of mine in the trade, Fred Poole, worked with many of the great companies at that time such as Austin and G Plan; he called Manny and his retinue 'Manny's Mafia' because they would breeze into the manufacturing showrooms wearing camel coloured coats and smoking cigarettes or cigars,' looking, I suppose like gangland criminals. Indeed those early days were colourful times: drinking, smoking, entertaining; furniture retail was very much a male dominated business. Fred was the person who introduced me to Cintique chairs, Hammonds Bedrooms and Karel Mintjens Belgian, solid wood, modern furniture, all of which sold extremely well. Some years later I met up with Fred early one morning at Manchester airport as we were going to visit Karel Mintjens HQ which was just outside Brussels. Fred was chatting away as we stood in the queue for check in when I homed in on the words, 'passport John'. Red faced and stupid I realised that I did indeed need my passport for a day trip and of course I had forgotten it. I called home only to find that Viv had gone out but fortunately lovely Susan, who helps Viv in the house, answered the phone: 'Susan, do you think you can help by hopping into your car and bringing my passport to the airport?' I begged. It was by now rush hour and we really were on the edge of time as she eventually arrived and handed my passport over. In fact our plane had lost its slot by the time we boarded and if looks could kill Fred and I would both be dead. Surprisingly the plane was only about fifteen minutes late when it eventually left but Fred had lost some weight I can tell you! Eventually we arrived at Mintjens which is a family firm and the quality of their furniture is excellent so we had a good buying session. The family own much of the land around the factory and had a herd of pedigree cattle that provided them with beef for their restaurant and Fred and I were invited to lunch to sample it. Eventually we tore ourselves away but by now it was the evening rush hour and due to heavy traffic we missed our plane, the gate had just closed as we got there. Unbelievable, we had only just made it on the outbound journey but we had missed the flight home altogether. Fortunately there was a later flight but we had to pay a premium price for a seat on it and didn't get back to Manchester until about midnight. I'm not sure why but Fred was always reluctant to take me anywhere after that trip!

February 1976 saw the opening of a Spring Fair in the brand new National Exhibition Centre (NEC) in the centre of England. Built by Birmingham council the original complex consisted of five large show halls and the exhibition has been held there every year since although it has to be said that things have undoubtedly got better and much bigger. The first event, which was opened by the Queen, was like a dress rehearsal where things often go wrong. As you arrived you were directed to huge car parks which surrounded the exhibition halls and the idea was to park your car then board a bus to take you to the main venues. The car parks were named and numbered something like South 1-2-3-4, North 1-2-3-4, West and East etc. and if you remembered which car park you had left your car in things were fine; if not you had a big problem which was made much worse on one occasion when it had been snowing and everything was a white out. Total chaos! Some people would leave their headlights on in mistake and often found the car battery flat on their return ensuring that the AA and RAC were kept busy. In fact one of the locals, an entrepreneurial chap, was making really good money by offering to jump start your car for

£5! As well as the creation of the NEC something of equally innovative importance in retailing had taken place in France and I just had to see it. Housing Units were members of NIH (National Institute of Hardware) who worked in coordination with National Cash, suppliers of cash tills and systems. National Cash arranged a trip for its members to visit the new Carrefour Hypermarket at Melun, which is not far from Fontainbleu, in France, and so I booked a place. It would turn out to be a long day as we set off in a coach from London to a remote airfield around the Margate, Herne Bay area. From there a plane was to take us to Le Bourget airport just outside Paris and I gathered from the state of the plane and the basic airstrip where we boarded that this was very much a budget trip. Upon arrival in France we were coached to the Hypermarket where we would have three hours to carry out our own investigative tour. Similar to the NEC there were numerous car parks and so we were reminded of the exact place where the coach would wait for us, and that it would leave at 3.30 p.m. prompt.

The Carrefour store was a mind blowing operation in those days and I became quite involved as I looked around. I thought it was fantastic although what really sank in was the fact that this was not the way I wanted Housing Units to go – 'stack it high sell it cheap' was their game but this wasn't quite what I had in mind. Back in England Tesco and Asda would be the forerunners of this type of selling and whilst it proved to me that people wanted to look and choose for themselves I felt that Carrefour's methods lacked real connection with their customers. What they had created was not a quality experience and was certainly not the vision for the future of our business. My visit concluded and, mindful of the departure time, I decided to head for the coach about 3 .10 p.m. Unfortunately I couldn't find the correct exit until eventually, at around 3.45 p.m., I arrived where I thought the coach should have been. It had gone. I got talking to a kindly French man who volunteered to drive me to the airport. Too simple. Although we had arrived at Le Bourget they had no information about a return flight to Britain and the plane wasn't there. I began to consider the idea that we must be using another airport for the return flight but I had no idea which one although obviously it had to be around Paris. Following a frantic conversation with another French man I was whizzed off at high speed in his car to Charles de Gaulle airport; twenty five minutes of nail biting driving but the plane had to be there. Together with my second

Good Samaritan we enquired about a flight booked under the name of National Cash UK but again they knew nothing. Now time was really running out; my passport was on the long departed coach, I had very little money and it was rush hour in Paris. My French friend conferred with a group of guys until, amidst a lot of arm waving and shouting, a decision was made: 'Ve 'av a man on motor bike 'oo will take you to Orly.' I was really amazed and appreciative of all their efforts; none of these men had been going my way in the first place but all were willing to help a distressed Briton. Well, the last car trip had been an experience but nothing had prepared me for the guy with the motorbike who seemed to see the rush hour as the ultimate challenge. With his headlights blazing we tore through struggling lines of automobiles, onto the kerb, off again, crossed lanes to beat the traffic lights; he didn't give a damn about anyone, it was like the Italian Job but on a bike! I was speechless when I got off at Orly whilst my driver was pouring with sweat but I gave him a French hug, he laughed and was gone. I entered the airport and enquired about the plane but once again there was no trace of it.

By now I had had enough; I was running out of airports and I was semi traumatised by the hair raising motorcycle ride. I made my way to the ticket desk in desperation. As I said previously my passport was on the coach, I had only limited cash and there was no such thing as a credit card then. However the ticket people were very helpful and after signing a couple of IOU papers and giving some convincing talk I found myself on an Air France flight within the hour, travelling in relative luxury with the extra comfort of a hot meal. In London I caught the airport coach to Victoria Bus Station which had been our original departure venue and, despite all my troubles, I was there a good half hour before the rest of the party and was feeling fresh and well fed. The guy in charge of my bedraggled companions nearly dropped through the floor when he saw me but quickly handed over my briefcase and passport. An interesting day.

A Learning Curve

Delay is preferable to error – Thomas Jefferson

So, things at Housing Units on Manchester Road, Hollinwood, had been moving along at quite a pace in the late 1960's and into the early 70's. We had been testing out the selling of lines which were not generally available to the public and we aimed to provide an even greater service by reaching those people who could not visit us easily for whatever reason. This was when the idea of a DIY mail order business came to me. Preferring to keep the trial operation separate from the shop to avoid any confusion, we purchased a small warehouse premises in Union Street, Chadderton, which had been formally occupied by Henry Hurdus Soft Drink Suppliers. We worked hard to clean it up and get it operational for our two members of staff who would be working there. Firstly there was the attractive Doreen Boyle who really helped us to get the enterprise underway, and secondly Little George, an older gent who was the caretaker at our Hollinwood site and who always had a pipe in his mouth reminiscent of Popeye. For some reason George would sometimes stay at the Union Street premises overnight and Doreen recalls that following such a night he would be boiling eggs in the kettle for his breakfast as she arrived and would then use the same water to make her a brew! He also had the disturbing habit of placing his discarded false teeth on the shelf in the office and they would be smiling at Doreen as she walked in. Nevertheless they worked well together and soon had everything ready. Our old friend Norman Bocking produced a brochure for us, we advertised in the *DIY Monthly* and *Mart Exchange* and by Christmas 1970 we were receiving orders and things were going well. As usual when things go well disaster struck; within a couple of weeks of our opening a mail order business the Postal Service commenced a strike which lasted for seven weeks and everything came to a standstill. It was January 1971 and in those days there were no courier services to use as an alternative so we had no option but to shut our whole operation down. I still believe DIY mail order could have worked but the strike dealt us a killer blow. Was it fate? We'll never know for sure but it was a real setback and we never tried again. We used the redundant premises on Union Street for much needed furniture storage as we continued to drive sales back at Housing Units. The shop was running well and we had more staff so my next venture was to explore the potential of a separate business under the title of 'Industrial Units' in an attempt to increase the 'heavy side' or trade sales. The name 'Industrial Units' sat well alongside HU I felt and so we purchased a brand new Morris Minor van, got it lettered with the new company name and a description of what we were selling: 'Allied Building and Timber Materials - Storage Systems, Special Paints.' I got myself togged up in a smart suit and clutching a briefcase called on all the mills and engineering businesses in the area trying to sell my wares. Enthusiasm was certainly not lacking but IU was only ticking over whereas the pace at Housing Units was not letting up and we were continuing to build and enhance the shop on Manchester Road. So whilst I was very keen to explore other areas of trade, eventually it was back to basics and Industrial Units was ended.

After the demise of the mail order business Doreen came to work with us at Housing Units, abandoning office work in favour of selling DIY products. However she later returned to administration and became our major multi tasker as she dealt with reception, phones, office work, and covering lunches on the shop floor. She always ran our stand at the various furniture exhibitions we attended and I remember how she would stalk the Tudor room set holding a 2' x 6" square lump of stained beam which she would toss to passing visitors; fortunately it was the lightweight Oakleaf polyurethane sample! It was around this time that David Johnson and his brother Michael left the yard sales to set up their own business and David's replacement was another ex APAS apprentice, Jimmy Goldthorpe. Jimmy was a timber machinist by trade and stayed with us from 1969 until 1975 when he handed over to Geoff Lees; both these guys did very well during their time at the business. The showroom sales had initially been managed by an enthusiastic lad named Trevor Barlow who also did well but he seemed to lose direction for a spell and planned to enter the church.

Unfortunately his new calling was short lived as he found out a young lady was having his baby and so he had to come back down to earth from heaven. He eventually went on to run his own DIY shop with his brother, Neville.

Regardless of changes in staff the business at Housing Units blossomed. Across the road from our premises was the mighty Ferranti works and our shop was very handy for the workforce to wander round during their lunch break when they would generate a steady trickle of business. Incidentally one of our most regular visitors from the works was Eric Taylor, Chairman of the local Conservative party who unfortunately lost his life in the IRA bomb in Brighton 1984, whilst his wife, Jennifer, was injured but fortunately survived. At Christmas as Ferranti packed up for the break the workers would drop into the nearby pubs, there were about six on the doorstep, and afterwards they would come to us to do their last minute shopping. Inebriated, these people would buy anything: huge pieces of Capo Di Monte worth around £100; wall clocks; mahogany gambling cabinets with a roulette wheel; or large chunks of Stewart cut glass. Antique style telephones were very popular and we would watch as they staggered out with the large instruments and wonder what their wives would think and know that after Boxing Day many of these 'gifts' would be returned! One guy came in with a wad of notes in his back pocket, bought the full size suit of armour we had on display and, as he was a huge fellow, he just picked it up and shoved it in the back of an old van. We had him down as a scrap merchant. Not everything was quite as amusing though. Someone appeared to be one step ahead of us as our lovely French wall clocks were disappearing one after the other; we had shoplifters and it was the greatest single problem. Fortunately we had a secret weapon in the form of Beryl Carney, a well built lady with a walking stick who worked for a well known security firm. I can still see her now in her Columbo style Mac, stick in one hand, and a large handbag in the other. Both items were actually props and she would use the stick to belt or trip a shoplifter whilst delivering a lethal right hand swing to the jaw with the bag! Above all Beryl's skill was to melt into the scene; she was a truly excellent undercover security person with a nose for the job, a second sense almost, so much so that she also caught several of our own staff.

One such was the nice guy working in the stores but nice or not she had her eye on him. He came across really well, in fact I loaned him Vivienne's small car for his holiday but he didn't fool Beryl: 'He's up to something, I'm sure Mr P.,' she would confide to me. 'No, he's fine,' I told her but one night she stopped him as he passed through the door after work and made him empty out his usual bag of sawdust which he would gather from the machine shop and use for his rabbit hutches. I got a call to come down from the office and there on the floor, between Beryl and the 'nice' man was a pile of sawdust surrounding a large piece of Capo Di Monte. I was absolutely astonished; I had really trusted this guy. There he was grovelling: 'I don't know what made me do it, never done it before,' etc etc. The police arrived and quick as lightening Beryl said: 'Come on Mr P. we're off to his house.' We all piled into the police car and travelled at excess speed to the bloke's house on one of the estates. As we walked in I was speechless; the place was like an Aladdin's cave, full of our tackle; he had obviously been at it for a long time and his wife must have thought every day was her birthday. I really felt like killing the guy but the police did not think that was a good idea. I identified the booty he had stolen from the shop and it came to a value of several thousand pounds; I didn't see any sign of his rabbits though! Needless to say he did not sleep at home that night and we refrained from continuing his employment. As well as the 'rabbit' man Beryl caught out many others such as the young lady working on the upstairs sales floor after a tip off from Yvonne Richards who was running the department. She was playing the game of two sales: one for the till, one for herself, but once Beryl was on to her she didn't last long. Another established sales lady would serve her friends and relations giving them the wrapped goods but forgetting to put any money in the till. The best safeguard is to always give a receipt with every sale; actually that might not be a bad thing in some pubs where mental arithmetic is not always correct! Always ask for and take your receipt, that's my tip. Beryl had great pride in doing a first class job; she believed in Housing Units and saved us considerable cash as she stalked her pitch like a lioness knowing just when to strike.

However there was another problem that even Beryl couldn't deal with. The finished shop front development of Housing Units on Manchester Road presented a fine display of plate glass windows which, in day time is great, but at night becomes a different thing. There was a night club about a mile away at the end of Broadway and our beautifully lit windows were very attractive to the drunken people emerging from there at chucking out time. Although the display lights in the window switched off automatically at 11 p.m. the road lights outside cast some illumination onto the windows thus highlighting the merchandise. I often deliberated if: a) the late night revellers didn't like the look of their reflection in the glass and so tried to head butt themselves; or b) they actually wanted one of our products. All our gifts were lined up charmingly on the windowsill and were therefore very accessible once the window glass was removed. Even merchandise that was towards the back of the display was taken although that meant reaching in through the broken glass and risking some bad cuts. The shop had an alarm system that went directly through to the police who would be on their way to the crime scene as I was receiving a phone call to get me out of my bed to attend the shop as the registered key holder. Undoubtedly this would be somewhere between midnight and 4 a.m., just as I was having a quiet snooze tucked up in my bed. We invariably got one call out per night at weekend but quite often it could be more and one night the second call out was only thirty minutes after I had boarded up the first broken window. Things got so bad that for my convenience plywood, already cut to size, together with nails and hammer were left out each evening by Bob the day time security guard. Good job I had done a bit of joinery! God knows how many windows I boarded up. It showed true dedication I felt, getting up in the early hours after a hard day at work so I began to time myself. My best time was twenty seven minutes. Out of bed on Copsterhill Road where we now lived (1), down to the shop, sort the police, board up the window and back in bed. An Olympic time. Eventually the night club changed hands and became a Church of all things; obviously the breaking of windows was no longer a problem but there were worse things ahead, needless to say nothing to do with the church.

Following a successful Saturday's trading I left the shop at about 6 p.m., set the alarm as normal, pulled down the door shutter and assumed all was safe. The next day I needed something from the office but as we always tried to keep Sunday free for family things I didn't go for it and so it was Monday morning when I returned to the shop. As I pulled up the door shutter and peered through the glass pane I could see papers and discarded food boxes scattered everywhere; looks like we had had serious visitors this time. Inside is a real mess; all the doors, both internal and those leading

Housing Units frontage circa 1970. The windows I had a ten year relationship with! Once, while boarding up at 4am a passing drunk stood swaying and watching me before asking 'What time are you opening?'

outside have been left wide open, the van has gone from the yard and the alarm is out of action. Eventually the police arrive and as we size up the damage it is apparent that several people have been involved. We assume they came in on Saturday night and worked right through until Sunday, possibly even throughout the day. As we move upstairs we see that the whole place has been ransacked; the offices and the showroom are strewn with food packaging indicating just how many meals the burglars have consumed whilst about their work. The shop floor has been used as a toilet, an unprintable message was written on a mirror, a cutlass has been stuck into the middle of a velvet chaise lounge and most other things have just been smashed up for fun. The place was such a mess I found it difficult to ascertain what was missing; goods had been taken from everywhere it seemed. The yard gate had been forced open with our fork lift truck but the thieves had closed the gate behind them, probably so that their work would remain undetected thus allowing several visits. It seemed this was a well planned job and I was puzzled about why the alarm had not worked. I have often thought since that had I slipped down to the shop on the Sunday I may have bumped into them and at least some of the loss and damage may have been prevented. Nevertheless we recovered and carried on.

I was always keen to enjoy the fresh air in the morning and had a thing about walking to work and back which became even more of a ritual when I got two Lakeland Terriers, Jamie and Jess. Once we arrived at work Jamie, Jess and I would settle down in my office above the shop where there was a large pedestal desk against the wall which the dogs would retreat under until lunch time. Any visitors I received would sit in a chair which was situated at one end of my desk and from where my quiet and well behaved dogs could not be seen. Unfortunately as conversation was underway a dreadful smell would often waft over us; it was the dogs of course who seemed to suffer from excessive flatulence every time I had a visitor! In the spirit of my Dad, practical joker that he was, I couldn't help myself, and as the noxious smell drifted around the room I would look at the red faced visitor and make my excuses. As I left the office I would close the door behind me, lean against the wall just outside and give Wendy, our secretary and receptionist, a wink. Together we would start to count knowing that within ten or twenty seconds the visitor would undoubtedly move and all hell would break loose as the previously undetected dogs would emerge from under the desk growling and snarling at the 'intruder'. As long as my victim stayed still the dogs would do no more than that but should he move they would be on him like a weasel down a hole. Wendy and I would crack up outside as we listened to the sounds of pandemonium in my office and I would eventually breeze in quite casually only to find the victim stood on a chair or on top of my desk with the snarling dogs snapping at his feet! As soon as I appeared the dogs would dissolve back under the desk, content to hand guard duty over to me. I wasn't too heartless though and only pulled this stunt on male visitors. One guy held the record of one minute without the dogs pouncing as he had not moved even slightly. When I finally opened my office door on that occasion the visitor was frozen in his seat having spotted the dogs eyeballing him from under the desk but because he hadn't moved at all, not even his feet, they had stayed put although they were emitting a constant low pitched growl! It has to be said that Jamie and Jess loved this sport as much as Wendy and I did.

In the mid sixties I was on one of my walks with the dogs when I spotted the abandoned Millgate Sunday School on Hollins Road which had been empty for some time and had a leaking roof. By now we had greatly developed the Manchester Road site and, with the introduction of extra products, we were running out of room so I weighed the old Sunday

School up and decided it did not seem mission impossible to convert it into a furniture warehouse and salesroom, similar to set ups I had seen earlier when travelling round the States. It was just what we needed. We could purchase the building reasonably cheaply but the cost of the repairs and shop fitting was the gamble, as was the location. Unlike Housing Units, the Sunday School was not on the main road although it was nearby; if we could promote it we would be in business, if not we would have a problem. We decided to give it a go, purchased the place, had some structural work carried out by my former employee David Johnson who now had his own business, and then sent two hardworking chaps from the furniture sales at Hollinwood to set everything up. Walter Denton, a complex but hard working guy, was to manage the operation whilst David Kennett was his 'staff'. They started there a couple of months before we were due to open and got stuck in, clearing and demolishing, building staging around the walls and creating centre isles. The old building was a maze of rooms and passages and it had loads of character but setting it up and sorting it out was really hard but rewarding work.

Once it was ready filling it was no problem at all, Derek and I had seen to that on our trips to the shows where we had purchased a great range of products. Whereas we had previously been restricted by space we now had the opportunity to promote our furniture sales and really go for it. Two hundred chairs came from Berry's of Preston; Stanley Woods mid priced range of oak finished tables, dressers and occasional furniture arrived in huge van loads; furniture suites of various styles shot the place to life as did the kitchen sets and wardrobe systems. Between the rooms on the ground floor was a narrow passage which we filled with twenty grandfather clocks all chiming and striking at once, prices ranging from Grandmother clocks at £300 to classics at £3000. Pictures adorned the walls, all carefully picked from Stansfield of Bolton: copies of *The Landlord's Story*; Constable's *Flatford Mill*; *The Haywain*; and various Monet's together with landscapes and pictures of waves and sea. For the bedding department we purchased a 'Bed of Ware' which was a huge four poster built by a firm called 'Old Charm'; cost – a clean £2800 including tapestry drapes! We also stocked other more moderately priced four posters as well as a full range of less decorative beds. As you walked into the new store at Millgate there was a splendid red carpeted staircase right in front of you which led to the world's smallest café comprising of four or five tables where you could have tea and biscuits – the start of catering for HU! Also in the entrance was a large, leather studded, Porter's Chair such as those found in the very best hotels in London, and opposite stood one of our full size suits of armour. We put signs on the low roof trusses where applicable reminding people to duck, whilst music and reasonable lighting rounded of the whole presentation.

The pricing plan was simple, another thing I had noted whilst in the States some years previously: we would dual price which meant displaying the retail cost as well as 'our' price which would be retail minus twenty per cent. Our stock and the prices were proudly displayed on handouts, which we delivered in their thousands, boosting up our advertising, whilst in one of the back rooms we installed a retired French Polisher, Mr Fowler, as I believed after sales service was essential in the furniture department as well as in all other areas of retail. Outside at the front the Sunday School had been altered by our architect friend, Reg Langton, who had designed and supervised the building of an extension which lifted the whole aspect of the premises. Finally we needed to ensure that there was adequate signage (2) as the old school was not on a main road position like Housing Units and at last we were ready to welcome the public in to test us out. We were not disappointed and made a steady start with sales accelerating almost immediately.

Over the last decade our staff had increased to somewhere between twenty and thirty and was still growing, particularly now we had the two sites. Derek and I, having moved on from our original roles, were fully stretched; it would often be about midnight when I returned home from a days work as there was so much to do once the two shops had closed. Even Mr Prebble, our accountant, was finding it much busier so we advertised for an accounting assistant. One of the applicants was Harry Fox and whilst he had not yet qualified as an accountant he was young and seemed to fit the bill and when Alf Prebble eventually retired Harry was ready to take his place. Later on Harry was joined by other Housing Unit stalwarts, Margaret, Nancy and Karen due to the great expansion of our business and by the mid 1970's the total number of staff would be about forty.

It was around this time that I came across Norman Motley, a character working with an advertising agency in Manchester. I had the idea that by using an advertising agency the job of promoting the business would be taken out of our hands thus relieving us of some of our workload so

Norman and I discussed using TV as an advertising medium in addition to the more usual press coverage. No one in our type of business had advertised on TV so far and it seemed a good idea although it was very expensive for a ten second spot. However, giving Norman a clear brief we decided on a buying package of about twelve adverts with a couple of prime time exposures guaranteed. Getting an ad in near Coronation Street was bound to mean good business and sure enough once the TV ads kicked in the show was really on the road. Our buying front was now huge and we stocked everything from a comprehensive range of building and timber products to a very extensive range of DIY goods; from houseware and gifts to lighting and fireplaces, not forgetting our extensive furniture collection at Millgate. All these products had been carefully chosen before being introduced for sale and if I had to put one skill forward as being vital in a sales environment it would be that of a multi product buyer which I had, out of necessity, become. Each product with its individual characteristics needs to be understood and appraised whilst being simultaneously assessed for the market place you are aiming for. Gut feeling and a degree of risk taking is the criteria for setting up a successful business and everything becomes much easier when you have captured the retail story you wish to tell. Once your merchandise is clearly identified and established the customer will respond – ours did, and although it was a hard slog we made steady ongoing progress which is what building a business is all about, and there are an awful lot of highs and lows. I recall the saying: 'experience is a good teacher but she sends in terrific bills!'

As is usual in life when everything is going well we once again suffered a tragedy. When David Johnson had been working with us, prior to him leaving to set up his own building business, we had installed his Uncle Jim who was semi retired. He worked part time during the week on maintenance and keeping the place looking good; a nicer kinder guy you could not wish to meet and even I called him Uncle although he was no relation. One day Jim and another chap were working together on some faulty guttering between the machine shop and the old smithy building. I had set the job up in the morning but as it was a Wednesday when I usually called to have lunch with Mum, I left them to it. Before leaving I had been up the ladder to check how the job was coming along and everything seemed fine so when I received a phone call at Mum's house to say that Uncle Jim had had an accident I couldn't understand it. Apparently he had fallen through the asbestos roof and landed on the floor near the circular saw and the ambulance was on its way. Luckily some of our staff had been sent on a first aid course and one of these was Yvonne Richards who tried to revive him whilst waiting for the ambulance. However her efforts were in vain for as I arrived at the hospital Jim's wife and daughter were just being told that he had been pronounced dead in the ambulance. My Cousin Michael's terrible accident flashed through my mind; like Michael I believed that Jim had been in my charge but there was no reason for him to have been on the roof. With age asbestos becomes brittle and if you have to walk on it you should only walk where the nail heads indicate there is a roof spar below, otherwise use a roof ladder. Jim knew this; also he was no lightweight and was in his late sixties I should think so I could not understand how he came to be on the actual roof. The accident happened immediately after his lunch break; did he have a funny turn? Did he reach for something? Did he fall backwards accidentally? It remained a mystery as the subsequent inquest could not determine what had caused the fall, there being no witnesses. Once again the guilt was overwhelming for me and it was a hopelessly unfair blow that had been dealt to a lovely old couple. When Jim had finished his days work he would return home to his peaceful cottage behind a farm at Park Bridge, sit down with a cup of tea and tell Mrs Johnson step by step all about his day. They were like Darby and Joan; their home flowed with the deep understanding love they shared within their strong Christian faith; the days and years revolved round one another, and their routine, traditions and absolute satisfaction with their lot in life shone through. Kindness radiated from this couple who never did a wrong thing. Once again I was questioning and doubting fairness through faith whilst Mrs Johnson was finding comfort in hers. The shock and suddenness of her husband's death was immense but she was lovingly supported by her daughter and family and I was asked to be one of the bearers of his coffin at the funeral, a tribute at a time of remorse I shall not forget. Mrs J. told me that Jim had enjoyed his time at Housing Units and had looked forward to his work every day and I remained in touch with her and called round frequently until she moved from her home to live with her daughter in Wales.

Despite the terrible accident the flow of business, merchandise and customers continued to increase and the advertising started to pay off as, amongst other things, Housing Units kept popping up on the TV screen albeit at an almost unaffordable cost. We now worked with a guy called Bryn Middleton for our advertising and together we came up with a brilliant idea about using all our products to transform an empty room. The advert began with the empty room and during the next ten or twenty seconds the makeover takes place before your eyes as fixtures and furnishings are brought in. Firstly there was the building of the fireplace and the fitting of the copper canopy on the chimney breast. Next it was the installation of beams on the ceiling and the light fittings, speedily followed by mirrors, pictures, sofa, occasional furniture, ornaments etc. The final bit of the advert showed the fire lighting, the lamps coming on and a cat curling up on the rug in front of the fire. The advert was absolutely fantastic and no one in retailing had ever done a TV spot like this before. It was risky because it was so expensive to air the ad, maybe around £1800 which was a fortune, and other retailers thought we were reckless. However it proved to be very successful and we were a year or two ahead of the others, even DFS were not advertising on TV then! To make this advertisement, that lasted only a few seconds, there was lots of filming and a very large crew. Bryn, who always wore a brown Trilby, did a great job and our effort was never matched. I have never regretted taking that advertising gamble which must have been one of Housing Units greatest moments as she launched herself at about six million people via the media of television. These days it is much more common and a lot easier to advertise although it still costs a fortune but there is big money coming through the door of most businesses. It is good to know that we were the pioneers of furniture advertising on television although the price did make my eyes water at the time! A fantastic event in Housing Units history.

The staff at Millgate grew as business increased and we had the room there to tell the real furniture story without fighting for space or cluttering the showrooms as we had at the Hollinwood site. We were selling good value lines alongside some high quality products and people were turning up to buy, so much so, that we had to purchase a larger delivery van and engage another driver as we were travelling far and wide into Cheshire, Lytham, and Warrington. But overall the good thing was that customers were happily visiting both of our stores with the aid of a direction sheet which would be handed to them at whichever of the two sites they visited first. Walter Denton continued to run the furniture depot; he was a conscientious, good and very hard worker but his restlessness could cause problems with some of his colleagues. Over at the Hollinwood store things were different. There we would hold 'customer nights' when all the staff would dress up in a particular theme to welcome the shoppers. We had French and Italian evenings and on one occasion we held a Burns Night complete with pukka MacDonald dress kits hired from Moss Bros in Manchester. We did the whole thing including hiring a bagpipe player who was also dressed in the full regalia and it was open house for our regular customers who were invited to eat Haggis which was on the buffet and to take a wee dram. The events went down very well and in my opinion that's making retailing fun!

So things were going well for us but eventually we began hearing a lot of noise from our 'friends' on Oldham Council about a proposed motorway going through Hollinwood. Whilst the Department of Transport were busy considering whether to give the go ahead for the plan the council were trying to 'help' us by inviting us to move to the ill fated St Peter's precinct in the town centre which went bust a few years later. In fact Councillor Crowther told us: 'you'll never trade here, move to Oldham,' a piece of advice that was of course proved wrong. We were resolute and in spite of their pleas I managed to keep my face straight as did Derek, the Saddleworth councillor, as we vowed not to get sucked into the sinking ship, *HMS Oldham*. Things were hotting up and the local people were greatly upset by the motorway plans and formed a 'Save Hollinwood' committee, the residents seeming to think that Housing Units would be a trump card in their case. We listened to them although I wasn't so sure we could change anything. The fact was that the blocked end of a motorway already existed nearby in Denton just waiting to be connected up to go somewhere and fortunately, or unfortunately, Hollinwood was in the way! The Government's proposed plans would require us to move our Hollinwood site which seemed such a shame when we were so well established and, even though we were not members of the Oldham Council fan club, we were unable to blame them for this particular problem. After much consideration we decided to sit on the fence and see what happened, meanwhile concentrating on funds as interest rates at the time were rising and would soon become massive.

A Learning Curve: Notes

(1) Once the children were a bit older we all moved to a new home, Copster House next to a park. Formally the home of Dr Hendry we paid £8200 for it to become ours and at last we had real space to live and entertain in. It was a great house and within walking distance of the 'shop' in Hollinwood. I loved grafting in the garden building walls and a new drive but the ultimate masterpiece was the circular swimming pool we built out of 3/8" tempered hardboard sheets with a plastic liner. It was a design published in the DIY Monthly by our old friend Barry Bucknell and it was around twenty feet in diameter and four feet deep. Every spring we would erect the pool in the garden and we all had great fun swimming around until the advance of winter would see us dismantling and storing it away again. Many years later it was replaced by a permanent, full sized, oblong mosaic tiled job which was professionally built and cost a fortune. Even so we were never able to exceed the fun we had in the £150 do it yourself pool which had now been passed on to our relatives, the Kelso's, who continued to enjoy it.

Whilst living at Copster House we had loads of parties: birthdays for Tim and Lou, various anniversaries, fete's, and a fancy dress ball which attracted Sheiks, Chimpanzees, Can Can girls, many TV characters, Roman soldiers, and even Cave Men! Many parties later, after about twenty five years, we decided to move to Greenfield with our retirement in mind so we sold Copster House to a man named Iqbal Ahmed, an Indian who had fled from Uganda when the country was under the terrible regime of Idi Amin. With little more than what he stood up in when he arrived in Britain, Iqbal went on to build a huge and prosperous business called Seamark, winning Queen's Award for Expert Achievement – a fantastic success story. Eventually, as always happens, things change and Redrow builders purchased Copster House, demolished it, and filled in the lovely swimming pool. They also bought the reservoir behind the house and the nearby Glovers Mill and the whole area is now a large estate. Hopefully Iqbal was well compensated; at any rate he moved to Cheshire where I believe he has a helicopter landing facility nearby!

(2) Howard Jones was an ex Oldham College of Art student who opened his own traditional sign writing business in 1977. Repetitive business is something we all look for and Howard was no exception when, in the summer of 1981, I wandered into his shop asking if he could help with some hand written show cards. He was already doing cards for James Brown Leather Market but felt it would be good to take on more work and so we became business partners on a small scale. Shortly afterwards I asked if he would take on all our signage requirements and the results of his work are there for everyone to see at the Housing Units 'village'. Howard recently wrote to me and recalled the time that I

1.

2.

3.

1. Tim's Christening at St Thomas' –
Godparents Joan, Bob and Ian a top team

2. Louanne soon arrived to occupy the
Osnath pram that Tim had by now left
vacant – a fine chariot pictured in the
back garden at 307 Windsor Road

3. Copster House, our second home –
Viv's dad – a great gardener fortunately

4. The do it yourself Barry Bucknell
swimming pool. Terrific fun

4.

invited him to look at the flattened site which was ready for the commencement of building Phase One:

J.P. called again ... and asked me if I would meet up with him at a place he had just acquired on Wickentree Lane. I met up with him the following morning in this rather barren looking fenced off wasteland and was rather bemused [when] he put his hand on my shoulder as we looked around this muddy patch of land and ... said '[We are] going to turn this into Housing Units 'village' ... [over] there will be a large building ... for furniture, with a second possibly there (pointing incessantly) which will probably be a fireplace centre and giftware store.' I have a lot of admiration for [J.P.] but I honestly thought [he] had lost the plot ... I personally could not envisage what the hell he was on about ... I still find it amazing when I am on the car park of Housing Units today – looking round in a 360 degree circle at the end result of one man's vision ... what a legacy.

Over forty years of trading we must have commissioned thousands of different signs from Howard Jones Signs as we were constantly upgrading them – thanks once again Howard.

Buy the Way

China now exports as much every six hours as it did in the whole of 1978!

In the late 1960's we were visiting most of the shows in the UK. Regionally there was the Manchester exhibition and a famous show at Blackpool's Winter Gardens which was popular for gifts, lights, stationery and art. Any overspill of goods would be displayed at several of the resorts larger hotels and, incredibly, full use was also made of the multi storey car park with displays on every level where cars would normally be parked. The higher the level the hotter it got as all the lighting displays were to be found on the top two storeys! The London venues, Earls Court and Olympia, were, however, by now old, high maintenance buildings and their days seemed to be numbered although of course we now had the NEC in Birmingham and it was mainly due to the great success of this easily accessible venue in the centre of England that the Blackpool and London shows eventually got killed off.

As sales at Housing Units grew I found it necessary to also attend European shows such as the Paris furniture show which was very big, and the lighting exhibition. There was the odd trip to Scandinavia and Brussels and just prior to the end of my buying trips I also visited Milan a few times and my very last trip there will always be remembered because the new model of the iconic Mini was just being launched and, unlikely as it seems, there was one hung on a slanting platform outside the entrance to the main hall! More recently the Far East became the place to go for buying although I never actually went there even though we were selling a lot of Chinese products by the time I retired. All serious buyers today are drawn to China and the Far East whether they like it or not as the goods are of a good quality and a reasonable price. Buying is a progressive business and in the case of Housing Units it grew and grew as it would continue to do with increasing sales. Also, for as long as I can remember we would attend the traditional Harrogate Gifts Fair which consumed all the hotels in Harrogate, not having a large enough singular building to accommodate everything. In my buying days I would do around eight or ten major exhibitions per year and sometimes I would take the relevant department head so they understood the range, as they would have to sell the goods and do repeat orders. Furniture sales were firstly attended with Derek Delhide then later Louanne. I also took Harry's lad, Nick, along briefly but overall I have always preferred to go on buying trips alone as I found that I could cover twice the ground in the same amount of time than if I had someone with me. Being in a retail business makes attendance at these shows absolutely essential if you wish to keep your customers happy with the very latest in style and design and these trips were therefore frequent. Even so our business was much different to today's rather impersonal trade; things were much more laid back and, as the bulk of what was traded were made in the UK, you often became good friends with the manufacturers. The many family businesses which we dealt with had close connections and continuity, unlike today's massive PLC's who out of necessity use agents and manufacturers around the world. So trading back then was a much more low key experience and there were many eccentric characters in the business such as 'King' Feather who was the Northern agent for a firm of gift merchandise suppliers called Anglex.

After the firm's autumn exhibition in London all the stock from the Anglex trade stand was transferred to the Feather's home in the Bradford area for his own 'road show'. How he managed to accommodate everything in his house remains a mystery for it was only of moderate size although it seemed to have an extraordinary number of small rooms. There were few signs of occupation by human beings in that house; everything personal had been removed: furniture, ornaments and pictures, all gone. Merchandise lined every wall and it must have taken Mr and Mrs Feather a week to display it all and another to take it away; the whole house resembled a network of Aladdin's caves with surprises everywhere. The only two rooms which were not transformed into a sales floor were the kitchen and the bathroom, both of equal importance as the former was used to make the alarming amounts of tea which was offered all day long, whilst the latter was, as a consequence, a very essential place. Once he was set up in his home all the customers on Mr Feather's patch would be given an appointment for a private viewing: one buyer in the morning and a second in the afternoon. In my case however, he would reserve the whole day as Housing Units was a substantial account although on one occasion I didn't manage to get to my all day appointment until around midday.

My delayed arrival was heralded as usual with Mr Feather stood in the doorway and his demure lady wife hovering in the background. She was beholden to the 'Kings' constant instructions which were fired from his mouth even when he was totally immersed in the scribing of numerous order pads which were strategically placed in every room. Following the usual formalities: 'Good journey? How is Mrs P?' I make excuses for my tardiness but spare the dear fellow the tale of bedlam I had left at Housing Units that day. What had happened was like a scene out of a film. The Gas board had their works behind our premises at Hollinwood and that morning they were holding one of their gas training evacuations during which they would demonstrate to visiting parties how they could contain a major leak. A gas pipe rupture is re enacted and because extinguishers are ineffective they apply a hugely powerful jet of air which goes off like an explosion. The whole of the surrounding area shakes as a consequence including our shop which feels like it is on top of an earth tremor. We had received notice of the test, which was usual practice, so that we could take precautions to prevent our products dropping off the display stands when the explosion hit, however on this particular morning not only did the glassware tremble and shake but an Alsatian dog, which was accompanying one of our customers, panicked and jumped through one of our crockery and glassware stands with a remarkable amount of success! Naturally his owner was very concerned and pointed out that his dog did not normally do this sort of thing, but we took it all in our stride as we were very dog friendly down there, more so than kid friendly sometimes! I can't say I blame the Alsatian as my own two dogs would growl gently in unison just prior to one of the Gas Board demonstrations; they seemed to instantly sense the changes in the air flow or something as they lay under my desk in the office anticipating the bang. Leaving someone else to sort out the dog, his owner and the mess, I made my escape whilst the phone line between Housing Units and the Gas Board became hot as we invited them to purchase some of our recycled glass!

And so I arrived, albeit late, for a peaceful visit with Mr Feather but as usual it turned into a marathon ordering session which lasted until about 9.30 p.m.

Following the traditional tea and biscuits we tackle room one, for all the rooms are numbered, and I scan every damned item calling out my orders to the scriber before moving on to the next room and the next. Now and again the 'King' chips in: 'one off hit Mr P., no repeats,' anticipating I will increase the order which I do. Room three done we knock off for a meal which is the same as last year and the year before that: ham, tongue, or cheese sandwiches on white bread with butter, sausage rolls and, thankfully, a small dressing of salad to relieve the calories. This repast would be followed by some 1960's confectionary and yet more tea, in fact I'm sure that half of Yorkshire's entire tea allocation was served up by Mrs Feather! It is hard to imagine now but what a stark contrast it was between a visit to King Feather's and the promenades of design and showmanship in Paris and Milan! It would certainly be very unlikely for such an experience as the Feather's tea party to attract today's serious buyers. Next we move on to discover the delights of room four before ascending the stairs where it suddenly occurs to me there are no beds so I ask where they sleep and am assured that both Mr and Mrs Feather have beds at hand although I can't see them. The theme in each of the show rooms varies: illuminated tackle, cats in baskets that meow, and astral oil bubble lamps in one; Jack in the Boxes and Murano glass from Italy in another; the next may be filled with shire horses in all sizes, either alone or pulling a cart. Remember them? Shaking snow scenes, tons of cut glass, Spanish wood ware, wine holders, shelves, cocktail globes, mega loads of pottery, ornaments, Toby Jugs; you name it and it was there. Volumes of totally useless stuff that seems to have multiplied in value when it appears on today's TV in shows such as 'Cash in the Attic' or 'Bargain Hunt'; almost every item shown is a legacy of King Feather and his colleagues. (1) I am flaking a little by the time we reach the final room but am spurred on as the 'King' tears off sheet twenty one saying: 'we might be ahead of last years total.' Now we are on the home straight as Mrs Feather flutters in with more carbohydrates and even more tea to fuel the power to order. As I pass the finishing post the 'King' asks if I would like to revisit anything which is easily done by starting at room one again. Hmmmm.

As I eventually stagger out into the night full of hospitality and tea and rubbing my aching eyes, the Feather's present me with a bottle of something and a diary for next year which I assume to be my Christmas present. My buying trip has produced just short of thirty order sheets which Mr Feather will price up and post out to me the next day. Nowadays traders use an electronic zapper which sends the order straight into the computer on the trade stand. You, the customer, walk away with a fully priced set of order sheets instead of having to wait for them to be written up. It is so much easier and more efficient with all the technology although it has to be said that a lot of the fun and the quirky characters of the business have been lost along the way. Enter Michael Ross Murphy, an associate I came across in the furniture business.

As well as being a furniture trader Michael Murphy was also a walker, dog lover and serious ex WWII soldier. I first met him when he called into Millgate to see me as a representative for Clements who were a London based leather furniture retailer. He also represented Charles Barr who supplied very classy mahogany and yew dining room ranges and, at this stage in the early 1970's, it could be questioned if we were indeed ready to handle furniture of the quality and high price level that Ross Murphy was selling. Nevertheless ahead we went and trusting instinct for what sells I ordered a Porters Chair from the Clements Leather range which was a tall, deeply buttoned leather model with a curved leather canopy 'designed to envelop and keep the servant relatively warm in his task of remaining at the door for long periods'. The chair came in Antique Green Leather and we stuck it in the entrance to the shop with a price tag of around £1200 and this was the 1970's! Would you believe it paid off and we sold it together with many repeat sales? Next to it was another of our quirky purchases, a full suit of armour with a price tag of around £1500; these also walked out steadily. Unbelievable, but I was lucky and obviously taking a gamble had paid off. The more we traded Michael and I became close friends and I would crack up as he told me about some of his exploits in the furniture business in earlier days when it seemed to be very much glamour and glitz. Prior to the war Michael had been the manager of the furniture department at Kendals, Manchester, a prestigious position in a very exclusive store where clients had their own personal accounts. A stickler for appearances, he would stalk around the sales floor dressed in a morning suit with carnation buttonhole. At that time furniture managers did much of their buying by going to visit the manufacturers themselves as this was long before the shows at Earls Court. In Michael's case a buying trip to a

London supplier would go like this: arrive around lunch time, take a mild sortie round the showroom followed by cocktails at the Ritz; move on to Rules for a very fine evening of wining, dining and passing the port round and then drinking the night away. After just a few hours sleep he would rise the following day and manage to squeeze in some business before getting a brief respite at an all singing lunch, probably at Langans Brasserie.

His business concluded, the long drive home would be broken by visiting one of his favourite hostelries in Derbyshire for another mammoth evening session of the finest cuisine and the appropriate tipples. That folks, was the way Michael did his buying in the pre war era, a time of tradition and the old boys club, rather different than today. On one such trip during the winter Michael pulled into his usual Derbyshire Inn on the way home and, together with his passengers, participated in yet another night's indulgence whilst outside it snowed heavily. Realising that the next morning his car would not be going anywhere he took a few hours sleep, arose at 4.30 a.m. and set off on foot through the snow to make his way to work in distant Manchester leaving his car to its fate with his colleagues. Fortunately he was aware of the time of the milk train having used it before, so he managed to meet a farmer that he knew from his numerous walking trips in the area and got a lift on his tractor to the local train station. Catching the 5.30 a.m. Manchester milk train he was on parade in Kendals, immaculately dressed as usual, by 8.30 prompt! Fortunately Michael could handle any drinking bout and be one hundred per cent fit the following day, or at least seem to be.

One of his good friends was John Patrick who produced some extremely nice occasional furniture. He had been in the Guards during the war as you could tell from his upright stance and when he had been on a drinking session with Michael it was seriously first division stuff and they would often be seen the following morning having a hair of the dog breakfast in the form of steak and a glass of port! Michael was also famous for his tales of endurance in other theatres of life. A serious walker, together with his two dachshunds he must have walked the equivalent of Britain's coastline twice over and he was also most knowledgeable of the high routes in the fells of the Lake District. He once asked if I would like to join him for a couple of days up there and of course I said yes. At that time I was quite fit as I was into YMCA circuit classes, running and playing squash, so I didn't foresee any problems. We booked in at one of his regular watering holes, The Derwentwater Hotel, with our dogs, Michael's two Dachshunds and my first

Lakeland terrier, Jock (2). Now walking drops into two categories, hard and easy. For one you need some supplies, for the other you don't so when I joined Michael for breakfast at 8 a.m. and he said we didn't need to take anything I understood it must be a short walk. We set off at 9 a.m. with no food, rucksack or water but he didn't stop all day long and we arrived back at the hotel some seven and a half hours later for some very welcome tea and biscuits! After this modest repast Michael read the papers, took a hot shower, dressed in suitable country attire including jacket, collar and tie, and was ready to take on the evening. Now my concern was would I be able to keep up with him knowing this guys drinking reputation and would I still be standing upright at the end of the night, after all we had just walked about twenty miles! Aperitifs in the bar start with a couple of Dubonnet's on my recommendation as surprisingly Michael was not familiar with the brew. Over dinner we handle a bottle of Graves red wine before embarking on some port with the cheese and biscuits. During dinner two very impressive middle aged sisters had appeared in the dining room wearing full evening dress and dripping with jewels. They commanded attention and would not have looked out of place on stage at the Garrick Theatre in a Noel Coward play! As they finished their dinner Michael asked the waiter to take over two liqueurs to the ladies and he placed a note on the waiter's tray asking them if they would like to join us. Now that is style! As we chatted he mentioned that we had to collect our dogs from the rooms and take them for a walk and asked if they would care to join us in a stroll to the local pub. They jumped at his offer and I can tell you that when we walked through the pub door those farmers were absolutely astonished!

On another occasion when it's just Michael and me we collect the dogs from our rooms to take them out for their evening ablutions which just happen to take us in the direction of the village pub again. Now the interesting thing in this pub, apart from the beer, is the presence of many dogs, all of which are cowering under the seats which line the walls. I soon realise why; the locals are playing darts and soon enough an arrow pings on the metal strip round the board, ricochets off in a random direction and, narrowly missing some poor pooch, impregnates the pine boarded floor. Pushing the dogs under our seats for their safety, Michael and I sit together in a mellow glow of alcohol, log fire and atmosphere, watching the dog's heads twist and turn as they follow the errant missiles. Later, on the way back to The Derwentwater Hotel, Michael notices the light is still on in the

Yacht club. 'Should we pop in there for a nightcap John,' he asks and of course I say yes. Falling over both my own feet and the dog I follow him inside and we soon find someone to reminisce and talk to for another hour or two. Eventually we get to bed. Breakfast next morning is 8 a.m. with our departure being scheduled for 8.30; this time maybe it's the Calderdale Round, Braithwaite, Grisedale Pike, Hopegill Head, Eel Crag and Sail, Scar Crags, or Causey Pike then back for the usual tea and biscuits before repeating the previous night's performance.

A truly enigmatic character, Michael's brand of culture, energy and company introduced many others to fell walking and the traditional celebration of the day's completed routes by copious imbibing in the evening. First to join us was John Marchant, a good neighbour of Michael's; next Bob West, a colleague in the furniture trade who was closely followed by Peter Honeywell, an ex police inspector and Harry from the shop. Brian Waywell, our auditor at the time, and my son, Tim, also signed up. Intermittently other guest walkers would be invited along and together we all formed the 'Michael Ross Murphy Boots and Bottle Club'. I designed a tie emblazoned ROSS MURPHY BBC (Boots and Bottle Club) which was available in two colours: green for informal wear and blue for more formal occasions and after a good dinner and drinking session we presented the ties to Michael and I rather think that pleased him. When we were not walking on the fells we would spend our time in the Lakes following the Blencathra foot pack with our dogs. Both the Huntsman of the pack, Johnny, and Barry his Whipper, were well respected members of that most traditional farming community where hunting foxes was a way of life. However I have to say that whilst I enjoyed following the pack it is a different matter once the fox goes to ground. The head to head fight between terrier and fox down a burrow, or in an underground chamber, can be intense and is often followed through to the death or serious injury of one or the other. In my opinion if the fox goes to ground that should be it, the hunt moves on. Nevertheless 'a hunting' we would go.

Over the years I would often ask Michael to write down some of his memories and experiences; he had served his country during the war as a member of Wingates Chindits in Burma and that alone would have made good reading. A small obligation and little to ask after a long eventful life, indeed you should do it for those you will leave behind, but he did not, and

1.

2.

4.

3.

5..

1. Some members of the Michael Murphy Boots and Bottle Club somewhere in the Lake District – left to right: Harry, Ian, John, Tim, Brian and Terry

2. Blencathra Hunt Pack – Johnny in the red coat was the Hunt Master until his death and Barry, the Whipper In has since taken over

3. The fox has gone to ground – study the dogs' body language

4. Ravenstones and our swimming pool just below – Tim please note – half my ashes chucked off here please – the other half in the River Dart – thanks!

5. God… talk about Last of the Summer Wine! Left to right: Terry Mundy, Peter Sellers, and Harvey Shaw just off the Holmfirth Road. Think they could use a little Jochem's piles pills!

Ross Murphy took his final walk just a few years ago; his tradition and tales departing with him. Kind, sincere, maybe one would think a bit aloof at times, Michael was a most genuine person and a hell raiser in his day. They truly don't make 'em like that any more.

A lasting legacy from my friend was my eagerness to do some of the longer route walks and consequently Viv and I covered much of the Devon and Cornish coastal paths. We also became familiar with the Cotswolds as well as doing the superb Dalesway, from Ilkley to Bowness. We would stay in Bed and Breakfasts en route and these were some of our best times together. With my daughter, Louanne, I walked the very popular Coast to Coast trail, St Bees to Robin Hoods Bay, which was a wonderful trip. Michael had always talked about hiking along Offa's Dyke', a walk which begins at Sedbury near Chepstow and ends in Prestatyn, North Wales so when he became seriously ill I completed the walk on his behalf as a thank you to him for the many good routes and the good times we had enjoyed together. Undertaken at the end of April through to early May it was an uplifting challenge; the wildlife and countryside is awakening at this time and you see, feel and smell the spring. Bursting with colour, lambs everywhere, Offa's Dyke must be one of the ultimate walks. Unfortunately the Pennine Way, which is right on my doorstep, remains unconquered as knees and ankle start to rust up! Perhaps someone will volunteer to walk this on my behalf!

1.

2.

3.

4.

1. This stone marks the start of the Offa's Dyke footpath. Michael Murphy said 'do it' so I did. A fantastic walk

2. Chepstow to Monmouth, the Black Mountains, Hay on Wye, Denbighshire, Montgomery to Prestatyn – splendid walk in the early spring

3. 182 miles later – Prestatyn – knees OK but my right ankle ain't!

4. Plenty of rivers to drop in for a cool off

1.

2.

3.

4.

5.

6.

7.

8.

9.

10.

1. A very wet Viv mid way on the Dalesway
2. The End – she's done it!
3. Hanging in there
4. South West Coastal path – Helford to Fowey with Jess, one of our terriers
5. Eleanor and Johnny O see us off on the North Devon coast path – Woolacombe to Bude stretch
6. Newton Ferrers – Viv tired and our B&B is the furthest house in the village at the top of a hill – but first we have to figure out how to get across the water!
7. Portloe – Lugger Hotel. Lovely dinner but we must have just missed David and Samantha Cameron
8. Walking holiday in Tuscany
9. Before you jump on to a plane to go abroad try Britain's coast
10. Top of the Haystacks – Wainwright's ashes are scattered here

1.

2.

3.

4.

5.

6.

7.

8.

9.

10.

1. Misty the cat and Meg – a great black and tan Lakeland Terrier. I let her down
2. Five puppies with no mother and no food. Thank God for Mrs Holland who saved the day
3. Viv was a real trooper – feed after feed – no sleep
4. We lost one but the remaining four were fine
5. Jamie and Jess, the two puppies that we kept. Jock and Ben went to another good owner.
6. Dartmouth – Jess on seal alert whilst Jamie is deep in thought – our 'cove'
7. Our little treasure from Manchester Dogs Home – Sally – an absolute star
8. Sally and I swim together – she is like an otter
9. Three of the fittest dogs in Saddleworth: Brig, Maisie and Sally
10. Jess – just started out at Grammar School

Buy the Way: Notes

(1) Unlike Gerald Ratner's jewellry – when he referred to his merchandise as 'crap' his business failed almost overnight. He has recently bounced back and launched an online jewellery company, which presumably doesn't sell 'crap'!

(2) We eventually lost our Lakeland terrier, Jock, in a road accident but very quickly decided to get a replacement so we approached Bill Brightmore, a farmer and breeder of terriers on the borders of Cumbria, the same man we had purchased Jock from. And so we met Meg, a great little black and tan bitch. Eventually we decided to breed from Meg and so on one of my trips with Michael to the Lakes I called in to see Bill and asked if he had a suitable dog for mating with her. He produced a big black Welsh terrier, much larger than Meg but pushing aside my concerns about the mismatch in size we allowed nature to do its work. In the course of time she had her puppies and it was very exciting watching as five tiny dogs came into the world. Unfortunately there was a sixth puppy that would not be born as it was too big and Meg remained in labour for hours until eventually we sent for the vet from Sayles on Manchester Road. It was late on Saturday evening by now and we were frantic with worry. He should have induced that puppy but instead he assured us that Meg would soon give birth and left her to it. We sat through the night with her as she struggled and got weaker whilst her other puppies were unable to feed. On Sunday morning we pleaded the situation again with the vet and he told us to take her to his surgery, which we did, but poor Meg died on the operating table.

The five puppies she had already given birth to had not been fed for twenty one hours and as we returned home from Sayles after losing Meg and the last puppy, Viv and I were distraught. Nevertheless we set to with the plastic syringe and milk that the vet had given us and tried our best to feed the tiny puppies who were now flagging. It was hopeless. I phoned Bill Brightmore, the breeder from whom we had got Meg but he wasn't able to give us any hope at all and advised us to let them go. By fate or desperation, after hearing that bad news I picked up a telephone directory and scanned through the list of dog breeders in the local area, desperate for help. I immediately spotted a Mrs Holland who bred Scotties in the Droylsden area so called her and asked for advice. Without any hesitation that Christian woman told us to keep calm and bring the puppies to her as soon as possible ensuring they were kept warm. We left Tim and Louanne, who were only children at the time, with our neighbour, Mrs Burke, and set off with the five limp but lovely puppies in a blanket covered box. As we drew up outside the house the lady was stood at the door and we hardly had time to introduce ourselves as she led us into a room containing a small kids playpen which was overhung by an infra red heat lamp casting a glow of reassuring warmth. Nearby were a couple of small Pyrex babies feeding bottles and Mrs Holland immediately got to work gently pushing the small rubber teat into the minute mouths. It was not an easy task but she persevered and managed to get a little of the life giving milk into each puppy, so tiny were they that one could easily sit in your hand. As soon as she had been round all the puppies once she started again but one of them was really struggling to take the milk. Nevertheless she persevered and as she continually fed them she taught us how to do it also and very slowly we got the knack. We had arrived at this kind ladies house around lunch time on the Sunday and it was around 2 a.m., after about fourteen hours of non stop attention, that she considered the immediate danger to be over and Viv and I qualified enough to carry on with the feeding. She dispatched us with the play pen, blankets, heat lamp, bottles and spare teats, and we were full of wonder at this saint of a woman as we made our way home.

Once settled we fed the puppies repeatedly as we had been shown and ensured they were snuggled on the blanket which was covering a hot water bottle. Mrs Holland had instructed us on all the things we needed to do which, amongst other tasks, involved gently massaging the puppies hind quarters in order to encourage them to defecate; a task their mother would have done instinctively. By now we hadn't had any sleep since Friday night but, as exhausted as we were, we felt jubilant that we were saving the pups that both the vet and Bill Broughton had given up on. Vivienne was terrific as she soldiered on until eventually we taught Louanne and Tim how to administer the milk so that they could assist. Mrs Holland would visit periodically to check that we were still on course as the puppy care took over our lives but we didn't mind, we had to do it for Meg who had been badly let down by both ourselves and the vet. I do not forget certain things in life and that vet from Sayles Veterinary practice on Manchester Road remains in my sights; we lost a super dog due to his incompetence as well as two puppies for despite our careful attention we lost one of the five survivors, the one that had struggled to feed. Fortunately the others grew nicely until they were ready for a new home when Ben and Jock II were both taken by a lovely couple whilst we kept Jess and Jamie who went on to have good lives with us. On that terrible Sunday the page of the directory had fallen open and my finger had gone directly to one name, Mrs Holland: fate? If there are angels amongst us I can tell you that this wonderful lady ranks amongst them. We were seriously on the edge of time as we took the puppies to her house.

Keeping the Show on the Road

Teamwork built this store – sign behind the reception in Phase One building

The writing was on the wall. There was increasing talk of the motorway coming to Hollinwood with Oldham council indicating that our main road site would probably be demolished to make way for it but I instinctively felt that Hollinwood was where we must stay. As well as the motorway threat we had several other things to consider. Although our Millgate store on Hollins Road was doing a good job with the furniture sales, the merchant's yard behind our shop at Hollinwood was overflowing with stock and needed more room to expand. If we could relocate that part of the business then the space could be used for customer parking, something which was rapidly becoming a very important facility. Looking around we were lucky enough to find a suitable site which was quite near to our existing premises, enter the fate factor. It was the old Beards Paint Factory just down the road on Wickentree Lane. Could we, I wondered, move our merchant's yard to the Beards site thus freeing up space at Manchester road for the parking facility we really needed? Could we afford to purchase the site and completely refit it? If the proposed motorway caused us to have to leave the Manchester Road site would it be possible to negotiate and convert the land surrounding Beard's for a new store? My imagination was going into overtime. The facts were that: a) we could not rely on the council looking after us and, as always, their running of affairs left much to be desired; b) we desperately needed more parking space at Manchester Road; and c) we may have to leave Manchester Road anyway if the motorway was going to affect the site. The decision was made and with Hollinwood and Millgate continuing to do a good job and generate income we purchased the Beards site and immediately got cracking with converting it. Getting our hands on all

1.

2.

3.

4.

5.

6.

1. The beginning

2. Night shot of Housing Units from original painting by Sonia Radcliffe

3. Millgate before it was Millgate!

4. Millgate Furniture Centre

5. Ex Beard's Paint Factory to which we moved our builders yard, DIY and the Fireplace Centre

6. Housing Units, Manchester Road – it was demolished shortly after we moved but it then turned out that the motorway didn't need the land 'you stupid boy!'

that space was like winning the lottery; I had always wanted to get everything onto one site and purchasing this land may well give us a foothold and opportunity to do so at some point in the future if all went well. No retailer would be able to successfully expand without the facility of adequate free parking, on that issue I had no doubt at all, and here was the room needed.

The Beards factory site was located well down the lane beyond the ex Ferranti's premises and consisted of a series of prefabricated buildings and some open land alongside a valley with a brook flowing in the bottom. Running behind the site was the railway line and there were some allotments, several garages and a smelly tripe works nearby. The existing, single storey paint works buildings could easily be converted into showrooms for the fireplaces and DIY, whilst the yard space could be concreted and laid out for the holding of the building materials. It was an exciting challenge and would be easily handled due to our construction background and I believed we could make the transition economically and in the minimum of time. The plan would also give us a base in Wickentree Lane but the big draw back was that our customers would then have three sites to visit: the original Housing Units on Manchester Road, Millgate Furniture and now the fireplaces and DIY on the ex Beards site. Also Wickentree Lane did not have the main road exposure of the original Housing Units and we would need to get permission to retail down there which, whilst it may be difficult, was not impossible. Outweighing these potential problems, however, was the fact that the ex Beard's site had plenty of room and seemed to be a heaven sent opportunity for eventual expansion on a grand scale.

Once the site was purchased, at an unusually low price compared to today's costs, we planned what was required and got on with it. Our first job was to concrete the yard and build ramps and bays for the aggregates and flags. Having pegged the positions out we flew at it as the sooner we got in there the sooner we got the tills ringing. The first concrete waggon with its rolling container arrived around 8 a.m. one morning and at 8 p.m. the last of twenty three loads arrived. We eventually finished work around 9.30 p.m., exhausted but jubilant. What a day! Wading around in the stuff for hours cost me a hernia later on but boy was it worth it. You know how it is when you go to bed and feel that something has really been achieved that day – well that was just such a time. As we surveyed our efforts the following morning we saw a whole yard full of set concrete – well done to all the chaps who worked so hard! We had a fantastic area of levelled surface which meant that we could start to build loading ramps for the builder or DIY enthusiast; the massive space awaiting us after our cramped yard at Hollinwood was unbelievable and everything would fit in with plenty of room left over. On completion of the loading areas we cleared out the existing paint sheds and shop fitted them with shelf and rack systems, ceiling systems, partitioned offices, timber racks, wood cutting machinery, counters, fireplace displays, lighting and music; always trying to beat the clock so that we could get the cash flowing. Once everything was ready it took much less than a week to transfer the yard, timber and fireside stock to its new home and we were back in business. Even more important was the fact that our customers once again followed us just as they had to the new Millgate store previously and it seemed it was worth it as they liked what they found down there: ten times the space we had previously, everything carefully planned with the customer in mind and plenty of parking. There was a super, carpeted, fireplace showroom which led into the DIY building where the walls were lined with stock. From there you could easily access the timber and boards cutting service area whilst outside we had enormous stocks of sand, cement, flags, bricks etc which seemed to have multiplied in quantity overnight. The first float was in the till and we were now trading on our third location.

Eventually our long term strategy began to materialise as we were soon in a position where we could consider getting everything in one place although certain quarters thought the rate we were moving at could mean financial trouble and whilst that is always a risk with a new venture I knew that we were sound on that score. We had dipped our toes in the water with the purchase of Beards and now it was time to turn our attention to Heginbottom's Tripe Works which overlooked the valley with the brook in the bottom, together with the allotments and garages.

Hegginbottom is a well known name in the Oldham area, in fact the family had been selling tripe on Oldham market for a great number of years and they had also previously owned the shop situated in one of our cottages next to the shop in Hollinwood. The factory owned by Heginbottom's emanated the most awful stench and eventually, to the immense relief of the nearby residents, we were able to purchase the place.

As soon as the deal was settled we demolished the lot but when we eventually came to level the vacant land the stuff we dug up was unbelievable! Cow carcasses and various other body parts were scattered around, together with bits of cars and iron work; it really was health and hygiene gone crackers and at times it was a bit like digging up the back yard of a serial killer who had used his garden to dispose of his victim's bodies! Next we turned our attention to the allotments and the garages which were on the other side of the valley. I was a little concerned about acquiring this site which may negatively affect the nearby residents but it turned out that things seemed to be on a decline in the allotments and an agreement was eventually, and courteously, arrived at. Housing Units now had access to a site of some three acres albeit with a big hole in the middle in the form of a valley with a stream in the bottom. To overcome this would mean some very difficult, not to say expensive, civil engineering work, but that did not deter us.

Then once again when everything is going well life deals another blow. I decided to go up to the Borders with Viv to look at a much talked about furniture store called Rob's which had recently opened. That evening as we were having dinner at the Inn where we were staying I received a phone call from Harry with some shocking news; apparently my right hand man Derek Delhide, had been found on the floor at his home and he was dead. It seemed that he had been having a meal when he suffered a fatal heart attack; he had not been in good health for some time and I had been encouraging him to cut down on his hours at the shop whilst his doctor had prescribed tablets of some form. Even so by the end of the working day Derek's face would be purple, possibly a sign of high blood pressure. His death was a terrible blow; we had been very good friends from day one at the tiny ex blacksmith's shop in Hollinwood and Derek's skills had been critical to the ongoing success of Housing Units. We had gone on buying trips together and had lots of good times over the years; I had always had great respect for him and tried my best to look after him once his health began to fail; in fact he went to run Millgate Furniture at one stage to try and make his workload a little easier. The really sad thing is that he did not see our big move to the lovely new building we had talked about and envisaged, the ultimate goal towards which he had given so much. I cannot thank Derek enough for all his assistance and patience.

As soon as we were over Derek's death and had readjusted it was back to business as we tried to sort out the large amount of land with the hole in the middle that we had purchased. David Johnson, who ran the builder's yard sales at one time, came across a couple of brothers based in Chadderton who were in the ground work business. Mike Winterburn and his brother quoted for a solution to the problem by proposing to lay a ten foot diameter Armco metal pipe culvert with a ventilation inspection shaft which would contain the brook. They did a good job although due to the access difficulty it cost us considerably. Incredibly I met Mike later in life in Antigua of all places. Viv and I were sailing with our friends, Anne and Stuart Carter, on their yacht *Orlanda* (1) when we ran into Mike who was then skippering a fabulous, massive yacht for a very wealthy German businessman. Turns out that Mike was Ocean Club Master material and a member of the Ocean Youth Club although I was completely unaware of this whilst I was working with him; it really is a small world sometimes. Back to Hollinwood and with the culvert finished we required someone to deal with the land fill of the valley and this job was eventually given to Reddish Demolition who levelled the site and handed it over to us for the next stage which was to plan our new building. For this task we needed to engage the services of an architect and I was determined we would have only the best as at that time the plastic shed era was moving fast with the likes of B & Q, Tesco, and Asda. In contrast we wanted to have a brick building of showpiece standard that, combined with great design features and a traditional feel, would send out the message that 'quality' was our watchword. I arranged to interview nine architects who would be thoroughly put through their paces. As well as looking at what was down on paper I was also looking hard for a guy I could bounce my design ideas off. Eventually the candidates were whittled down from nine to two; one was an architect from a good practice who at that time was designing cinema complexes and was in the process of erecting one in Bury; the other was a local practice in Royton called John Gaytten Associates. John Gaytten put forward a good presentation and he also seemed to fit the bill as a guy with whom I could get along with. On a second interview I told him what a long journey it had been to get to this point and explained how it was vital that I work with someone who could interpret my dreams. I remember him looking right at me with his honest blue eyes and saying: 'I will not let you down.' Later that evening as I shared a bottle of wine with Vivienne at home I told her who I had chosen but was wondering if I had made the correct choice as the other guy was also good. I need not have doubted; John went on to do a super job and we worked well together. On our final meeting before the commencement of the project, Phase One as we called it, Tim and Harry came along to meet John's team along with the Quantity surveyor, Bill Roadhouse who was a key player, and the mechanical and electrical designers. The fees for this extended team were higher than if we had just had a design and build project but their presence meant that the quality of the work was not compromised. It would be down to John Gaytten and these guys to produce the magic – and without doubt they certainly did.

When all the preparatory work was satisfactorily completed we were ready for the ultimate challenge – submitting our plans to Oldham council. We proposed to build the best retail complex possible with plenty of car parking and every other facility. The finished store would probably be one of the finest buildings in the area, offering much needed work and utilising old, tired land; surely the planning department would not refuse permission. But they did. I wasn't greatly surprised to be turned down by this shambolic authority (2); after all we had never received much in the way of help from them. Even with our fantastic plans, the promise of more jobs, and the knowledge that our base at Hollinwood was under threat by the motorway they refused us but we were undaunted and immediately appealed. Everything hung on this. Why on earth were they hell bent on stopping us? Their main reason for objecting was simply that they wanted to keep the retailing in Oldham centre, which is understandable, but history had shown us that the council could not be relied on to give good advice and the lack of town centre parking was a great mistake in my view. On the day of the appeal hearing we attended the appointed venue ready to fight our case only to find that Oldham council had lost or misfiled the documents with the result that the appeal was automatically granted in our favour. The incompetence of Oldham Metropolitan Borough Council was nothing new but I still ask myself if it was fate that gave us the helping hand; had the planning department presented their case properly on that day their objection to our plans could have been closely contested and HU may have been denied the opportunity of expanding. It is so hard to explain how difficult all our dealings with the council were over the years and to describe their inadequacy, including the fact that they once again got it wrong: our land on Manchester Road still remains unused not having been required for the motorway after all! So, by some fluke, we had our planning permission and could now finalise the plans and put the team in place; it was all systems go. John Gaytten and I worked up the building design in detail and put out the job to tender with five or six builders. George Dews of Oldham quoted but just missed the job which went to Jarvis, the same company that were to build Phase Two four years later.

Everything was ready and work was about to start so, in order to celebrate, the design and building management teams met for bubbly one evening in the ex Beards, now Housing Units builder's merchants store, before setting off to an Italian restaurant in Oldham. It was a great night with some serious drinking and bonding although it has to be said that we did get carried away. At one point 'someone' holding a large tray of Italian trifle decided to mimic Manuel of Fawlty Towers fame resulting in several people getting dessert whether they wanted it or not! But that night out got things off to a good start and we met socially on quite a few other occasions during the contract. It's good to combine friends and fun and our socialising must have paid off as Phase One went absolutely according to plan. There were no extra charges incurred and Jarvis the builders, under the foreman Dave together with his number two Richard, a giant of a fella, did a great job. I was particularly indebted to the architect, John Gaytten who delivered as he said he would. At the monthly site meetings he was always positive and kept the job up to speed; he was on the same wavelength as the builders and myself which was great because not all architects are and then there can be problems. A few years later, after working with me on Housing Units Phase Two, John retired to go and live in Ledbury with his wife, Liz. Sadly some seven years later, in November 2002 he passed away. Bill Roadhouse, the Quantity surveyor, and I drove down to Ledbury to attend a wonderful thanksgiving service at St Michael's church which was very well attended and many people gave tribute to this colourful, charismatic character. One little tribute, read by John's granddaughter, Sophie, went like this:

Where do people go when they die?
Somewhere down below or in the sky?
'I can't be sure,' said Granddad, 'but it seems
They simply set up home inside our dreams.'

Whatever happens to Housing Units in the future it should not be forgotten that it is all down to the initial concept of what was put together using John Gaytten's understanding and design. I will always be grateful to him and the team.

Maybe catch up with you one day John.

Two Johns at The Olive Branch doing the other thing we were good at
as well as putting up buildings

1.

2.

3.

4.

5.

6.

7.

1. Housing Units new home

2. Building work commences – in the far left of the photograph you can see the ex Beards premises

3. Taking shape

4. Signs go up – note matching van!

5. The clock tower shows the date 1947 – the date Dad started Housing Units

6. And 7 Getting there, note the lovely lighting columns

1.

4.

3.

5.

1. Millgate finished – a gamble that really paid off

2. The winning room set – note the fireplace, beams, cottage suite and reproduction furniture – this was used for the TV ad.

3. Princess Alexandra opens the Manchester Ideal Home Exhibition – Louanne is waiting to make a small presentation whilst the suits of armour stand at the ready!

4. On with building Phase Two. From front: Tim, me, Louanne, Geoff and Harry

5. John and Paula Wallace over from Tenessee to open Phase Two. Canon Stuart Driver is to my left. Note the commemoration plaque which is now to the left of the entrance to the Fireplace Emporium

6. Autumn Leaves race – team H. U. and our bespoke replica van

7. Job done – Phase One building complete. Great design and lovely lighting standards – not a plastic shed!

6.

7.

A Few Facts

First and foremost I arrived at Housing Units as a builder – not a retailer. It was that knowledge that allowed the original shop on Manchester Road to be developed.

Millgate was brought back to life having been empty for a long time with a terrible leaking roof. Similarly Beard's Paint on Wickentree Lane was rescued – it would simply have been demolished today, an affordable and automatic process.

The formula always was:

1. Purchase property – never rent or lease.
2. Convert quickly and economically
3. Generate maximum income
4. Good housekeeping, good staff, good rewards
5. Trade; save; invest; spend: no debt

We did not kid ourselves and it was the ongoing, endless belief and investment in the three sites that gave us the finance and spring board to pass on our dreams and vision to John Gaytten the architect who created what is on that site today.

Keeping the Show on the Road: Notes

(1) Anne and Stuart Carter still own the fabulous yacht named *Orlanda* and Viv and I once joined them for a sailing holiday in the Caribbean. Following that I would also join Stuart on boy's only trips such as sailing round Gibraltar to Sardinia. As well as being an excellent skipper he is also an excellent engineer and if you are down at the Lowry complex in Salford note the lifting bridge and the wheel that turns it on the canal. It was made at Stuart's engineering business in Cleveleys. Stuart and Anne are both semi retired now and disappear for six months every year to take *Orlanda* to new cruising grounds, seeing and experiencing things that we may never have the opportunity to.

(2) It wasn't all bad at Oldham Council so it is only fair to mention the popular one time Head of Planning and friend, Les Coop, who was excellent at his job whilst the system got in his way.

1.

2.

3.

4.

5.

6.

7.

8.

9.

1. Great cruising on Stuart and Anne Carter's yacht Orlanda
2. The crew celebrate in the Harbour Club, Antigua. Left to right: Stuart, Anne, Uncle Arthur, David, June, Viv and me
3. We berth next to the Astrid who, at that stage of her life, was being used by the 'Youth Ocean Sailing' organisation. The bearded Brian Blessed lookalike gives us a tour
4. Then we party with them 'til late
5. Orlanda alongside Astrid – our skipper – 'Pugwash'!
6. Lunch on shore. Stuart and I decided to swim back to the boat – I had forgotten that my wallet was in the back pocket of my swimming shorts. Luckily Viv spotted it floating as she made her way back to the boat in the dinghy
7. Money laundering?
8. A few years later – lad's only trip from Gibraltar to Greece
9. I have to leave them at Sardinia – pressing matters back home

Millennium Handover

It would never be the right thing to do, but the most practical for the future

Close of business on Saturday the 14th September, 1991, was the final chapter of the story of Housing Units at Manchester Road, Hollinwood where we had traded for over forty four years. Similarly our sister site, Millgate Furniture on Hollins Road, which had previously been the old Sunday school, was also closing its doors after twenty one years. But it wasn't the end, oh no, rather it was a new beginning as we were moving to our new, larger site at Wickentree Lane, just a short way from the existing stores. Phase One, as we called it, consisted of a brand new building which would house everything that had previously been contained in the two stores resulting in Housing Units in its entirety existing on one site. The existing DIY and Fireplace showroom in the ex Beard's factory would continue to trade next door and in fact this part of the business was then managed by Tim. (1) There was also plenty of land left over for extensive car parking which I had learned was an invaluable asset whilst travelling around the more advanced USA in the late 1950's and I am thankful that we hadn't listened to Councillor Crowther and his ill advised colleagues when they wanted us to move to Oldham town centre where parking is at a premium; we would definitely have been on a kamikaze course to failure had we complied. So, complete with plenty of car parking, Phase One was eventually finished and ready to receive all the existing Housing Units stock as well as the launch of some new lines.

At the time my daughter, Louanne (2), was managing the Millgate business and, together with Jeff Hughes, the manager of Housing Units, and Harry who handled the office, they planned and executed the move. I remember quietly walking around both redundant sites on that last afternoon in late summer and, between bouts of selling, had a last look at my life's work so far. In many ways it was very sad; both sites were emanating retail excitement as I reviewed and recognised every inch of development carefully put into place over the years. It was a pity to let it go. However, to cheer me up, I only had to look at the new building which was just waiting to come alive. It was stunning and reflected real quality with its open car parks and the wonderful traditional outdoor lighting we had gone to so much trouble to have made. In another five short days, Friday 20th September, this brand new store would open in readiness for the busy Saturday traffic. The whole experience of the new site had been a journey; it was at times like climbing Mount Everest whilst being oxygenated by customer comments from the past such as: 'our house is full of Housing Units stuff,' and 'we love to shop here.' Right then, 'let's see what they make of this as they drive in through the gates to the new site,' after all everything we did was aimed at improving customer experience.

On the Sunday morning after closing our doors to the public for the last time at Millgate and Manchester Road there was a real Dunkirk spirit to be found in Hollinwood and it was all hands on deck for the transfer of stock from old buildings to new. We rounded up as many vehicles as we could muster and Anne, from the lighting department, commandeered her husband, who worked in haulage, to bring the largest pantechnicon imaginable. It was so massive that it was a route march just to walk the length of it! Everyone rolled up their sleeves and worked hard, even burning the midnight oil on occasions and by some miracle we were ready in time for the following Friday's opening of the stunning new building at Wickentree Lane, due entirely to the efforts of all the staff for which I thank them. Selling commenced and the only real interruption was a couple of weeks later when a fire alarm went off in the middle of a Saturday afternoon rush resulting in the Fire Brigade turning out. Apparently there was a fault on the system due to a wiring error but it had necessitated the evacuation of the whole store whilst the firemen, suitably attired, took twenty minutes to check through the whole building. We joked about it afterwards suggesting that maybe it was the heat generated by the large amount of customers piling in that had instigated the alarm, but in reality it was most frustrating having to close the store at peak trading time and watch as our customers got in their cars to leave. Nevertheless things continued to go well over the next couple of years and turnover accelerated, so much so that it wasn't long before I sat down again with our architect, John Gaytten, as he got out his pencil to pave the way for Phase Two.

This second phase would see the building of another new store which would allow Tim's operation to move out of the converted paint factory. By this time we had decided to discontinue the builder's merchants and DIY goods as we did not choose to compete with the rapidly expanding B & Q. Actually this was rather a sad decision to make as it was thanks to those goods that HU had really taken off in the beginning and I was sorry to let it go although the decision turned out to be the correct one. Instead we added other departments alongside the fireplaces which created a wonderful mixture as we sourced occasional and conservatory furniture from around the world together with mirrors, gifts, pictures and rugs. The premises Tim had vacated would in turn be demolished and much needed warehousing would be erected there. In 1994 we made the move into the second, quality designed building as well as getting our new warehousing up and running. Rather like Frank Bruno, we had been ducking and diving our way around the Hollinwood area for years but finally everything was together in one place. We had a grand opening service in the newly built warehouse which was conducted by a friend, the Canon Stuart Driver, whilst the Dobcross Brass Band added good music to the occasion in the best northern style. Trading progressed well and on Saturday's the two stores were overflowing as was the traffic outside. We had defied the plastic shed era and instead erected a retail experience that would stand the test of time and would soon employ over two hundred staff. 'Quality' was our message and this was reflected in our lovely buildings, the excellence of the stock, our replica Asquith delivery van and, of course, the installation of the famous Housing Units doorman. Also in our favour was the imminent opening of the motorway link at Hollinwood which would bring many more customers from the north and south of Manchester. Business was booming; a thankful tribute to good staff, customer support, luck, and something called the pyramid.

I came across the pyramid via a friend that I made quite by accident. In the mid 1960's I visited a house in Bamford, Rochdale, to give a Flymo demonstration as we were agents for the company at the time. The demo was scheduled for the evening after the shop was shut and the customer

1960s – the show is on the road

and

Housing Units
NEW
Home Furnishing Store

The Store of the Year!
Over an acre of shopping on a five acre site.

THERE'S NO PLACE LIKE IT!
WICKENTREE LANE, FAILSWORTH. TEL: 061 681 5678

We get there in 1991 with Phase One followed in 1994 by Phase Two with a large free car park for over three hundred cars.

And so the great story goes on – a huge distribution warehouse together with an administration building have been added and the warehouses have been converted into 'The Crescent' retail units – all this after my retirement. Housing Units is still professionally operated with first class marketing as the story of one of the UK's top shopping experiences continues.

was a Scotsman with the broadest of accents called John Nesbitt. It turned out that John was the manager of Scottish Widows Manchester Branch as well as being chairman, or president, of Sale Rugby Club. We hit it off really well and at a later date HU would set up some insurance business with John's company. We would often discuss the future strategy of Housing Units until late into the night at John's house fuelled by tea and sandwiches served to us by his wife, Joyce. These visits were very much appreciated by me as John was a good sounding block and a good friend. It was he who emphasised the pyramid principal, a management theory which was based on example and leadership from the top, down through the different levels of management to the team at the base of the structure. Success meant having all the blocks in place and working hard to avoid weakness or failure at any level as every tier relies on those above and below and each one must be productive and stable. It isn't rocket science, but in those earlier days businesses were noticeably vulnerable to anything less than good management and the number one enemy was debt for at that time interest rates were an astronomical 13-17%. Fortunately we owned everything outright, buildings, land and stock; we had money in the bank and had never needed credit, a practice that I had always avoided. Also as we had cash on deposit we actually benefited from the high interest rates instead of going under as many companies did. We had good staff and introduced performance related pay to ensure everyone's involvement; things were going well and we were well equipped to face the future.

In the 1990's the world was rapidly changing as technology and the use of credit cards by our customers began to move at a pace. The computer age was about to alter traditional habits in business and buying was now a global concern with aeroplanes offering a virtual bus service to anywhere in the world. China was developing at speed and building factories quicker than we were building houses; the Far East and Asian markets would dominate quickly. Buyers were flocking out there purchasing innovative, well made products and fuelling the growing trade in shipping container traffic which meant that businesses could order in huge quantities from the other side of the world and receive the goods within six to eight weeks. World technology and manufacturing was really ramping up and Housing Units needed to get on track. In the early 1990's we researched the talents of various computer companies eventually selecting one who assured us they could handle our, not uncomplicated, requirements. Unfortunately they failed to deliver and this resulted in a difficult and expensive court case which Harry, Tim and several of the staff took on in tandem. They eventually won the case but it was a time consuming first entry into technology. The next computer company we hired were successful, thankfully, and steadily things fell into place. The endless stock sheets became a thing of the past and Housing Units IT system was now professionally operated by the new Director of Computer Systems, Neil Anderson. The pace over the years had never slackened and in fact seemed to have speeded up even more but suddenly it seemed time to step back and take stock.

I am sure many of us have at some time reached a crossroads in our lives or had to face a life changing event where it is necessary to pause and reflect before continuing on the conveyor belt. A John le Carre quotation comes to mind: 'A desk is a dangerous place from which to watch the world,' and, whilst it had not been my favourite location for over forty years, a certain amount of dedication to that item of furniture had indeed taken place. For some the desk may symbolise a commitment for life whilst for others it is good to look out of the window and think about other things that could be passing us by. By now I was sixty seven, well topside of Dad's departure at the young age of fifty two. I found that this fact was increasingly on my mind and whilst I had always refrained from smoking, as this was Dad's downfall, I was maybe not quite as sharp as once upon a time although in general I felt OK. In some respects it seemed that my real journey was over having moved HU to her permanent base after being scattered around various locations; yes from that point of view there was a feeling of mission accomplished so where do we go from here I wondered? I reflected on being dumped outside the Carrefour Supermarket in France in the mid 1970's and being mind blown by the space and the huge car parks. Also previously, in 1957 I had visited the shopping centres in the USA and Canada which were a great contrast to what we had at home. Stunning lighting and décor, a place to sit and have coffee or eat, comfort and warmth, retail was promoted as a leisure experience in those places and the seed to 'one stop shopping' had been planted although I hadn't known it at the time. Now such an experience had been brought to fruition here in Hollinwood.

Whilst always thriving on the excitement and challenge of moving the business forward I suddenly began to feel tired and, although this later turned out to be a thyroid problem which is now fortunately under control, I was also aware that I was not pumping out the Vincent Peale stuff, positive thinking, quite as well as I had in the past. I felt I had run out of steam. Also at this time Louanne had left her managerial post in the Furniture Department to have her first child, Eleanor, so I was fulfilling her role as well as my own as it was the high ticket furniture items that were creating the main growth at that time. True I was not a computer buff; nor at my age was I over excited about adding to my forty years of buying experience by jumping on planes to fly round the world as buying was by now very much a global business. My thoughts turned to the staff and it was true that everyone had ensured success through good teamwork. Indeed many of them, particularly the girls, were excellent multi-taskers, a skill for which I was very much appreciative. We had ridden the waves well so far but I sensed some tricky water lay ahead. I pondered the situation in relation to both myself and the business. Regarding the business, Tim was settling in well in the Phase 2 building but due to the speed of events over the years I had not worked closely with him on the broader front of the overall business. I blame myself for that, yes I was wrong there. There's a saying in the north: 'look after the man who looks after the brass,' and true to that I had gifted shares to Derek Delhide when he was running the office side of things and had done the same for Harry in appreciation for the support he was giving to HU. By now Harry had worked with me for twenty years during which time we had liaised well together, made decisions, controlled the funds and generally got things done. Some time previously he had asked me if he could bring Nick, his eldest son, into the business which I agreed to. A couple of years later he expressed a desire to work alongside him and one can read into that as they wish but indirectly the water was being tested here bearing in mind my age, and, should we say, opportunism? Thinking back I remembered the tumultuous time at APAS caused by Dad's untimely death for which little provision or planning had been put in place. As a result of this lack of planning Mum and I had suffered considerable difficulty in sorting out his business affairs and it took two to three years to fully settle. Also I had to consider the question of Tim and Harry having to work together if I popped my clogs. Would it work? Above all I began to wonder if I had the appetite for it any more as I felt I was underperforming. We talked things over at home, particularly with Tim, on the way forward but meanwhile, now the site was well established, we would have it valued.

After lengthy consideration and talks it seemed I had three options: 1) settle on the shares which I had given to Harry as he had indicated that he wanted to go his own way which was understandable with two sons in the wings; 2) press on and work closely with Tim, getting him involved in the whole business rather than the specialised and allied departments he was familiar with. This option would mean postponing any thought of retirement for the foreseeable future; 3) negotiate with Harry to achieve a workable agreement for him to take the shop on. He had a good overall knowledge of the business having been my right hand man for many years and so he was in position at the right time to be able to move things on with staff numbers now edging well over two hundred. This plan was not without its problems for either of us but it was a lifetime opportunity and he would be able to maintain staff continuity which was very important to me as well as anchoring the ongoing investment that must never stop. I then had to think about benefits and opportunities for my family. Selling Housing Units would offer security for everyone and allow me to ease off and no longer have to worry knowing that the HU story would continue smoothly. This option would also give Tim the chance to do his own thing in his own way, not overshadowed, able to face his own challenges as indeed I had done. After a really hard time spent soul searching, asking questions of myself, and considering everything, the third option seemed to be the solution although it would involve a squad of expensive legal people, valuers, and accountants. This decision heralded an unsettling time for all concerned and I would not choose to face such trials again.

In the early summer of 1999 Viv and I were due to take a week's oper holiday based at Lake Garda in Italy, a break that had been booked man months previously. Although we were very unsettled and the sale was at th due diligence stage which is near the finishing post, we still made the tri whilst back home the negotiations continued. I had never been to an ope in my life but here we were at the spiritual home of great operat experience ready to listen to the outdoor performances spread over tl week. The productions were atmospherically charged and stunning as 1 sat in the warmth of the gentle *pianura Lombarda* which surrounds Veroi But there was a big problem. I was seriously unsettled; so much v running through my head I was finding it really difficult to sleep a resorted to pills for the first time ever. Previously if things were on i mind and stopping me nodding off I would get up, write down i

So Viv and I are thankful of 50 years.
Lots of talking amidst a few tears.
Tryfan Mountain in Wales where our engagem
was made on firm rock.
Sometimes I guess that has helped to stand
up to life's shocks.

Now the trick is this, our friends take note.
Follow this advice, and you will not get too remo
Take a mid-week tipple on a Wednesday night
Give up when the bottom of the bottle is in sight.
Repeat the same at weekend too.
This way you will see most troubles through.

John & Viv.

thoughts, go back to bed and fall asleep immediately. But not now. I had a lifetime's work on my mind; what in God's name was I doing sitting around listening to opera? I could not get out of my mind the fact that after forty years I was considering any alternative other than cracking on. What my Grandfather and then his sons had carried on I was now in the process of selling after all that bloody hard work. It is a well established fact that it is the third generation that will sell or move out of the family business .... flashbacks in my mind.........after my father's death I parted company with Arthur, his brother, and I had carried on my side of the inheritance successfully whereas Arthur eventually handed APAS to his two sons with a reduced staff and before long that side of the business sadly folded. The fact was I was well out of order to even consider selling the business. We returned home where all the paperwork was continuing and there was a sense of being in a no mans land, things were on hold; it was rather like watching a clock ticking away whilst everyone involved holds their breath until the final hour. Things were so near the edge but a change of mind was very possible.

Prior to signing the final documents in August 1999 we went down to Dartmouth to try and get some respite. Tim had popped down to visit for the weekend but returned home late Sunday. On the Tuesday evening there was a knock at the door and there stood Tim. He had driven back three hundred miles and before he uttered his message I knew what he was about to say: 'Dad, I don't think we should go ahead with the deal.' We returned to Oldham the next day. This must have been a difficult time for Harry, he knew I had problems with my decision as we had chatted things through and I was causing further uncertainty whilst I had put myself on an emotional roller coaster. Mishandle a life changing situation or take a wrong turning and it will stay on your mind until the end. I considered the many mistakes I had made throughout life and revisited the fatalities that had happened to people entrusted to my care. I was really questioning myself and my actions whilst quietly trying to come to terms with it all. If there is anyone reading this book that has not had to reflect on a past decision whilst thinking that given another chance you would handle it differently I would be very surprised. Like you I made a choice for the right reasons whilst they were not 'my' reasons and another saying springs to mind: 'if in doubt do nowt.' On the final August morning Viv, Tim, Louanne and I parked up in the miserable, dimly lit basement of a towering glass office block in Manchester where I would sign on the dotted line. As the lift door opened to take us upstairs I wavered for a moment, feeling in unison with our dismal surroundings and as we exited into the bright lights and wealth of plush offices and suited people, there were plenty of legals and paper wavers bringing loads of documents to be signed so they could submit their accounts promptly. I felt I had placed myself in a 'Dragons Den' as a simmering anticipation of people surrounded me; however I had started this so would see it through. That was truly a life changing day and it certainly wasn't a happy one although I had no one to blame but myself. Thus I would hand over to a guy who, to use his own words, had a passion for the job, a quality that would be proved in the future years.

In 2007 Housing Units celebrated their 60 year anniversary although it has to be said that the founder's name was not mentioned for some reason. However, continuing the tradition of creation and vision, it is good to see Harry, his sons, and the excellent staff at HU making splendid progress and winning top UK store awards for fireplaces, houseware and gifts. It does not come better than that– well done. Yes, the business has come a long way from the tiny builder's merchants, the old Sunday School, and Beards Paint Factory and for that I must thank my dad and his building company, APAS, for the foresight in establishing HU in 1947. Oh and something called a 'Building Apprenticeship' as I was after all a builder by trade and only a retailer by accident.

Millennium Handover: Notes

(1) Tim is a chip off the old block and lives life right at the edge of time just like me and his Grandfather, Lewis Pellowe, who unfortunately he never met. Whilst some of our approaches to business differ, Tim is a super guy with a big heart. After attending Grammar and Boarding School he applied to join the Marines and was accepted but I foolishly talked him out of it as I considered signing up for five years to be a bit too long. Instead he enrolled on a Business Studies Course in Stoke where he discovered, amongst other things, lager! Following that debacle he went over to America for work experience. Using contacts I had made in the trade Tim was made welcome wherever he went and often stayed at the store manager's home. After he had completed one or two postings I contacted John Wallace of Wallace Hardware Company which was a large company operating state wide from its base in Morristown, Tennessee. I talked to John on the phone and thought he was a sound guy; he told me to send Tim along when he had finished at his present work placement. 'We'll shape him up', was his comment as he offered a two week posting which actually turned out to be the best part of a year. At one time Tim was working at 'Henry Surates' down town store which proved to be a revelation in retailing. Hill Billy's wandered in, picked something up, waved it at Henry and said: 'just book it up Henry,' and they were gone! No cash ever seemed to change hands and needless to say this is one practice we have never encouraged at Housing Units. John also set Tim up with a car and sent him off to hardware conventions around the USA. John Wallace had a great sense of humour and on a couple of occasion he would get the local police to pull Tim over whilst he was driving – one night he even arranged for Tim to be put in a cell! Towards the end of his time abroad Tim hitch hiked up through America and into Canada – following in my footsteps – and although he didn't get to South Africa he did travel around Europe and North Africa which was where we found him when, with an uncanny coincidence, he was recalled home. His maternal Grandfather had died.

Kindness and Christianity knew no boundaries in John and Paula Wallace; they lived deep in the bible belt of America and were very religious. Following Tim's visit Viv and I were invited over to stay so we combined the invite with a berth on the QE2 which was to be our first cruise ship experience. We really enjoyed ourselves and looked forward to returning home on her a couple of weeks later. John put us up at his hotel, part of The Ramada chain, which was situated next to his house in Morristown. No alcohol was served there, it was iced tea and cake that was the order of the day, but we were treated like royalty. Every day a different member of John's senior staff would take us somewhere as well as showing me round the retailing side of his businesses. On Sunday's the whole day was spent in church followed by a special treat of ice cream and sodas after the evening service. All too soon it was time for us to leave and make our leisurely way back to Boston where we would pick up the QE2 again. John produced a Lincoln, the American Rolls Royce equivalent, for us to make the trip in. It was an automatic and it was also computerised; the headlights operated themselves and it was like driving on a cloud. 'When you've finished with the car just leave the keys at your hotel and my man will come along to pick them up,' John Wallace casually said! We arrived in Boston one day before we were due to sail and went to look at the QE2 as she floated easily in her berth. The next day we hired a taxi to take us to the pier for our departure but we were delayed by a road accident in which a helicopter landed on the road to collect injured people. We lost a lot of time and when we finally got to the pier head the ship was not there. I looked at Viv who was totally shocked and as I turned to the taxi driver he started to cry! We checked the tickets to make sure we had the correct date and that she hadn't sailed the day before but no, the dates were correct and she wasn't due to sail for another few hours so our delay hadn't caused us to miss her. Well the QE2 was rather a big boat to lose and it occurred to me that she may have been moved for some reason so I went to enquire at the nearby warehouses. I asked several men but no one could help me. I was absolutely astonished that no one seemed to know where this gigantic ship had gone. How would I tell Viv? As I dejectedly made my way back to the vacant berth a dock worker caught up with me. Having seen my predicament he asked if I was looking for the QE2. 'Sir, she's three or four down East End, they moved her yesterday.' I felt like hugging him. Viv and I often laugh about it – such a huge thing to move!

In return for the generous hospitality the Wallace's had shown, particularly to Tim, we invited them over to the UK on two occasions and tried to reciprocate. In fact they were in attendance at the opening of Phase Two at Housing Units where a commemorative plaque in their honour was unveiled which can still be seen near the main doorway. John Wallace sadly passed on a few years ago.

(2) A question that often crops up is 'where did the name Louanne derive from?' When we got engaged Viv decided to put in some serious pre mother in law time in order to cement her relationship with Mum in case I took off again. On one occasion we took Mum and Ethel, Kelvin's mum, down to the Praa Sands Hotel in Cornwall for a couple of weeks and it was there that we met a Canadian couple who had a daughter called Louanne so we banked the name just in case; you're something of a Canadian export Lou! For the second week of the holiday Viv and I slipped away to Dartmouth as one weeks

bonding was deemed to be enough – little did we know that Mum's company would last for another forty years; something Viv in her flush of youth had probably not anticipated!

Louanne was rather 'talked into' getting involved with the furniture at HU. After boarding school she went on to do a secretarial course followed by some secretarial temping before joining Neilson's Travel as a ski resort manager for a couple of years. Lou and I had done a trip or two in the Dellow when she was very young and spent some time rattling round the Brittany coast where she got a taste for the French language which she appears to speak fluently when I listen to her! As a result of this interest in all things *Francais* at one time she went to work as an *au pair* for the family of a Parisian doctor which also allowed her to attend the Sorbonne. However the family treated her rather badly giving her a room stuffed up in the attic space whilst the whole house was dark and depressing. She was expected to visit the Doctor's grandmother in hospital *every day* and in short her time there was not very uplifting. Viv and I popped over to see her at one point and realised that she was living a Dickensian life in this mausoleum and so her stay was cut short. Following that experience Louanne went on to complete an interior design course at the Inchbald College in London and later, following some persuasion, she came to work in the Millgate Furniture Centre. After learning her trade there she eventually took over as manager and we did the furniture buying for the business together. She is infectious and popular; so much so that doing the buying rounds at the shows with her took three times as long as normal. She is organised and efficient, sometimes actually *ultra* efficient. She soon sorted out the overstocked warehouse at Millgate and put in place a good system for the office which improved customer after sales service. The difference of a woman doing the job to a man! She is a great girl. Outgoing with lots of friends, she has grit and spirit.

One of my very best holidays was when we did the coast to coast together, Louanne navigating. Another occasion, when she was younger, saw us motoring through France in the Dellow which I had found and bought back after many years apart. As we were heading for the return ferry we pulled into a village market which was full of really fresh vegetables, superb patisserie, pate's and cheeses and as we looked round we noticed some small ducklings. On impulse we bought four of them who were put carefully into a cardboard box and stowed in the tight confines behind the seat of the Dellow. As we approached England on the ferry I remembered about customs regulations and wasn't sure how we stood so we decided not to mention anything and I told Lou to sing loudly if the ducklings started to make a noise. As it was we sailed through and were soon on the road again. Some distance from the ferry terminal we stopped at a farm for tea and we let our new pets out for some exercise. The farmer noticed them and when we told him we had bought them at a French market he seemed concerned and disappeared for some time before returning looking very authoritative. He told us that he had phoned the customs but was able to inform us ducks could be imported freely in contrast to other livestock. Of course I was apologetic and told him how I was ignorant of such things and waffled on but it was a near do. Those little ducklings went on to have a happy life at Copster House where they grew to be huge and fertilised the whole garden for free as they mingled with the hens and the ever breeding rabbits that we had.

Taking Stock

Laziness is nothing more than the habit of resting before you get tired -
Jules Renard

The terms set up for the handover of Housing Units would be spread over four years during which time I would tick along as Chairman although with hindsight maybe this was a mistake. If you pass over the rudder perhaps it is best to get off the bridge but it was a time of readjustment and if it made the passage smoother so be it. Cash flow continued to be good for Housing Units which allowed them to complete the sale in a little over two years rather than the four years we had originally set up. Harry, as Managing Director, together with his two lads, Nick and Stuart would extend the management team whilst being quite capable of taking HU on the rest of her journey. Without reflecting on matters too much the change proved to be as difficult as I had anticipated. I really missed the interaction with the staff and customers as well as the buzz and adrenaline rush that comes with making things happen. Yes I had created a void for myself although I kept busy by serving on several committees although I was not really a committee type of person. One of these was The Prince of Wales Trust who mentor youths who have been awarded start up loans to set them up in business. The Trust does good work although personally I would like to see more time being put into promoting apprenticeships as we need practical people in this country thus lessening the need to import tradesmen.

Although I kept myself busy and had many interests I became depressed. Depression was a foreign word to me. I had heard about it but never taken much notice being the unsympathetic b****r I am. But no one is immune as I was about to find out. You can take pills, see a shrink, sing your way out of it, train till you drop, but eventually one day you just have to have a talk with yourself and re-programme in the style of Ninette De Valois, one time Director of The Royal Ballet, who said: 'respect the past, herald the future but concentrate on the present.' Whilst I am no authority on ballet I found her words very meaningful so I sorted myself out and got on with things.

Tim stayed on to manage his side of the business at Housing Units but after a couple of years he left when he bought a small, quality picture framing business in Harrogate. It was a very hard learning curve as he travelled to and fro, often staying overnight but as he specialises in long hours (a chip off the old block) he could handle it. However, as he was to find out, manufacturing is a much harder business to run than anything in retailing! Eventually Tim bought the shell of a 20,000 square foot new factory in Dukinfield, Cheshire to where he eventually transferred the Harrogate production and whilst he was still dealing with things in Harrogate I helped to get the place fitted out for production which was a welcome project. Hence the company called Artko Ltd was formed at The Birches on Park Road alongside the River Tame. Tim had completed a hard deal for the purchase of the building and adjacent land with an Irish demolition contractor who turned out to be rather a tricky customer to deal with, but eventually the business was up and trading. Artko produce quality designed pictures for trade sales with prints constantly arriving from publishers all over the world. Mouldings and materials are sourced in the UK, Europe and the Far East whilst the Design Studio turns out two collections a year, the first in January at the Furniture Show, then for the Spring Fair followed by associated trade shows. Design is the key and this is ongoing with more of their own photographers and artists coming to the fore whilst Tim was also very fortunate in meeting Nigel Glassbarrow who formerly owned a top picture framing company called Manuscript; he has been a good mentor and they work well together on company policies. Production at Artko is exciting and stimulating and good agents throughout the UK and Ireland are supplying the trade and galleries as well as many of the larger stores such as John Lewis, DFS, Fenwick's and Housing Units. Staff total around forty and the business has recently seen an extension of 6,000 square feet added. I put my two penneth forward now and again whilst frequently our views may differ but Tim is moving the business successfully forward in these tough competitive times in his own way. What a change from his first career - well done son. Tim works alongside his partner, Susan who assists with the marketing and design at Artko. Together they have a son, a fine little chappie called Sam. Meeting him will not be a dull experience I can assure you; we may well have the future Peter Kay here!

Time heals and now life is settling into a routine although this is something I am rather suspicious about. God how the years fly: 'age shall not weary us,' but looking about I'm not so sure. However the positives now far outweigh any negatives and, as the lady says, 'concentrate on the present.' First and foremost right across the family we have good health, an appreciation for which cannot be expressed in mere words; a gift that allows us all to share the great benefits of being together – you cannot buy that. Louanne and her husband, Dennis, went on to complete their family and now have three children, Eleanor, Johnny Oscar and Roberta. Had Louanne returned to work full time at Housing Units after having her first two children the last one, Roberta, may not have happened and there is no way we could do without this highly organised little trooper! Louanne also got the opportunity to be a full time, hands on, Mum and the whole lot of them have a great family life which Viv and I are privileged to share. At home Vivienne sees more of me than she ever did before although I am not sure if this has enhanced our relationship! We are not day trip types nor do we go to the Garden Centre for afternoon tea but we share good times when we go to our house in Dartmouth where we can relax. Whilst at home in Greenfield we always seem to be busy and whilst Viv enjoys being at home I have a tendency towards itchy feet, there is so much to see and do. Like my father I need my own space; I am well past the three score years and ten and time must be running out! We are, however, pretty good at sharing a bottle of wine over an Italian meal at the end of the day; you do after fifty years of practise! In 2006 having been without a dog for a few years, we visited Harpurhey Dogs Home with our grandchildren and returned with a crossbreed bitch called Sally. For £60 we got the dog, already chipped and fully inoculated, a feeding bowl, collar and lead, identity disc and a bag of food. That purchase has turned out to be the best value ever; she is an absolute star; aged two or three when we got her she has a nose that will pick up prey when it is well up wind. She swims like a seal and walks to heel, no lead required; she is great with everyone she meets and has cheered our lives up considerably. According to Viv, Sally is more house trained than I am but I can live with that – she's probably right. Viv does the early morning walk as I am now most definitely a night owl just like my father, and later in the day Sally goes out with my neighbour and friend, Richard Holden who walks for hours with his prize Welsh Collie, Brig. Dedicated dog walker, historian and raconteur he keeps me entertained when I manage to accompany them – Hmmmm thought I was retired! Sally and Brig have to be some of the fittest dogs in Saddleworth as they regularly go for a six, eight or ten mile walk which, with all their detours and running around, must actually relate to about twenty or thirty miles for them per trip. Brig comes from Welsh Champion stock whilst Sally comes from God knows where! However both are no trouble at all and give to us as much, if not more, than we give them.

Vivienne, now in her mid seventies, still attends two aerobic classes every week which were initially run by my spirited cousin, Joyce Kelso, herself a super fit person who has made teaching aerobics a career over many years. Joyce has handed over to her daugther Josie and Viv has now moved to the back row and may be the oldest swinger in class whilst still working to the beat but there is no mention of easing off. It's an important part of Viv's weekly routine and my money is on the fact that you will have an eighty year old in your class one day Josie! Quite a contrast to my mother's band of thirteen 'keep fitters' who were all great friends and whose training comprised of tea and supper every Thursday night! If any keep fit ever came into it they retired from it well before the age of thirty five is my guess! In those days the concept of old age was quite different to that of today, people took life more easily but it certainly did Mum no harm, this lack of exercise, as she lived to be ninety nine! Meanwhile Viv and I try to work at keeping young and fit as we apply oils and lotions to our shifting bodies. Whilst I push Viv out for the early morning walk with Sally I do a sharp fifteen minute bathroom work out followed by a hot then cold shower avoiding soap. I owe a debt of gratitude to the YMCA having been a member for sixty years and applying the 'no gain without pain' theory via circuit class there: weights, swim, steam room. After the work out it is the best feeling in the world (well almost) and I am so thankful to still be able to partake. Also I am not the only aged person at the Manchester Y for there you will find the fittest bunch of mid sixties to late seventies men in Manchester. The Y has one of the best gyms with great facilities and ongoing classes through the day and evening. Call in sometime and ask to be shown around.

1.

2.

3.

4.

5.

1. The morning of my sixty fourth birthday I was awakened by the Dobcross Band playing When I'm Sixty Four. Thanks Harry

2. Richard and I on a stone wall building course – he can now add this to his other attributes – historian, dog walker etc!

3. I built a studio onto Dyehouse Cottage… one day… you never know… buy now!

4. John McCombs holds evening painting sessions during the summer – many a good painter started out with his classes

5. Staithes Gallery run by Al Milnes holds very good three day residential painting classes. Here we are painting with David Allan – pastels this time

Weekend walks with Richard, Brig and Sally round off the weeks that now fly by and I am appreciative and thankful both Viv and I are still on track. There have been highs and lows, mistakes and repairs, sadness and sunshine, but it is rather a long time and we appreciate much amidst some regrets along the way. In December 2010 we celebrated fifty years together which is around 18,000 days! I thought about buying a few gold shares for Viv to mark the occasion but realising she couldn't hang them round her neck my grandson, Johnny Oscar, and I toddled off to the jewellers and looked at the silver jewellery which I thought was more modern. However Johnny intervened and guided me to the gold counter where he subsequently helped with the purchase of a Pandora bracelet by chipping in a whole pound! Meanwhile any jewellery in the safe is just waiting for the return of an era for such clutter when Viv will burst back onto the social scene again all a glitter! Incidentally I heard recently that Tesco were about to sell gold – they never let up do they? Perhaps one day they will be the first supermarket to sell body parts so don't lose your points card which will really mount up if you live until the age of ninety.

Now we come to the million dollar question – would I do it all over again? Well with hindsight and some adjustments you betcha!

Magic Moments

Family Holidays

Throughout our married life holidays have been important and we never tried to compromise this essential break. When the children were small we would have two annual trips to Abersoch where we hired a great house above the beach called 'Pendorlan' which belonged to the local grocer, Mr Evans. Christine and Dennis Heywood and their two boys, John and Stephen, would join us there and we would all spend our time on the beach running, swimming and playing football; all the necessary beach tackle filling the hut that we hired. On one occasion we added to the collection with a Campari inflatable canvas boat which we were selling at the shop at the time. It was a substantial thing, unlike the plastic blow away ones of today, and Tim rowed it for miles whilst later I raced it against Bob Lees from the bottom to the top of Lake Windermere. We really tried to get good varied holidays and later we hired a caravan, hitched it to the back of my Reliant Scimitar and raced down to Cornwall where we had a fantastic time.

Nothing stops progress though and as the age of charter flights began to increase in the 1970's we decided to try a holiday in Tenerife. At the beginning of the fortnight the weather was overcast so we abandoned all thoughts of sunbathing and hired two scooters, Tim and I at the handlebars with Lou and Viv on the back. After about an hour our pillion riders pleaded for us to drop them at the hotel as they were cold and miserable so we did and then Tim and I scootered off to travel right round the island. We didn't arrive back until about 8 p.m. and Viv really tore into me for being so late as she had us written off by that time! A few days later we transferred to another hotel on the other side of the island in a resort called Los Americanos where it was sunny. What a surprise we had when we bumped into good friends of ours, Ruth and Peter Wild and their two lads, Stephen and Andrew; so with plenty of humorous company and lots of sun at last we all proceeded to enjoy the hotel's amenities one of which was a poolside buffet. It looked splendid and we all tucked in but unfortunately it caught Lou and me out and we suffered a severe bout of food poisoning ensuring that we returned home much lighter than when we set off!

Christmas

Of course holidays aren't always spent away from home and Christmas is one such time. In fact the only Christmas we ever spent away from home was when my cousin Michael died in the terrible accident in Llandudno. After my Dad died, Mum and I would spend the day with my mother's sister Joan and her extended family, and of course once Viv and I were married we would also visit Joan and Joe in their spacious house on Kensington Road. This Christmas venue would continue for years and years, the family expanding all the time; Joan and Joe's children, Bob, Anne and Joyce, grew up and married, Bob meeting a girl called Pat Moon one romantic evening whilst Anne added a little Russian aristocracy by marrying Michael Pesteroff, an accountant. Joyce made her move for John Kelso who later qualified as a doctor and is of course a benefit to us all. Viv and I added to the numbers even more when Tim arrived and we would wheel him in his Osnath pram to Kensington Road for the annual Christmas Party and as the snow outside fell heavily the hospitality within would flow. Much later, still laughing, we would wheel the little fella back home as he slept soundly in his pram on that crisp, cold, clear evening with a sky full of stars. The family numbers continued to grow as many other babies begin to arrive. Pat and Bob seem to be first past the post with Nicola followed by Richard and Alex, whilst from the Pesteroff camp emerge Roger and Mark. Joyce and John do a good job with Emma, Robert and Josie and of course we soon had our second child, Louanne. Consequently there was a lot of coming and going with carry cots and extended sleepovers but soon enough the kids were at an age where they could be left to perform a pantomime or a play whilst us parents slowly sipped the champagne cocktails. Also, as they grew in stature, the kids abandoned their separate table at the Christmas dinner and joined us in our black tie effort, taking their place at the top table at last. Many years later the Christmas venue moved to the home of Joyce and John, 'Parkhill' at Lydgate, another lovely spacious house with live fires roaring away in the rooms. Top of the table was still under the command of Joe but time as we all know takes its toll and all you are left with is a legacy of times gone by and memories and we lose him first. His place at the top of the table is then occupied by Joan until she goes to join Joe when it's Gran's (my mother's) turn. Miraculously Joyce and John continued to fit everyone into their home for many years as they carried on the tradition of passing round the bottles of wine whilst everyone gave their annual opinion as to how well the turkey was cooked. Some guests with large appetites would go for a second helping before the Christmas pudding is brought in, flaming with brandy, followed by the port decanter as it starts its journey around the left hand side of the table. Once everyone is full it's time for the banter, laughter, and singing as tongues loosen and some of us fall off our chairs in all the fun. Time moves on and things change and when the grandchildren of the Lees' and allied families continued to increase we could no longer all get round the table at 'Parkhill' and we had to split up for the festive dinner. Forty years of Christmas happiness will not be forgotten though and we have all been privileged and appreciative of such magical times.

Louanne's School Ball

Louanne was 'packed off' as they say, whilst with the best intentions, to Howells School in Wales where she soon seemed to settle to enjoy the experience. Some friends of ours, Shirley and Lees Firth, had a daughter called Claire who was already at the school so we would take it in turns to run the girls to and fro as holidays dictated. There is one particularly memorable visit to Howell's school that I still have to smile about. The occasion began quite normally with Viv and I booking into an hotel near the school in order to attend the end of term ball which, for many of the girls, would be their final one – something of a 'passing out' I suppose. Dressed in our finest we left the hotel together with Shirley and Lees and made our way to the school where there was a live band knocking out the 70's stuff. Everyone was very nicely turned out in black tie or ball gowns; amongst the youngsters were some imported boys from a suitable school nearby and we were really getting into the swing of things when, invited or otherwise, Tim, 'Chappie' Chapman and Bob Smith arrived to swell the young men's numbers. Three nice lads out for a bit of sport, where's the harm? It was after this evening that Bob became known as a bit of a Champagne Charlie for as well as sporting a white silk scarf he also had a full case of Champagne stowed in his car. As the night's festivities progressed the three lads managed to smuggle the champagne into the building and establish a hidden base from which to dispense free bubbly to the girls. They had every intention of spreading a little happiness and indeed that is what happened – for a while at least. It didn't take long for the bush telegraph to work and more and more girls made their clandestine way in the direction of the three most popular boys in the place. As Viv and I were innocently dancing we kept noticing girls disappearing behind the enormous black stage curtain whilst others, having already enjoyed Bob's hospitality, were moving out into the grounds to avoid teacher patrol. All was going well for the young folk until one teacher decided to pull the stage curtain back and then the balloon went up. Also it was about the same time that some of the girls decided to be sick and by midnight the whole thing came to an abrupt halt as many of them were also passing out or being shepherded back to their billets. Lou reported that the next day several of them were still in the sick bay and there was serious dialogue between teachers and casualties. The three musketeers had disappeared meanwhile, beating a hasty retreat north. I wonder if Howells have had a passing out to match that since!

Who Could This Be?

Road Closed sign – seems to hold a challenge for him to investigate, preferably with the Dellow to climb over any obstacle! This and other such 'deviations' lead to Vivienne continually breathing 'divorce' under her breath and she expects to get totally lost on every outing.

No Swimming – an immediate signal to take a dip usually in a reservoir, which often includes Sally, his dog, and her boyfriend, Brig.

Keep all Dogs on a Lead – this instruction often leads to Viv returning hurriedly to the car having witnessed an overdose of terrier dog sheep chases. Out in the hills his walking colleagues would place bets on his 'terrier recovery chases'. Sally, the current dog, really does not need a lead but no one believes it!

Traffic Signal Compliance – such a sign has led to the man in question having to attend two compulsory driving courses in order to avoid points on his licence. It is thought he must have added colour blindness to his dyslexia and other shortcomings!

Closing Times – living on the edge of time as he does he believes if he makes it in there even seconds before the deadline he will not be refused
… and so goes the favourite saying in the Pellowe household – 'and you wonder why I'm a nervous wreck? You've made me like this'.
That's one credit the man in question can log with absolute certainty and totally accepts responsibility for!

Sketch by Louanne Pellowe-Bailey

FAMILY, FRIENDS

AND GOOD TIMES

1.

3.

4.

5.

6.

7.

8.

9.

Socialising

1. A family gathering at Copster House
2. Great Christmas dinner at Joyce and John's home
3. La soiree du Master Vintner
4. After the meal the carpet is always rolled back and Greenfield goes Greek style! Left to right: Pat, Bob, John, Joan and me
5. And another do at The Alpine – left to right: Peter, Margaret, Melwyn, Aunt Joan and Uncle Joe
6. January fancy dress parties at Copster House
7. This could be your Doctor – my God it is! Dr Kelso topped up with medicine
8. Sheila, Francis, Austin and Terry – good friends all
9. We briefly lived at Fernlea on the other side of the valley to where we are now. Tim and Susan now own the house

10.

11.

12.

13.

14.

10. Mum's 90th – still had another 9 to go! Left to right – Tim, Viv, Mum, Joan and Joe Lees

11. Another 'do' at the Alpine – this time it's my 50th – Diana and Bob West with Derek reading Louanne's home made present to me – a book on the 'Moron'!

12. Maureen and George Warburton (ye s the bread people) we met on a couple of cruises. Here they are inspecting the ship's galley as George was very interested in how they made the bread on board.

13. Good Dartmouth friends one New Year's Eve at the Castle Hotel in Dartmouth. Peter the Rasta man, Mary as Minerva McGonagall, Viv does the Charleston with Columbo

14. Fun off shore as Bob picks up the beat with John, Joyce, Viv and Anne at sea level

1.

2.

4.

3.

6.

5.

Trip to Nepal

7.

The Annapurna Range via CAN who raise money for the hill people of Nepal. Run by Doug Scott CBE. Paul Braithwaite, a local mountaineer, is one of the trustees.

8.

1. Kathmandu Hindu temple – cremation ceremonies are constant – the ashes will go into the River Ganges

2. Each evening camp is set up, tea is served. All the food is vegetarian – go and do it with CAN (Community Action Nepal)

3. Machapuchare the 'fish tail' holy mountain 6993 metres high – climbing it is not allowed

4. Tomorrow's Sherpas and Gurkhas

5. One of many holy men at the temple

6. Girl porters wearing flip flops! They carry loads of around 60lb whilst the male porters carry 80lb

7. I try a porter's pack and my mobility immediately ceases!

8. Had to fly over Everest whilst I was out there – better climbed!

1.

2.

3.

5.

4.

Moving with the flow of life

1. Boys stuff – joined Malcolm Miller, Sail Training Association (STA) as second purser on a three week voyage out of Leith on the north east coast 1973

2. Rougher going in the channel

3. We pass our sister ship *STA Winston Churchill*

4. Then follows the party! David in sunglasses and Tommy Cooper hat. Lou's husband, Dennis, sat next to me. All the crew got smashed so it was left to me and a guy from the Army Sailing Club to motor home through the night. When Skipper David and his crew woke up we were off Portsmouth. A good weekend

5. A weekend race Cowes to Caen with a pal from the furniture trade, David Ruddiman. Here we are at the finish and docking in Ouistreham

As Time Goes By

1. The rear of our first home – 307 Windsor Road– mixing concrete with the kids
2. We had many holidays in Guernsey where we would hire bikes at St Sampson and cycle round the island
3. A bag full of mackerel – easy – there were shoals turning the water silver – Isle of Man
4. It will be OK son (believe me I.O.M. water cold in spring!)
5. Solution to boggy Lancashire Show
6. Tim and Louanne outside Gran's bungalow– ready for their first school
7. Abersoch – another place where we had many great holidays. Tim rowed the Campari dinghy round like a good 'un
8. Louanne – first day at Prep School – she seems pleased about it
9. Tim at Rossall School – coming in to win the cross country

1.

2.

3.

4.

5.

7.

6.

8.

Four Weddings and a Baby!

1. Lewis and Mildred Ena Pellowe – a good looking couple
2. Such style – 1930s. Dad's brother Arthur to the right of Mum. Her sister Verna is on the left and Joan is on the right
3. Vivienne's mum and dad, Tom and Edith, on their wedding day
4. Our turn – Viv and I at St Thomas's – Vivienne carries out the warning she gave me!
5. Left to right of the happy couple – lads: Ian, Jimmy, Phillip, Bob, Peter, Kel. Left to right girls: Susan, June, Joyce, Anne
6. Louanne and Dennis choose Barbados, can't say I blame them
7. Then when home, party time at The Alpine, Delph – again
8. Four generations of the 'girls'

1.

2.

3.

4.

5.

6.

7.

8.

Dartmouth Days

1. Outside our flat on Ridge Hill – Back: Lou, Gran, Viv, John, Joyce. Front: Emma and Robert. Years later we moved next door to the gated house

2. Tim on water skis with a backdrop of the entrance to the River Dart and Dartmouth Castle

3. The Red Arrows whizz in for the Regatta and every thing stops moving on the river

4. Johnny Oscar in fancy dress (well nearly!). He is actually dressea as 'The Naked Chef'

5. Roberta in a pavement artist's competition

6. And another year… Johnny O and Sam as the famous 118 people – unfortunately someone else had the same idea. Roberta's outfit represents a pavement artist.

7. Magic times – Lou, Eleanor, Roberta and Johnny O – a trio of water loving kids

8. We may have changed a little but here is Viv going about carrying out her promise… and for me??

1.

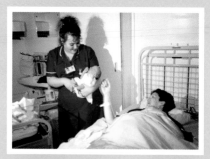

2.

3.

4.

5.

6.

7.

8.

The passage of life – 1 hour to the 99th year!

1. Christmas 2004 'Look what we have bought you for Christmas Gran'! Eleanor demonstrates; Johnny O's wondering if this is a good idea while Roberta enjoys her thumb. Gran's ninety ninth year

2. Eleanor the Princess arrives – 1 hour old

3. Johnny O practising for the next Harry Potter film

4. Tim with Sam aged eighteen months

5. Johnny Oscar makes an early exploration!

6. On a recent cruise ship Tim and Sam tackle the 'Flowrider'. If you come off it's like being in a washing machine!

7. Sam is doing fine – just about to kneel up on board

8. Bantham beach car park – uncalled for! (Dennis and Lou)

1.

2.

3.

4.

6.

5.

7.

8.

9.

Home and Away

1. Nice ship, good company – cruise with John and Joyce Kelso – Pyramids and Jerusalem run
2. East Coast USA. Lincoln car that John Wallace kindly lent us for ten days
3. Corsica holiday with Dennis, Louanne and gang. We hire bikes… puncture – roadside tactics chat!
4. That's the problem then! Jamie and Jess raring to go
5. Lovely Dye House Cottage where we now live and Higher Kinders behind
6. Summer – Roberta and Sally on fish watch, Dyehouse Cottage
7. We love 'Strictly Come Dancing'… midnight tango arrives at The Lowry to meet Flavia Cacace
8. What a woman – we embraced and kissed – it left me in shock! (Must learn the Tango)
9. Louanne's sketch of the family up to their antics whilst watching a Christmas edition of 'Strictly'

2.

3.

1.

4.

5.

6.

The Folks

1. Tim
2. Viv
3. Louanne
4. Christmas Day so out comes the hat box
5. Outside 4 Cats Restaurant in Barcelona – a must if you are there – famous and good. It's where Picasso met his friends – Susan, Sam, Tim and Viv
6. Yanks weekend in Uppermill when WWII comes to the village… a pause for a treat
7. Love this shot – eeny, meeny, mo – shoes look very clean – must be the start of term at Oldham Hulme Grammar

7.

This is Tim's business, Artko, a modern facility with a hi-tech printing and design studio based in Dukinfield, Tameside. Selling pictures directly to stores and galleries throughout the UK, EU and Ireland, the workforce includes dedicated artists and photographers enabling Artko to provide exclusive images amongst the great variety of wall art on offer. Business is going well but it's certainly harder than retailing!

Acknowledgements

I would like to thank John McCombs N.D.D.; R.O.I.; R.B.A.; F.R.S.A.; M.A.F.A. for his painting, which has been used for the front cover image

Chapter 3 – The Cornish Connection
Gill of Gill Bolton Books; Leonora Johnson, Falmouth Library (Local History); Kim Cooper, Cornish Studies Library, Redruth; Margaret Bauer, Cornish Ancestors Rootsweb; Myra Cordrey, OPC Genealogy, Calstock, and St Dominick, Cornwall

Chapter 7 – The Turning Point
Thanks to: Ian Holt, Archivist, Oldham Hulme Grammar School; Peter Wood and David Washington, Oldham Hulme Grammar School; Geraint Morgan, Llandudno Library; Conway Library; Samantha at Llandudno Tourist Information

Chapter 8 – Everyone Needs an Apprentice
Thanks to Freda Millet for the photograph of A. Pellowe and Sons in the 1930's

Chapter 11 – Two Year Holiday Part Two
With many thanks to Maurice Nicholls and the late David Carter of Britain's Small Wars (BSW) Cyprus section; Richard Callaghan RMP Museum

Chapter 13 – MV Baron Inchcape
Lynne Crawford, Archivist, Mitchell Library, Glasgow; Emma Yan, Archivist, University of Glasgow

Chapter 17 – One of Life's Crossroads
Mrs G. Hampton for references from Trevor Hampton's unpublished biography and kind permission to reproduce a photograph

Chapter 19 – You Make Your Bed You Lie in It
With thanks to William Porter for the image of the bridge at Mumps, Oldham and to Wendy Johnson for the photograph of David and Sheila

Chapter 23 – Keeping the Show on the Road
Liz Gaytten for her kind permission to reproduce a photograph and poem

Artko Ltd for all their help and for selling this book through their website, thus ensuring that all profit from sales will go directly to the Pellowe Family Charitable Trust.